THE FRIENDSHIPS AND FOLLIES
OF OSCAR WILDE

Oscar Wilde (1854–1900), poet, dramatist, and wit. (Picture Post)

THE FRIENDSHIPS
AND FOLLIES OF
OSCAR WILDE

LEWIS BROAD

THOMAS Y. CROWELL COMPANY · NEW YORK

Manufactured in the United States of America
by the Vail-Ballou Press, Inc., Binghamton, New York

Library of Congress Catalog Card No. 55-5619

First printing January 1955

The quotations beneath the chapter
headings are, with one indicated
exception, from Oscar Wilde's writings.

TO THE READER

*"Nothing can be more absurdly untrue than the asser-
tion which is invariably made by about half the reviewers when a new book about Wilde comes out is that
the subject is exhausted and that nobody wants to hear
any more about it. The subject will never be exhausted
just precisely because of its human and dramatic interest."*—LORD ALFRED DOUGLAS.

THE life story of Oscar Wilde has become one
of the folk tales of the world, one of the tragic
legends of the ages.

His history has been much misrepresented by the chroniclers. Their vision has been obscured by the moral miasma of a
Victorian scandal. Many have not penetrated from the Old
Bailey dock beyond the gray bricks of Reading jail. Such have
seen only the sorry figure of a police court case.

Others have praised the playwright and the wit. They have
sought to minimize, to exculpate or reprobate the conduct that
was the immediate cause of the man's ruin.

The Wilde who has joined the legends of the ages is another figure than these. Wilde the wit and dramatist has taken
his place among his peers of English letters. The Wilde of
legend is the man who was the architect of the spectacular
catastrophe that ended the dramatist's career.

His comedies and his offenses against the law are not the essential basis of the fame of this Wilde of legend. By his plays
he rose to fame, by his conduct he was involved in ruin. The
essential basis of his drama is that of the classic tragedies of
ancient Greece.

v

His history awaits the dramatist who, in a modern setting, seeks a manifestation of the fate that befalls the mortal who, by his recklessness and his folly (ὕβρις) brings down upon himself the penalty (νέμεσις) reserved for those who tempt the wrath of the immortal gods.

Oscar Wilde splendidly contrived his own catastrophe. He presented himself as one to whom the gods had given everything—genius, a distinguished name, high social position, brilliancy, intellectual daring. He stood at the zenith of a glittering career. The theater was opened before him for further triumphs. Everything was in his grasp. Then, by one insolent act of folly, he ruined all. He pulled about him the pillars of the temple of his own fame. In one short week he passed from the pedestal to ignominy and infamy.

The simple purpose of this book, that is published in this centenary year of his birth, is to tell the story of his rise and fall.

I count it to be my misfortune that, since I began to write eighteen months ago, cases in the courts have directed public attention, sensationally, to offenses of which Oscar Wilde was convicted. With these I have considered myself, as biographer, to be concerned only so far as they provided the occasion for the fall. I have sought neither to emphasize nor to shirk any of the facts, although avoiding, as far as possible, the technical terms some authors seem to relish.

I make no apology for adding to the many books on Oscar Wilde. I have written for those who are not acquainted with the turns and twists of the Wilde story, disclosed piecemeal fashion, in half a century of writing. The authors, in particular the principal actors in the drama of his life, and Wilde himself were not richly endowed with the quality of truthfulness. Omissions, evasions, distortions, inventions and downright prevarications have confused their record of events. The narrative here presented, based on the evidence of Wilde himself and of his friends and of the reports of the various trials, is the result of these varying and sometimes conflicting testimonies, produced on a mind unguided and unbiased by acquaintance with any of the characters in the case.

CONTENTS

ix

LIST OF ILLUSTRATIONS

THE FRIENDSHIPS AND FOLLIES
OF OSCAR WILDE

1. THE EVIL NETS OF FATE

Actors are so fortunate. They can choose whether they
will appear in comedy or tragedy, whether they will
suffer or make merry. But in real life it is different.

Scenes from a double drama were being enacted
that night at the St. James's Theatre, London.
Within, a brilliant audience were assembled for the presenting
of a comedy that was to confirm the fame of Mr. Oscar Wilde.
Without, a few London policemen and theater attendants were
witnesses of an act in the comedy from life that was to end in
Mr. Wilde's ruin and the touching off of one of the most grievous scandals that shook Victorian Society.

It had been snowing that day and the streets were unpleasant
to walk, treacherous for carriages to drive on. Nevertheless,
beautifully attired women and their squires faced the cold to
attend the first night of Mr. Wilde's "The Importance of Being
Earnest." Already two of his pieces had scored successes. A
third had been put on not many weeks before at the Haymarket,
the Prince of Wales himself gracing the première with his presence. So the wintry streets did not prevent theater-goers from
turning out for a society and theatrical occasion. And the brilliant audience was most brilliantly entertained.

Outside in the snow a man had tramped from door to door of
the theater. He was seen to be carrying a bunch of vegetables,
carrots prominent amongst them. At each theater entrance he
was turned away, expostulating. For an hour or more he
prowled around the theater, but finally gave up his mission and
went off into the wintry night gibbering like an ape.

The carrots were to have been hurled at the playwright at the moment of his acclaim. Balked in his purpose of affronting the author on the stage, the man with the bunch of carrots meditated on other means of accomplishing his purpose. A little later a visiting card, more sinister in its implication than the carrots, had been left with the porter at Mr. Wilde's Club. The Marquis of Queensberry had accomplished the first step in bringing to book his enemy, that "brute" Oscar Wilde.

For many months past the Marquis had been pursuing the playwright, devoted friend of his youngest son, Lord Alfred Douglas. He had warned the two of them to break off the association that had become the talk of all the clubs and gossips in London. The scandal of their conduct was notorious. It had been made the subject of a novel that was the talk of the town. With his own eyes the Marquis had seen the pair of them "flaunting their disgusting relationship" before the world at the Café Royal. He would have liked to shoot them. When he ordered his son to give up the playwright, Alfred sent him impertinent letters and telegrams, openly defying him. Meanwhile this man Oscar Wilde was being applauded by idle audiences in the theaters. If he killed the fellow he would be perfectly justified in his own mind, such was the mischief he conceived him to have done.

While the Marquis was planning the means to expose Oscar Wilde, Lord Alfred, with unfilial purpose, was plotting the ruin of his father. They were Douglases both. The mad, bad blood of Scottish clansmen was their common heritage. The Marquis in his detestation of Wilde was matched by Lord Alfred in his hatred of his father—the parent who had neglected his children, the husband who had persecuted, bullied and betrayed the children's mother. The fond son saw himself as the champion of his mother, whose wrongs must be avenged. The quarrel between his friend Wilde and his father offered the means for the accomplishment of his purpose. The attacks on Wilde could be used to get the Marquis shut up in prison.

The outcome of the conflict between these implacable, elemental forces, the Douglases, father and son, was the catastrophe of ruin and infamy that befell Oscar Wilde. A few weeks after the man with the bunch of carrots had been turned away from the theater, he stood in the dock at the Old Bailey accused of criminal libel on Mr. Oscar Wilde. A few weeks more and Wilde himself stood in the Old Bailey dock charged with offenses against youths.

From that dock he was removed to serve two years in jail, castigated by the judge who had sentenced him, his career in ruins, while the women of the streets, outside the Old Bailey, danced in their delight at his fall.

With a sense of the theater, Wilde had made his greatest triumph the occasion for exposure and disgrace. After years of endeavor he had established himself as a dramatist, the wittiest since Sheridan. The notoriety of his fall eclipsed the fame of his success. His name became a by-word. No scandal of our time has produced anything approaching the execration that he aroused. This is no matter for surprise considering the state of opinion in England in the closing years of the reign of good Queen Victoria.

Oscar Wilde, at the time of his fall, was forty years of age, a man of big build tending to corpulence. He was a figure in society, was more proud indeed to be a figure in society than a man of letters. He moved amongst what were still termed the best people, or almost the best. Wherever wit was the passport he had the entrée. His social charm was not to be questioned and hostesses had come to regard his presence as a guarantee for the success of their parties and their dinners. The pleasure of his company was the one point about him on which they were all agreed, even his inveterate enemy, Lord Queensberry. Frank

Harris, a good enough judge of a man at the table, pronounced that given the wits of all the ages to choose from he would have selected Wilde to be his companion for an evening—"I would rather have him back (from the world of the dead) than anyone I have ever met. I have known more heroic souls and some deeper souls—souls much more alive to ideas of duty and generosity. But I have known no more charming, no more quickening, no more delightful spirit. The most charming man I have ever met was assuredly Oscar Wilde." To which you can add the testimony of Alfred Douglas:

> *in music measureless*
> *I heard his golden voice and marked him trace*
> *Under the common thing the hidden grace,*
> *And conjure wonder out of emptiness,*
> *Till mean things put on beauty like a dress*
> *And all the world was an enchanted place.*

Wilde had to a superlative degree the quality he admired— the detachment of a mind that enables a man to toy with ideas, no matter how unorthodox, without feeling outraged in his moral, artistic or professional senses. It was what he termed the "Oxford temper." He was tolerant, he was easy going, he was good tempered, even sweet tempered, and, as a consequence, he was not given to earnestness and zeal. You should no more expect your jester to be a moralist than Calvin or John Knox to indulge in idle jesting. We suffer the defects of our qualities and, perhaps, are enriched by the qualities of our defects. To the straightforward character of the easy-going exhibitionist, nature added the tendencies to abnormality that, developing after his marriage, turned him from his wife and set him seeking the society of young men. From this sprang his association with Lord Alfred Douglas, who, reversing the experience of Oscar Wilde, grew beyond his youthful tendencies to seek the society of women.

Douglas, in character, was most things that Wilde was not. In place of a soft-natured Irishman stood a fiery tempered, rancorous, venomous-tongued Scot; in place of a natural exhibitionist, a small-minded egoist, nourishing a vanity that ranged from the petty to the colossal. He was, says Harris, distinguished by aristocratic insolence. He was, says Wilde, burdened with the terrible legacy of the fatal Douglas temperament. There was charm about this Douglas in his genial moods and the appeal of youthful beauty to which all who loved him paid tribute.

From the meeting of these two ill-matched natures there developed an association that repeated the story of David and Jonathan, except that Jonathan had no father to denounce David. The chroniclers have no good to say of John Sholto Douglas, 8th Marquis of Queensberry. No son has given his father a worse character—inhuman brute, crazy lunatic are among the epithets lavishly bestowed. The father thought no better of the son—miserable, misguided, white-livered, sickly looking son. The Marquis has a title to remembrance as the legislator for the sport of boxing, who drew up the Queensberry rules. The son left claim to fame in the sonnets that rank him with the minor poets.

Oscar Wilde placed between these truculent, turbulent Douglases was a pouter pigeon between two hawks. By common consent he was the mildest natured author who ever coined an epigram. Malice was as foreign to him as it was natural to the two Douglases. In his easy-going, Irish fashion he was not easily aroused to anger. Rancor was unknown to him. Even against those who worked for his downfall and those former admirers of the days of success who turned from him after his fall he bore no resentment. Emotionally and intellectually he and Lord Alfred were utterly dissimilar.

Over a period of years these two, the falcon and the dove, consorted in strange and uncomfortable association. Many times the turbulences of Douglas, his ungovernable furies, caused Wilde to determine to break off a friendship that tormented him beyond enduring. But such was the bond between them that he suffered himself to forget and to forgive.

ⅤThe glitter of the paradox was one of the ornaments of Wilde's wit. It is the paradox of his career that the offenses which were the occasion of his prison sentence were not the primary, originating cause of his downfall.

He placed himself in jeopardy to oblige his friend. He went to the law with the object of having his friend's father sent to jail and, the tables being turned, he found himself in jail instead. With the lamentations that were raised afterwards about the oppressiveness of his sentence I find it difficult to identify myself. The law had not gone out of its way to ferret out Oscar Wilde. It was Wilde who offered himself to the law. With full knowledge of the penal consequences involved, he presented himself in the courts, courting exposure. He accepted Queensberry's challenge. He set the processes of law in motion. Prison for one of them was the stake for which they played. Wilde, not Queensberry, was the loser. Wilde, in fairness be it said, made no complaint against the law. His complaint was against the friend for whom he had placed himself in peril.

For his own generation Oscar Wilde was beyond comprehension. Abnormalities such as his were outside the pale of decent reckoning, although, in fact, the Victorians were not so rigidly limited to normality. Wilde was one of the three abnormals of Victorian letters. There was Lewis Carroll whose mild friendships were with Alices of his own wonderland, girls barely reaching the years of incipient womanhood. Ruskin cultivated a romanticism for the virginal in women, and could not conquer his revulsion for the spectacle of the womanly form of the wife he had wedded. Wilde, who came to share Ruskin's distaste, began his married life with a zestful and proclaimed delight in his wife's charms. Lewis Carroll remained peculiar. Ruskin, avoiding all indulgences, became mentally deranged. Wilde, reaching prison and infamy, was to the end splendidly sane.

To what extent he was to be held responsible for the line of conduct that resulted in the prison sentence has become, since Wilde's death, wide open to argument. The psychologists, or psychiatrists, who try to grapple with the problems of the un-usual in man's mental and emotional make-up, challenge the view that the abnormal of his type has freedom of choice over his conduct. Nature (or the genes), they say, gives a man his character and this determines in broad outline the course to be pursued in life. Only within the general form of character has a person freedom of choice to follow this or that line of con-duct. It is a conception that raises as many problems as it solves. Under the old idea a man was held responsible for his character as well as his actions, and you knew where you were. If he turned out to be in the wrong then he was to blame. Now, nature, or the genes, or his parents are found to be responsible for what a man is, and so if he turns out a wrongdoer these days, then he can shift the responsibility onto his progenitors. This is very satisfactory for the wrongdoer, but it is a system that, for society at large, lacks the satisfying simplicity of the old arrangements.

Added to this is the difficulty of identifying wrongdoers. Formerly Oscar Wilde was to be put in that class, but now, under the new dispensation, he is to be classed not as wrong but as different. It adds up, I suppose, to the same thing, a fact described with the moralizing omitted. I do not find it possible to class myself with those who have reached that altitude of moral perfection which enables them to pass judgments on other men. That is better left to the bishops and other professionals. Observation and the Sunday newspapers do not foster any sustained faith in the strength of human morality. As far as my observation goes men, and women—irrespective of age or class—remain moral for so long as their desires and passions find reasonable fulfilment. Man is not so richly endowed with strength of character that he can for long sustain conflict between desires in their strength and moral force in its weakness. Nevertheless half the world spends half its time censuring the other half. Any Tom, Dick or Harry who can find himself a pulpit is ready to speak in judgment on better men.

Some exercise is needed in toleration to accept the inverted values of the unfamiliar world of inversion. One must school oneself to acquiesce in Wilde writing to the "Dearest of all boys," assuring him that he cannot live without him, so "dear and wonderful" has he become. One must tolerate expressions of extravagant endearment and strangely sounding phrases between men such as "those red rose-leaf lips of yours should have been made not less for music of song than for madness of kissing." One can smile at the warnings Wilde so solemnly gave to a boy friend on a trip to Paris not to expose himself to the temptations of the siren women of the Moulin Rouge.

It needs less effort of the imagination to comprehend something of the pathos of the last lonely years of disgrace and ostracism when Oscar Wilde, exile in other lands, wandered from place to place in search of the consolation of the companionship he could never find. He had championed the love that has no name but it did not bring to him the comfort of enduring companionship to assist him in bearing the burden of living.

The man besotted by the spectacle of his own brilliance is a character well enough known to the world. But for the rash courses upon which such men have entered there has customarily been some glittering prize to lure them on. For Oscar Wilde there was nothing except the beckoning hand of doom. That he, with his aberrations, could have so deluded himself as to face an infuriated father before a British jury is an act of folly as incredible as Lord Scroop's treason. All the circumstances of forty years of living are needed to reach some understanding of how, when the world seemed to be at his feet, he came to involve himself in the catastrophe of his career, caught, as he conceived himself to have been, in the evil nets of fate. For the first causes we must revert to his ancestry.

2. HEREDITY

*Heredity, the only one of the Gods whose real name we
know . . . brings gifts of strange temperaments . . .
and impossible desires.*

THE essential facts about the birth and parentage of Oscar Wilde can be briefly stated. He
was born in the City of Dublin at 21 Westland Road, on the
16th day of October 1854. The date of 1856 is wrongly given
sometimes, an error that arose from his own misstatement in
the particulars for his marriage. His father was a surgeon, and
eye and ear specialist of renown, who was also an archaeolo-
gist and antiquarian. His mother too was a writer of some
note in Irish circles. There were two other children of the
marriage—William two years Oscar's senior and a younger
sister, Isola, who did not survive her childhood.

The Wildes were of the Protestant faith and the boys were
educated at Portora Royal School and Trinity College, Dublin, where Oscar distinguished himself in the examinations. In
1874, at the age of twenty, he graduated at Magdalen College,
Oxford, at which college he won a scholarship. His Oxford
record was a brilliant one and he went down in 1878 a double
first and winner of the Newdigate Prize for verse.

How far do a biographer's duties extend? Can he content
himself with stating the bare facts of the birth certificate? Or
must he go delving back in the ancestral past? The answer is
not in doubt in these days when heredity is called upon to
solve the mysteries of the ego and when a man's failings are
placed upon the shoulders of his forbearers. How far pre-

cisely heredity may be made to serve is not as yet outlined.
Any faults, clearly enough, may be passed off as attributable
to ancestral influences. But what of the virtues? There is not
so much readiness, as far as I can observe, to attribute a man's
achievements to his parents, grandparents and so back into
former generations. I have yet to see it argued, for example,
that Shakespeare's genius is to be explained by the brilliance
of his father.

It is only in their weaknesses and their ill humors that men
hark back to their parents as Cassius of his mother:

> *Have not you love enough to bear with me,*
> *When that rash humour which my mother gave me*
> *Makes me forgetful?*

To which Brutus gave the assenting answer:

> *Yes, Cassius; and, from henceforth,*
> *When you are over-earnest with your Brutus*
> *He'll think your mother chides.*

Heredity in the Wilde case has been made to work wonders by skilled and partial manipulation. Robert Sherard, the
first biographer, realized the possibilities and exploited them
to the full, and his example has been followed by later chroniclers. Wilde's parents are pleaded as extenuating circumstances
for Oscar's development. They have been put frequently in
the dock before the judges of posterity and the verdict has
been entered against them. Wilde's guilt has been transferred
back a generation because his mother was dominating and eccentric and his father given to lust. It is not, however, argued
that Sir William and Lady Wilde are to receive any of posterity's bouquets for the epigrams, paradoxes and comedies of
their younger son. Patently enough rules of heredity will have
to be worked out for the guidance of biographers. Lacking

this guidance we can do no more than assert that heredity and environment (as parentage and upbringing are otherwise styled) while not sufficient to excuse Oscar Wilde, yet go some way towards explaining him.

First then of his race. Oscar Wilde was born an Irishman. For a man with ambitions to be a wit it is a proper step to take, an insurance at life's outset. More epigrams have come out of Dublin than London. Of the comic dramatists, Goldsmith, Sheridan, and Shaw as well as Wilde were Irish born and bred, while Congreve's early years were spent in Ireland. For the development of the comic spirit, it is a further advantage if Saxon be mingled with the Celtic blood. Wilde like Sheridan and Shaw (but unlike Goldsmith) had English ancestors.

The Wildes have no length of pedigree behind them. They are said to have originated from a Dutchman who came to England with William of Orange. There was a Wilde in business in County Durham when George II was King, whose son decided to seek his fortunes across St. George's Channel. This emigrant, Ralph Wilde, was Oscar's great-grandfather, source of his English strain. The ladies who were his great-grandmother, grandmother and mother were of Irish blood, linking the Wildes with the O'Flyns of Roscommon, the Surridges and the Ouseleys. There was talent in these families. One Ouseley, a noted Oriental scholar, was sent as Ambassador to Persia; another, a General, served with distinction under Wellington. Gideon Ouseley, the Methodist, was the John Wesley of Ireland.

Oscar's mother was an Elgee of Wexford, grand-daughter of an Archdeacon who was "one of the saints of the Wexford Calendar." One of her uncles, Sir Charles Ormsby, was a member of the old Irish Parliament; a cousin was Sir Robert M'Clure, seeker of the Northwest Passage. The famous Maturin was her grand-uncle.

Charles Maturin is an author whose novels are sought today by readers of literary curiosities. He was much esteemed in his own time for his blood-curdling tales of the grotesque and fantastic. He was esteemed also by his great-grand nephew. Oscar's mother and Oscar in his turn were both influenced by this eccentric person. His most successful novel, "Melmoth the Wanderer," is the story of a man who made a pact with the devil. The young Thackeray read it trembling with apprehension. The great Balzac read it and praised it as a work of a genius to be ranked with Molière and Byron. Posterity has not endorsed this verdict, but Oscar accepted it, for Balzac was one of his gods. As a youth he gazed in admiration at the bust in his home of his great-grand uncle, a man of impressive personality, who dressed in strange attire and whose writings were "those of a madman glowing with burning eloquence and deep feeling."

The marriage that united Oscar's parents brought varied qualities together—talent, eccentricity, degeneracy. Dr. Wilde was then thirty-six and his bride twenty-five. Whatever differences of opinion there were about Dr. and Mrs. Wilde, on one point there was agreement—they were in appearance a singularly ill-assorted couple. He was short, she tall. He was insignificant, and shuffled about like an ambling ape. She was well built, with a stately bearing and a distinguished air. With her dark hair and flashing eyes she was attractive enough to have made a match with a better man than this doctor, who was not overly clean in his habits—"a pithecoid person of extraordinary sensuality" as one of his descriptions runs. He was one of those libidinous Irish characters of the type that had impressed Father Bernard Campion a couple of centuries before—"the lewder sort, both clerks and laymen, are sensual and loose to lechery above measure."

Despite his appearance little Dr. Wilde had a way with the

women. His gallantries were numerous, his ardors unrestrained, of which indiscretions Jane Francesca cannot have been wholly ignorant when she agreed to become his bride. Professionally Dr. Wilde was a person of distinction. As eye and ear specialist he had won a reputation that was known beyond St. George's Channel. He was appointed Surgeon-Oculist-in-Ordinary to Queen Victoria, the first time such an appointment to the Royal Household had been made in Ireland, though Her Majesty is not known to have required his services. He did, however, treat Bernard Shaw's father with the result that he "squinted the other way for the rest of his life." Despite the pressure of his other affairs, the doctor found time to devote himself to investigation of Irish folk-lore and antiquities, undertaking field work and embodying the results in half a dozen published books. So despite his looks and his amours, he was reckoned to be quite an ornament of Dublin society.

Dr. Wilde can easily be seen for what he was—a man with literary and professional talents, with sex well developed, morals undeveloped and no particular force of character. Was this the man an aspiring genius would choose for sire? The question is easily posed. Who can determine the answer?

The mother, Jane Francesca, was a woman out of no common mold. There was a distinction about her, some loftiness of character, so that had she not been lacking in balance she might have joined the company of those matrons for whom Rome was famous. She had no more morals than her husband, but less sex, more force to her character, and a contempt for the world's opinion. This sprang not so much from lofty disdain as from an imperfect sense of the world's realities. She did not live life in the world around her but dramatized herself on a stage of her own imaginative creation. As a girl she saw herself in the role of Irish revolutionary, a Joan of Arc of another race and a later day, inspiring Fenians to throw off the hated Saxon yoke. Rhetoric flowed from her facile pen, sometimes in verse, at greater length in prose, always pseudonymous. Rhetoric, not reality—how could there be reality behind the vaporings of a girl of nineteen? It was the sort of stuff that can turn the heads of romantic youth. She gained her moment in history with a more than usually inflammatory piece—"Jacta Alea Est," which she signed in her nom-de-guerre of "Speranza." Appearing in the "Nation" of July 29, 1848, it won for that publication the notoriety of immediate suppression by the order of the Viceroy, and the prosecution of the editor for treason-felony. When the prosecutor read passages from the article in support of the charge, Speranza rose from her place amongst the spectators in the public gallery to declare herself to be author of the piece—hers was the blame, if any blame, and hers the place in the dock. She was silenced—not as a criminal and sedition-monger, but as a chit of a girl who was disturbing the dignity of the court.

It was not long afterwards that Dr. Wilde made her acquaintance and Speranza, the parlor Fenian, lost her identity in the wife of Dublin's leading eye specialist and mother of his lawful children.

It was Oscar's misfortune on the doorstep of life to have been scheduled in the mind of his expectant mother as a girl. As her firstborn was a son, a girl was postulated as her second contribution, a girl she prepared for and, despite the contrary provision of nature, it was a girl she at first proceeded to rear. Oscar the child might be named, but it was in girl's clothes in which he was attired, with appropriate gew-gaws making him look, according to one observer, like a miniature Hindu idol. The mother disguised her disappointment as became a lofty mind. The baby's arrival was announced to a friend in Speranza's own style—"A Joan of Arc was never meant for marriage, so here I am, bound heart and soul to the home hearth. Behold me, Speranza, rocking a cradle at this present writing in which lies my second son—a babe of one month old the 16th of this month, November, and as large and fine and healthy as if he were three months. He is to be called Oscar Fingal Wilde. Is not that grand, misty and Ossianic?" To these names two more were added, O'Flahertie and Wills, to mark the connection with W. G. Wills, dramatist, painter and poet. When he reached years of discretion the object of this baptismal prodigality reduced himself to the simple Oscar.

Incalculable are the influences of heredity and environment. Those who transfer the aberrations of Oscar Wilde to the parents who begat him might think on the Irishness of his origins. Dublin born, Ossianic in his naming, son of the revolutionary Speranza—here, you might have thought, were the makings of an Irish patriot. Never was a son of Dublin—not excepting Bernard Shaw, who was in process of being begotten a street or two away—less of the Irishman than this son of Dr. Wilde and Speranza. The Irish in him was forgotten once he had crossed St. George's Channel. The fight for Irish independence was to continue throughout his days. Never, so far as the record goes, was Oscar to identify himself with the struggle of the land of his birth, but he was not the man even in the reckoning of his loyalist friends to champion an unpopular cause and the Irish were not popular in England. His were the times when advertisements for domestics had the warning "Irish servants need not apply." Irish acquaintances were treated with limited confidence in the London clubs and Irish cousins were looked upon as decidedly dangerous. Oscar Wilde did not parade his Irishness. Once he had left school and college the Irish phase was complete. He took his place in English society as a cosmopolitan.

Dublin did not make an Irish patriot of Oscar Wilde but his upbringing had a determining influence on the development of his character. What youth could have emerged unaffected from the atmosphere of the Merrion Square home? It was the gathering place for the Bohemians and the wits. The former gathered at the call of the Doctor, who at an early age had become persuaded of the benefits of alcohol medicinally prescribed. The wits assembled to enliven the drawing room of his wife who, yielding Joan of Arc, had decided to be the inspiration of literary genius in her salon as a second Madame Récamier. There were gatherings of literary and artistic folk at her At Homes, celebrities, notorieties (particularly welcome) and eccentrics. It was generally agreed that the hostess was the most eccentric of them all. Every description includes some comment on the strange qualities of Speranza—"an odd mixture of nonsense with a sprinkling of genius," "resembling a tragedy queen at a suburban theater" and more to the same effect. Her dress was of baroque magnificence, voluminous skirts, crimson flounces, Limerick lace, Oriental scarf, six feet of highly decorated womanhood, decorated with jewels, gems, brooches and cameos, the whole surmounted with a crown of laurels. The casual observer regarded her as odd. The more discerning saw purpose beneath the spectacle—"She exaggerates whatever is unusual about her because she likes to make a sensation." This demonstration that notoriety can be the first step to fame was not lost on the young Oscar who was paraded at his mother's salon. She knew by intuition that he was going to "turn out wonderful," and she brought him out at her parties. Before he had reached his teens he had been much exposed to effects of Irish talk and Irish wit.

On the other side of the hall, later in the evening, there were his father's Bohemian dinners. It was a house of deep drinking, loose talk and no morals in particular. The Doctor's gallantries were the talk of the town. Francesca was indifferent.

That she did not follow his example was to be ascribed to mere disinclination without moral backing, for it was her view that "There has never been a woman yet in this world who wouldn't have given the top off the milk-jug to some man if she had met the right one." Oscar had so far developed that by the age of eight he had "already learned the ways to the shores of old romance and had seen apples plucked from the tree of knowledge." In after time Oscar was to declare—"Morality does not help me; I am one of those who are made for exceptions not for laws." It was the heritage of Merrion Square.

It is common experience that the children of men who rise to eminence come (like their chauffeurs) to regard themselves as being superior to the common clay. Oscar was very sensible of the distinction of both his parents. They had bequeathed to him a name made "noble and honored, not merely in literature, art, archaeology and science, but in the public history of my own country." When he was a child of ten his father was knighted by the Viceroy. He had received the Order of the Polar Star from the King of Sweden. His work on Celtic culture had gained him the Cunningham Medal of the Royal Irish Academy. The father's fame built up in the boy's mind the notion that as a Wilde he was apart from and superior to ordinary folk and the rules governing their behavior.

Then came the notorious lawsuit. How strangely the experiences of the parents anticipated the fate of the son. A libel action, scandal made publicly notorious—the Dublin trial of 1864 was the forerunner of Oscar Wilde's action in 1895. None but the foolhardy would have been enticed into court. It was the same consciousness of being superior persons that was the undoing of Sir William and Lady Wilde and of their son thirty years later.

The action of Travers *v.* Wilde and Another that diverted

Dublin in December 1864 has been so frequently told amongst the causes célèbres that a summary outline will suffice here, but to those unacquainted with them I recommend the proceedings for their rich Irish humor and the magnificence of the forensic bathos of counsel for the plaintiff, who sailed dangerously near burlesque. It arose from one of Sir William Wilde's affaires. The lady, then about thirty years of age, was Mary Josephine Travers, daughter of a medical professor at Trinity College. She had been treated as a patient by Sir William and then seduced. When he broke off the liaison she made her ruin and her wrongs known to the world in a printed pamphlet, copies of which were sent to Merrion Square. Lady Wilde wrote an indignant remonstrance to the lady's father protesting at the disgraceful conduct of Miss Travers and accusing her of blackmail. "The wages of the disgrace she has so basely toiled for and demanded shall never be given to her," was Lady Wilde's parting thrust.

On this letter Miss Travers issued a writ for libel against Lady Wilde, joining Sir William as co-defendant, and claiming £2,000 as damages. Not the lady's good name but Sir William Wilde's reputation was the real issue and, in view of the inevitable disclosures, Sir William was encompassing his own professional ruin when he allowed the facts to be publicized in court.

The case presented to the jury for Miss Travers was that she had been ruined by Sir William while she was under the influence of chloroform. It was not difficult in cross-examination to discredit the plaintiff's story of the seduction of an unwilling patient in the doctor's study.

Counsel for Lady Wilde: Did you tell anyone of what had taken place?
Miss Travers: No.
Not even your father?—No.

Why not?—I did not wish to give him pain.

But you went back to Dr. Wilde's study after the awful assault?—Yes.

You went again and again did you not?—Yes.

Did he ever attempt to repeat the offense?—Yes.

After the second offense you went back?—Yes.

Did he ever repeat it again?—Yes.

Yet you returned again?—Yes.

And you took money from the man who had violated you against your will?—Yes.

As to the chloroform, Miss Travers was vague in the extreme. She did not know what chloroform was like, did not know what it smelled like, could not even swear that chloroform was in fact used. Her only reason for suggesting chloroform at all was that she had lost consciousness.

When it came to the turn for the other side, Lady Wilde did her case harm by protesting too much with too much disdain. She did not believe a word of the allegations against her husband; he was above suspicion; he would not so demean himself. Miss Travers had written to her about her husband's attempt on her virtue. She had not replied. Why not? "I took no interest in the matter" was the answer that plainly shocked the court.

Lady Wilde had antagonized the jury. Sir William declined to go before the jury at all. And the girl was not to be believed. The jury found a solution that disposed of both parties. Damages for Miss Travers to the amount of one farthing. Costs to be assigned against the Wildes.

Sir William's reputation could not survive the verdict. Lady Wilde might put a bold front on it, but he was never quite the same again. When he withdrew to his country estate, Dublin said that it was because of the scandal. Then his health began to fail. That, they said, was due to the life he had led.

√The ill-natured never have difficulty in identifying the acts of providence designed as chastisement for man's sins. This is to outrun the chronicle by a dozen years, for Oscar was an Oxford undergraduate when Sir William died in 1876.

There was about Lady Wilde the appearance of loftiness of mind. But it is with her character as with her son's prose —always there is the suspicion that the noblest sounding passages did not spring from sincerity of feeling. They were poseurs both, the son and the mother.

The influence of this mother in the development of this son is scarcely to be exaggerated. No woman was to influence him more, not many men as much, certainly not his father, for all his distinction. It was not the dressing up as a girl baby and such things that gave a twist to his personality. It was his submissiveness to her, he in his easy-going, self-indulgent weakness, submitting to her in her greater strength of character. There was not the possessiveness shown by his mother to D. H. Lawrence, leading to the unhappiness of a clash of wills. Oscar's was the deference naturally yielded to a force that was not exercised but which existed. It is a problem for the psychiatrists to determine whether the man with his strange tendencies became what he was because of the workings of his mother-loving; or whether this mother-loving was the earliest manifestation of the Oscar Wilde that was to be.

It is beyond question that the early impressionable years gave the first mold to the youth's mind. Before his schooldays had begun his outlook had been tinctured in the Merrion Square circle in which brilliance mattered more than truth, wit was prized more than morals, in which the artist was encouraged to disdain the Philistine, and the person of distinction to despise the multitude, in which the realities of the common world were looked upon as commonplace and commonly held opinions were dismissed as vulgarities. The son who began his education in Lady Wilde's drawing room became the master of drawing room comedy. But for the saving grace of his native wit he might also have developed into a tediously superior person.

3. PORTORA TO OXFORD

Education is an admirable thing, but it is well to remember from time to time that nothing that is worth knowing can be taught.

THERE has been much poring over the records of Oscar Wilde's years at school and university. It has been an unrewarding labor when undertaken to produce evidence of his youthful aberrations. This was not to be found. It does not mean that everything in the young Wilde's life was pure and innocent—few men can claim to have lived twenty-five years in complete continency. But, as the police phrase goes in the courts, nothing was known against him, so that Frank Harris, wanting a schoolboy touch or two, was driven to invent them. Wilde is entitled to all the benefits of a blameless record.

Oscar Wilde at all stages of his life was described as overgrown, tending to flabbiness, lethargic, clumsy in his movements. He had none of the surplus energy that drives youth to vigorous athleticism. Even his intellectual development proceeded without bursts of mental activity. He had an easy facility for absorbing knowledge on subjects in which he was interested. He passed through the examination room with the appearances of effortless distinction. At school and university his record was one of sustained brilliancy. He was never seen to be exerting himself.

Portora was his school, one of the four Royal Schools of Ireland, which had in the Royal Charles of England its founder, patron and benefactor. It had as Chairman of Governors the Bishop of Clogher.

Wilde at Portora from 1864 to 1871 laid the basis of his classical scholarship. There is something unexplained about the schoolboy years. There is every reason why he should have been plagued by his fellows for he was everything the average schoolboy detests. He was bookish, he would take no part in sports, he wore his hair long, his dress was out of the ordinary. The top-hat school custom required for Sunday he, and he alone, wore all week. This is the type that schoolboys, most conservative and intolerant of creatures, go into action against with persistency and without mercy. Individuality is ironed out into uniformity. Oscar escaped these ministrations. It would have been to his ultimate advantage to have been reduced for a space to the level of the average. The presence of his elder brother ("Blueblood" Willie as they called him) may have served for his protection and always he had the shield of his wit. They teased him once—it may be apocryphal, but it is good enough—that his skin showed signs of dirt, to which he replied that it was dark not from dirt but from the blue blood of the Wildes. Nothing is known to have disturbed his youthful ease, except the austere Protestantism of the school.

In his final year he won the Portora Gold Medal, the best classical scholar of the year, with outstanding distinction in the *viva voce*—he simply walked away from the other entrants. His name was inscribed in letters of gold on the tablets of the schoolhouse. In after years, when disgrace befell him, order was given for the inscription to be erased. There was no need. Nature had anticipated authority. A crack had developed in the slab and this had struck at the very place, obliterating the gilded letters of his name.

There was one cause for sadness in his schoolboy life—the

death of his sister Isola. He was twelve at the time and he
suffered her loss most keenly. He had felt for the child unusually strong affection. For a time he was inconsolable in his
grief. He made frequent and long visits to the grave of the
girl who had been "a little ray of sunshine dancing about our
home." When he took to writing verse he mourned the lost
Isola in one of the few poems of simple sincerity that he was to
write:

> *Lily-like, white as snow*
> *She hardly knew*
> *She was a woman, so*
> *Sweetly she grew.*

When he came to take a woman to be his wife, he chose
one who in kindness and gentleness brought back memories
of his lost Isola.

At Trinity College, Dublin, young Wilde continued as he
had begun at school. For all his shortcomings in mathematics
he placed second at the matriculation examination in 1871. In
classics, on the first of the two days, he did no better than
fairly well in grammar and the rudiments. On the second day
in higher classics, he outshone all the others. It was characteristic of him. Groundwork and detail was not his strong point,
he was never a grammarian.

A year at Trinity was sufficient for Oscar Wilde. He had
won a scholarship that would have paid his fees for his remaining years, but he preferred to try his chances across the
Channel. The enchantment of Oxford had cast its spell upon
him. He took little with him from Dublin but the Berkeley
Gold Medal, and the friendship of his tutor, the great Mahaffy.
The Rev. John Pentland Mahaffy, Precentor and Junior Dean
of Trinity, was the greatest Hellenist of his time. Ordained
priest of the Church of England, he was a sceptic whose spirit-

ual home was Greece. He dropped the prefix "reverend" from his name. The pulpit of Trinity College Chapel was barred to him. There was no conflict in his mind arising from divided loyalties. His allegiance was wholeheartedly surrendered to Greece. In Wilde he was to set up a mental conflict between Greece and Rome that was never to be resolved. At Trinity the friendship was begun, Wilde's Hellenism was developed and Mahaffy's book on Greek social life received "improvement and corrections" from Wilde.

Apart from Mahaffy, Oscar found no companionship among Trinity men. He continued, as at Portora, to stand aloof. It was as a superior onlooker that he uttered his opinion of his fellows. "They thought of nothing but running and jumping; and they varied these intellectual exercises with bouts of fighting and drinking. If they had any souls they diverted them with coarse amours and women of the streets. They were simply awful." There were no regrets on either side when Wilde left Trinity College to pursue his university career in England.

Oxford—sweet, gray city that nurtured him. There are no words of rhapsody that would be too strong to express what Oscar Wilde felt for Oxford. He caught every accent of the voices from the towers that "whisper the last enchantments of the Middle Ages." It was an Oxford that men of later generations were not privileged to know, the city before the vandals came, before Cowley was noisy with the din of the machine and the High was polluted by the dust and fumes of myriads of cars. Later he saw that there had been two turning points in his life and one of them was when his father sent him to Oxford.

There has been much delving into Wilde's Oxford days to discover the origins of his later aberrations. What need, what reason to put the blame on Oxford? If every Oxford man who

took a classical degree were infected and corrupted by reading
the Greek authors, then the Church, the law and other professions would be staffed by peculiar persons. Common observation attests the contrary. A man does not take to poetry
because he reads Shakespeare, though Shakespeare may make
a better poet of him. Not all the textbooks of Euclid would
have made a mathematician of Oscar Wilde, nor would all
the sonatas and symphonies of Beethoven have changed him
into a musician. He was as well acquainted as the next man
with the Restoration comedies that puritans have denounced
as iniquities, but Congreve and Wycherley did not make of
him a libertine. It takes more than a reading or misreading of
Plato to transmute the normal into the abnormal. Earnest and
diligent inquiry has failed to establish that Wilde while up at
Oxford evinced any abnormality more censurable than a liking
for blue china. And on going down he showed his good sense
by falling in love with beauty in an actress.

Wilde went up to Oxford in October 1874. He won a demy-
ship at Magdalen of the value of £95 a year. He repeated with
the same ease his previous successes, taking a first class in Mod-
erations in the Honors School in 1876 and a first in the Honors
Finals in 1878. He was given the best rooms in the college and
his paneled walls were decorated with nudes and blue china.

It is to be concluded that he lived the life of an average undergraduate with inclinations towards art rather than athletics.
At least, in after years, when men set their memories going
to recall him as an undergraduate, they were able to produce
little of note. He emerges from their recollections as the host
of the blue china rooms, with a circle of acquaintances who
shared his love for poetry and art. Nor did he disdain to interest himself in some forms of athletics. He did not hunt, but
he rode. He did not play cricket, but he was seen on the
cricket field. He did not undertake the labor of the oar, but

he was always in his place on the Magdalen barge to see, even
to cheer his college Eight. More to his taste were languorous,
sunkissed hours sprawled in a punt:

> Moor'd to the cool banks in the summer heats
> Mid wide grass meadows which the sunshine fills
> And watch the warm green-ruffled Cumnor hills.

It has been thought necessary to establish that he was not
effeminate and so there is Max Pemberton's often quoted account of the rout of the Philistines who came to raid the
blue china. One invader was kicked out, another pushed out,
a third thrown out and the fourth borne out—a baby vainly
struggling in the arms of the all-powerful Oscar. Strong men
are known to have their moments of weakness. There is no
need to deny Oscar a lapse into muscular aestheticism.

On occasions he was to be seen with road-makers toiling at
Hincksey as laborers never toiled, under the inspiration of
John Ruskin. He gained the special honor of filling the Professor's own wheelbarrow and of being shown by the Professor himself, how it should be trundled. The experience did
not make an honest working man of him nor, despite the presence of a professional stonebreaker, is he known to have become skilled in the craft. But there was a lesson to be drawn
from the presence of journalists and cartoonists whose attentions gave wide publicity to the proceedings and drew curious tourists to watch young England at labor on the Hincksey marshes. The road that was made was incredibly bad,
but the attendant publicity was altogether admirable.

Showmanship—that was Ruskin's gift to Wilde. In his apprentice years it was by the arts of showmanship that he sought
to foist himself on the world. Aesthete—the very title betrays
the origin and indicates Ruskin as the model. In 1874 during
Wilde's first term at Oxford, Ruskin was lecturing twice a

week. His subject was "Aesthetic and Mathematic Schools of Florence."

Ruskin was then at the height of a career that would serve as a glittering beacon to point the way for ambition. Only four years before, he had come up to Oxford to deliver his inaugural discourse as Slade Professor of Fine Arts. The company that gathered to hear him overflowed the ample limits of the lecture room at the Museum. With the Slade Professor at their head, all moved off to the ampler accommodation of the Sheldonian. Such scenes of enthusiasm were not customarily associated with university lectures. The Slade Professor lived up to the requirements of the occasion his reputation had created. A magnetic personality was revealed on the platform. His lecture, we are told, was a studied performance. Voice, gestures, even the clothes he wore contributed some distinctive detail to the final and impressive effect.

In the four years that had passed since then the lecturer had learned how to perfect the processes of his showmanship. Wilde was never to persuade the knowledgeable that his knowledge of art was more than superficial, but in showmanship he proved himself to have been a receptive pupil. Never, however, was he able to catch and echo the lofty moral strains that tinctured Ruskin's eloquence. Art without morality was as impossible to one as art with morality to the other.

Did Wilde ever detect any suspicion of a hint of Ruskin's strange reactions towards women, of the repulsion the Professor felt for the female form that anticipated the distaste to develop in Wilde? Ruskin during his Oxford visit made calls on his friend Dean Liddell, of Christ Church, and spent idle moments entertaining little Alice Liddell and her sisters, who looked forward to seeing him nearly as much as they did Dr. Dodgson with his tales of Wonderland. It was a coincidence that the University of Oxford at that time had within its venerable walls the three great abnormals of Victorian letters.

Following Ruskin's example Wilde made a pilgrimage of art in the vacation of 1875, visiting Milan, Padua, Venice and Verona. There are a few letters which he sent home to his parents recording his impressions of the masterpieces he saw. Already he foreshadowed the felicities of his mature charm as a writer, light, fanciful, witty. Frequently his letters ended on a financial note as did many another letter in later days. His companions were continuing their journey, but as he had no money left he was forced to leave them. He was hopeful that in Paris there would be a genial five pounds for him. So he returned to Oxford and to poetry.

It would be an exaggeration to say that Italy made a poet of him but his visit moved him enough to set him tuning the lyre. He recalled his approach to Italy in a sonnet:

> *I reached the Alps; the soul within me burned*
> *Italia, my Italia, at thy name,*
> *And when from out the mountain's heart I came*
> *And saw the land for which my life had yearned,*
> *I laughed as one who some great prize has earned.*

He remembered the sunsets, turquoise sky turning to gold. He remembered the pine trees that waved "as waves a woman's hair." In the November issue of the Dublin University Magazine in the year 1875 he made his bow as author with his "Chorus of Cloud Maidens," an adaptation from Aristophanes. Thereafter, during the remainder of his Oxford days, he was engaged as poet. Except for the "Ballad of Reading Gaol," his poetical works were written—begun if not completed— at Oxford or in the year after he went down. It was not a large output. Thereafter he expressed himself in prose.

Religious impulses began to stir in him. By the usual reckoning he was not a religious man; no more was Charles the Second. But these two worldly men, the jesting king and the jesting playwright, were attracted by the faith of Rome and both found a Catholic's consolation at the last. Wilde had been chilled by the austerities of Portora and Protestantism. He responded to the ritual in which the most pagan presentment of the Christian creed is backed by the appeal of scent, sound and color.

His intentions were halted by family opposition. There was an uncle who died leaving Willie Wilde one thousand pounds while Oscar was given a mere one hundred pounds, and that on condition he remained true to the Protestant faith of his fathers. The uncle had been a poor fellow, lamented Oscar, bigotedly intolerant of the Catholics. "Seeing me on the brink he struck me out of his will. Fancy a man going before God and the Eternal Silence with his wretched Protestant prejudices and bigotry still clinging to him."

It would be an exaggeration to ascribe to Wilde any of the torture of the hours of doubt that have beset men of deep religious faith. But, on the evidence of his poems, there were times when he was troubled and felt the need to be at one with God. He was disturbed by his continuing faithlessness:

> *well I know my soul in Hell must lie*
> *If I this night before God's throne should stand.*

He felt the longing for the vision that was denied him. Sir William Wilde had rejoiced when his son went to Oxford away from the corrupting influences of Catholic Ireland. But Oxford had faltered in Protestant orthodoxy. It was some years since Manning and Newman had gone over, but others followed them on the path to Rome. It seemed at one time that Wilde would join them. His friend in these days was David

Hunter Blair, heir to a baronetcy and to a fine place in Scotland, who was to surrender wealth and position to become a Benedictine monk and Abbot.

It was in Wilde's second term as a freshman that Hunter Blair was received into the Catholic Church and his friend was greatly impressed. Wilde confided his troubles, speaking of his leanings towards Catholicism and of his father's opposition. "I am sure," he said, "that if I had turned Catholic at the time my father would have cast me off and that he would do the same today. He rejoiced at my winning a scholarship to Oxford where I should not be exposed to pernicious influences, and now my best friend turns out to be a Papist."

Wilde began to accompany his friend to various Catholic gatherings. They went together to hear Manning, raised that year to the purple, preach at St. Aloysius's. The outward and visible sign of what Roman Catholicism could make of a man must have impressed a mind that responded to personal example rather than to general principles. Wilde a Cardinal— he would have found his place amongst the great figures of Rome of the Renaissance. Religious pictures and other aspects of devotion began to adorn his rooms. There was a picture of Manning himself. His friends began to jest over his intentions and his ambitions. "While your eminence is preparing to fit the red hat on your sacred head" one correspondent teased him.

Wilde unburdened himself to a priest, who urged him to become a convert. "In the meantime," was the shrewd advice, "pray hard and talk little." Another priest was not so sure about the sincerity of his intentions. "At present he is in earnest about nothing except his quite laudable ambition to succeed in the Schools and even that he keeps in the background. The finger of God has not yet touched him."

Hunter Blair arranged to devote the Easter vacation to a pilgrimage to Rome. Would not Oscar join him? It was not possible, Wilde explained with regret, he was absolutely and irretrievably broke. That was not necessarily a bar.

"I am going to stay with my people at Mentone," said Blair, "on my way to Italy and I will stake a couple of pounds for you at Monte Carlo. If it is predestined that you are to go to Rome I shall certainly win the money."

The gods of chance smiled on the words of faith. The £2 became £60. Wilde joined the party at Genoa and traveled with them to Rome. He set out with the expectation of a crisis in his life, hoping for a new vision such as had been seen on the road to Damascus. It eluded him. The predestination of Monte Carlo remained incomplete. It was the Rome of history, with its monuments of antiquity, rather than the Rome of Christian and Catholic, that claimed Wilde's attention.

Hunter Blair was able to secure an audience with the Holy Father. The circumstances of the reception by Pio Nono were vividly impressed on Hunter Blair's mind. "I am sure," he wrote years afterwards, "that my companion remembered to his dying day the words of the venerable father as he placed hands of benediction on his head and expressed the hope that he would soon follow his condiscipulus into the City of God. Wilde spoke no word as we drove back to our hotel in our open carriage. Arrived there he locked himself in his room. When we met later he presented me with the MS. of a poem which he had written with the impression of the visit to the Vatican still fresh in his soul:

> *Oh! joy to see before I die*
> *The only God-anointed King.*

"That April day was, I think, the high water mark of Oscar Wilde's rapprochement to the Catholic Church."

While in Rome Wilde made a pilgrimage to the Protestant cemetery to kneel in homage beside the grave of Keats. He thought of the boy-poet and saw a vision of the boy-martyr as he sang:

> *Rid of the world's injustice and his pain*
> *He rests at last beneath God's veil of blue,*
> *Taken from life when life and love were new,*
> *The youngest of the martyrs here is lain*
> *Fair as Sebastian and as early slain.*

Others could say with him that Keats was the poet of the "sweetest lips since those of Mitylene." But who but Wilde would have confused the boy-poet with the boy-martyr of the arrows? The prose note to the sonnet explains the inspiration of the thought:

"As I stood beside the mean grave of this divine boy I thought of him as a Priest of Beauty slain before his time; and the vision of Guido's San Sebastian came before my eyes as I saw him at Genoa, a lovely brown boy, with crisp clustering hair and red lips bound by his evil enemies to a tree, and, though pierced by arrows, raising his eyes with divine, impassioned gaze towards the eternal beauty of the opening heavens."

Sebastian the Martyr—the image was vivid in his mind and so remained. In later years in his prison cell there were arrows to mark his convict dress and it was as Sebastian, Sebastian Melmoth, that he came back into the world.

While Hunter Blair's finger pointed the way to the Ark of St. Peter, Mahaffy, pagan Mahaffy, beckoned him to the shores of Greece. "Stop this nonsense," Mahaffy wrote. "Come away with me to Greece and I will make an honest pagan of you."

They sailed across the sapphire-colored sea and came to the land whose very names make music. From the prow Wilde

marked Zacynthos, Ithaca's cliff, Lycaon's snowy peak, the
flower-strewn hills of Arcady. And then

When 'gan the west to burn
And a red sun upon the seas to ride
I stood upon the soil of Greece at last.

No diary records the impressions of his explorations in
Athens and his travelings through this classic land with Mahaffy
at his side to bring back the past to life, Mahaffy, the man for
whom "all culture culminated in Greece, all Greece in Athens,
all Athens in its Acropolis and all the Acropolis in the Parthenon." The storied past came back to life and pagan gods peo-
pled the Pantheon. The vision of Rome faded. When next
they met at Oxford Hunter Blair found that Wilde had
changed, had become Hellenized, somewhat paganized perhaps by the appeal of Greece to his sensitive nature. Wilde was
always dominated by the last vigorous personality that he con-
tacted.

Walter Pater was the other and more abiding influence of his
Oxford days. A few years later the freshness had faded from
Pater's prose and Max Beerbohm was pained to boredom by
"the sedulous ritual wherewith he had cut every sentence like
a shroud." But in the Seventies they saw the apostle of a new
gospel of beauty in this unimpressive don, a small, rock-faced
man, with his top hat and gloves of bright dog-skin that Max
found to be so discordant. Pater preached art for art's sake
and the duty to embrace what experience offered in new sensations, and pulsating exquisite moments. He lived dismally in
rooms of monkish austerity, lamenting his own lack of looks.

"I would give ten years of my life to be handsome," he
said. When the offered bargain was not accepted he grew a
moustache that gave him a false-military air. His appearance

was not such as to rouse Wilde's admiration, but though the preacher was unattractive his creed offered everything required by a young man in search of a cause to serve. In his later Paris days Wilde could drink the waters from the original springs. But had he never read Baudelaire or Gautier, the secondhand version of Pater would have sufficed him.

Art for art's sake, that was better than Ruskin, who could not dissociate art from morality. Art the supreme business of life—it followed that the artist was the supreme exponent of living. Ruskin's heroes were the Old Masters. There was a greater than these—the master of imaginative criticism of whom Ruskin was the living example. The highest creative role to which man could aspire was the artist, and the greatest of these was the imaginative critic. It was a pass of admittance for Wilde to the highest rank of the hierarchy. To this Pater added the siren inducements of the new gospel of living:

To burn always with a hard gemlike flame, to maintain this ecstasy is success in life. . . . While all melts under our feet we may well catch at any exquisite passion, or any contribution to knowledge that seems by a lifted horizon to set the spirit free for a moment, or any stirring of the senses, strange dyes, strange colours and curious odours, or the work of the artist's hands, or the face of one's friend. . . . With this sense of the splendour of our experience and of its awful brevity, gathering all we are into one desperate effort to see and touch, we shall hardly have time to make theories about the things we see and touch. What we have to do is to be for ever curiously testing new opinions and courting new impressions.

Pater was content in his monkish rooms to realize in thought the ecstasies and pulsating moments of his prose. For Wilde there would be no such detached and distant way with sensation. Before he had taken his degree he had made known his intention to a friend. He wanted to eat of the fruit of all the trees in the garden of the world. He was going out into the world with that passion in his soul. By then he had traveled far along another path since he had journeyed with Hunter Blair to Rome. Mahaffy and Walter Pater had made of him a pagan and a sensualist.

Oxford ended in triumph. The Newdigate prize, since it was founded by the 18th-century antiquarian whose name it bears, has been the occasion for the outpouring of some reams of undergraduate verse and one immortal line—"Rose-red city half as old as Time." The poem that Wilde submitted is claimed to have been rather above the average in its merit, but then he was placed above the average at the start by the advantage of personal acquaintance with the subject set by the examiners. Ravenna was the appointed theme and Ravenna, city of the Caesars, Dante's last resting-place, had been visited by Wilde during his travels in Italy. He sang:

> *O lone Ravenna! many a tale is told*
> *Of thy great glories in the days of old;*
> *Two thousand years have passed since thou did'st see*
> *Caesar ride forth to royal victory.*
> *Mighty thy name when Rome's lean eagles flew*
> *From Britain's isles to far Euphrates blue;*
> *And of the peoples thou wast noble queen*
> *Till in thy streets the Goth and Hun were seen.*

Later the poet was able to introduce a personal note in lines recording how he himself had ridden through Ravenna's olive groves and noble forest pines.

> *On and on*
> *I galloped, racing with the setting sun,*
> *And ere the after glow was passed*
> *I stood within Ravenna's walls at last.*

The sceptic who knew him well protested at this. "You went there lounging in the comfort of a stuffy railway carriage. You know you never mounted a horse in your life. You would have tumbled off at once if you had." The judges accepted the personal touch.

Sherard, whose admiration for Wilde did not stop this side idolatry, considered the poem to be a very fine piece of work, with many beautiful lines. A sterner critic dismissed it as a "rhymed dictionary of mythology." It is not of much consequence now. It served Wilde well enough. It won him the Newdigate. Together with his success in the Schools it secured for him remission of the £45 fine that the dons had imposed on him for having overstayed his vacation during his last wanderings in the South.

"Ravenna" is not memorable as poetry, but its delivery before the assembled members of the university was an occasion. The winner of the Newdigate is required to recite his verses before the assembled university in the Sheldonian Theatre. For a diffident, shrinking poet the occasion is an ordeal. It was not so for Wilde. He faced his audience with assurance and delivered his verses in a manner that, we are told, won rapt attention and frequent applause. The rhetoric and diction of the piece were admirable material for declamation. "Ravenna" seemed a poem of rare quality to those who heard the author deliver the lines in the most melodious of tenor voices, that June day. It was a fine curtain on the opening act.

4. THE NATURE OF A POET

A great poet, a really great poet, is the most impoetical of all creatures. But inferior poets are absolutely fascinating.

FOR the celebrity he destined himself to be Oscar Wilde was incredibly careless about the records of his earlier days. He looked on youth as the pinnacle time of life, mourned in later years the youth that had deserted him. Yet he neglected to provide memorials to his cherished past. For a man so conscious of his own personality, he was curiously lacking in an autobiographical sense. Some history about himself he gave in his "De Profundis" prison letter, but these were merely sidelights of autobiography.

The prison cell was not his first confessional. In the poems he wrote in his later years at Oxford and when he first entered upon the wider world, he disclosed the workings of his mind. The verses betray the strange nature of the poet.

The poems have been frequently examined. No writer on Wilde with pretensions to be a critic has failed to mark the deficiencies of his meter and to trace his indebtedness to other (always better) poets. Wilde's work, if the critic is favorably inclined, is allowed to be derivative, rich in imitations; if the critic is hostile, it is replete with plagiarism. The sources are set out—among them Milton, Keats, Browning, Swinburne, Arnold, Marlowe and Rossetti. The technical criticism of the poems is complete, but the critics have not passed beyond the technical to speculate very deeply on the nature of the man who wrote. There is need for no deep penetration to discern that the mind at work was not that of the normal young songster hymning love and beauty. There are hints of strange impulses, promptings of mysterious desires.

The earlier pieces inspired by visits to Rome and Greece tell of his conflict over religion. Then the temper of the verse changes. There are outpourings of eroticism that end in the tainted images of "The Sphinx" and "foul dreams of sensual life." Sensual, always this poet's verse is sensual. Even in moments of religious longing the sensual note is there. It is the appeal to the senses, the pageantry of color, the symphony of sound, the ecstasy of the realization of sacrifice that moved his religious instincts.

Wilde manipulated words, as a musician uses notes, to produce euphony in sound and color. It was not the sound echoing the sense. The sound not the sense was dominant in this purple rhetoric in meter. You can feel him lingering in ecstasy of delight over the phrases—sleepless souls and anodyne, poppy drowsy, amber asphodel, ivory-horned Tregelaphos. No painter splashed color upon his canvas with the abandon of this poet in his verse. I chose one piece at random and found:

SILVER jar.
WHITE lilies.
GOLD bees.
YELLOW lotus.
PURPLE lidded sleep.
GOLDEN vestured sun.
CRIMSON haze.
WHITE feet.
SAFFRON dust.
BLUE Ionian air.
WHITE feathered snow.

RED toothed lightning.
VIOLET hidden waters.
CRIMSON sun.
BROWN fields.
RED spear.
YELLOW buttercups.
CRIMSON stained mouth.
WHITE narcissus.
YELLOW eyed lions.
SILVER gossamer.
CRIMSON lamps.

A kaleidoscope of shimmering color. The sweetness of the sound completes the cloying, sensuousness of the verse—the sibilant "s," the murmur of the "m," the lingering languorous "l." The poet put his thoughts to sleep in beds of honeyed words. Amidst the caressing sensuousness of sound one is startled now and again by a more sinister note. The spectacle of lily-white flesh on which the poet lingers is disturbed by the image of the arrow—lily-white flesh, the piercing arrow, the crimson splash of blood. In the poems of his early years there are touches foreshadowing the mood that produced the bloody images of "Salomé."

There are, curiously enough, few signs of boy-love in the verses, not more than can be found in, say, D. H. Lawrence, less than in Tennyson or Shakespeare. There is the shepherd boy of "Endymion."

> *You cannot choose but know my love*
> *For he a shepherd's crook doth bear,*
> *And he is soft as any dove*
> *And brown and curly is his hair.*

There is also the sonnet that on its original publication began "A fair slim boy not made for this world's pain." Later the lines were made to change their sex when the author had hurried need for a sonnet of homage to his lily girl, but this belongs to the record of his courting days.

There was a time when the poet's rooms above the Cherwell were decorated with nudes and the fascinations of the female form were amply displayed upon the walls. He experienced the normal impulses of young manhood. Following the fashion of his fellows he experimented and was dismayed. He turned away with some sense of shame. In future he would not "mesh his soul within a woman's hair." Let his companions mock him, they were mere slanderous fools. Better to stand aloof than to

> *go back to that hoarse cave of strife*
> *Where my white soul first kissed the mouth of sin.*

The poems tell of the strife of the succeeding phase. There were the stirrings of his religious sense, times when he yearned for the consolation of conversion and sought in vain for any place of rest. There were the splendid moments at Rome when the silver trumpets rang out and he saw, borne upon the necks of men, the Holy Lord of Rome. Then Mahaffy and Greece and pagan days. There was the clash when he returned in Holy Week to Genoa:

> *The young boy-priest passed singing clear*
> *"Jesus the Son of Mary has been slain,*
> *O come and fill his sepulchre with flowers."*
> *Ah God! Ah God! those dear Hellenic hours*
> *Had drowned all memory of Thy bitter pain*
> *The Cross, the Crown, the soldiers and the spear.*

Back at Oxford he sought to preserve the afterglow of Rome against pagan Helas. A little while he strove, and then the tide of doubt came flooding in. In "Santa Decca" he has almost reached capitulation. He begins with the declaration "The Gods are dead,"—

> *All the wantoning*
> *By secret glade and devious haunt is o'er:*
> *Young Hylas seeks the watersprings no more;*
> *Great Pan is dead, and Mary's son is King.*

And yet—the faint voice of doubt obtrudes itself—he was not so certain after all. Perchance in this sea-tranced isle, some God might yet be hidden in the asphodel.

As he wandered on solitary walks, he found himself looking for some stirrings in the leaves. He would strain his ears to catch in Nuneham meadows the tread of some long-hidden God. He listened for the sound of Atalanta's horn blowing across the Cumnor hills. Proserpine, forgetful it was not Sicily, might perhaps be leaning across mossy Sandford stile.

Within a year his capitulation was complete and he was pronouncing, quaintly, that the English Thames is "holier far than Rome." The English poppies were twice as fine as the sight of some crimson Cardinal. By now Fra Giovanni, "bawling at the Mass," was out of tune as he listened to the singing of the lark overhead. Sing louder, he called, to the singing bird so that his memories might be drowned in song:

> *Why must I still behold*
> *The wan white face of that deserted Christ*
> *Whose bleeding hands my hands did once enfold,*
> *Whose smitten lips my lips so often kissed,*
> *And now in mute and marble misery*
> *Sits in his lone dishonoured House and weeps,*
> *perchance for me?*

The vision of Rome had faded. His verses tell of other preoccupations now. He passes from religious doubtings to write of the burden of profane love.

There is an intensity about the feelings of the poet of these later verses, an urgency about the reckless questing of which Eros was the inspiration. He wanders in the garden where every flower is amorous—"to me flowers are part of desire." The very earth itself has passions hymeneal. He conceives himself with all lovers to be a part of "sensuous life." The fields men till will be "more fruitful for our love tonight." The hot hard flame "with which our bodies burn will make some meadows blaze with daffodil." He is too young to live without desire; to feel is better than to know, one pulsed passion is worth all the proverbs of the sage. He calls out to his unknown:

> *Vex not thy soul with dead philosophy.*
> *Have we not lips to kiss with, hearts to love*
> *and eyes to see?*

Was she, this sweet unknown, a creature of reality or the phantom of his dream? At times his mistress was no more than the spirit of beauty. But was this all, was there no beauty of flesh and blood? Surely there was something more tangible than a spirit however beautiful. There was a moment when they took their hearts' "full pleasure." It was surely the voice of experience that told of the lover rising and lingering over his last kiss—

> *They who have never seen the daylight peer*
> *Into a darkened room, and drawn the curtain*
> *And with dull eyes and wearied from some dear*
> *And worshipped body risen, they for certain*
> *Will never know of what I try to sing'*
> *How long the last kiss was, how fond and late his*
> *lingering.*

The joy of passion, that "dread which not to know is not to live at all"—it was a joy spoken of from experience. But experience did not consume all the impulses of his imagining. So when he went wandering in the Oxford woods, he was possessed by longings, being "drunk with the trampled vintage of my youth." Visions came to him of the loves and passions of the gods and goddesses of old. "Wooing that drifting imagery which is no sooner kissed than broken," he had thoughts of Salmacis

> *Who is not boy nor girl and yet is both*
> *Fed by two fires and unsatisfied*

Through their excess, each passion being loth
For love's own sake to leave the other's side,
Yet killing love by staying. . . .

His thoughts were over-peopled with famous lovers of the
past. He pictured nights of passion for himself:

O for one midnight and as paramour
The Venus of the little Melian farm.

Then his imaginings presented him with the strange conception of a marbled paramour, the warmth of passion kindled
from some cold block of statuary. Did stifled longings often
give birth to imaginings like these?

O that some antique statue for one hour
Might wake to passion and that I could charm
The Dawn at Florence from its dumb despair,
Mix with those mighty limbs and make that
giant breast my lair.

A faint shout from a boat at Sandford lock brought him
back from his dreams. Across the flats he saw Magdalen's
tower tipped with the tremulous gold of sunset and the sound
of the curfew came booming from the bell at Christ Church
gate, recalling him from his wanderings. But the thought of
that imagined tryst with marble come to life did not leave
him. In "Charmides" he told of the Grecian lad whom he
created to realize the strange dreams he had been dreaming.

The setting of this experiment in eroticism was simply contrived. A young Greek boy concealed himself in the temple
at Corinth and by the departing priest was locked in for the
night. When the marble floor was lighted by the moon he
came from his hiding place and stood fearfully before the
goddess ready for death if he had to die for his impiety—

well content at such a price to see
That calm wide brow, that terrible maidenhood,
The marvel of that pitiless chastity.

His fears passed. Growing bolder he threw off his cloak, approached, touched the throat and with hands violate—

Undid the cuirass and the crocus gown
And bared the breasts of polished ivory
Till from the waist the peplos falling down
Left visible the secret mystery
Which to no lover will Athena show,
The grand cool flanks, the crescent thighs, the bossy
hills of snow.

.   .   .   .   .

A little space he let his greedy eyes
Rest on the burnished image, till mere sight
Half swooned for surfeit of such luxuries,
And then his lips in hungered delight
Fell on her lips, and round the towered neck
He flung his arms, nor cared at all his passion's will to
check.

.   .   .   .   .

Never I ween did lover hold such tryst
For all night long he murmured honeyed word'
And saw her sweet unravished limbs, and kissed
Her pale and argent body undisturbed,
And paddled with the polished throat, and pressed
His hot and beating heart upon her chill and icy breast.

.   .   .   .   .

It was as if Numidian javelins
Pierced through and through his wild and whirling brain,
And his nerves thrilled like throbbing violins

In exquisite pulsation, and the pain
  Was such sweet anguish that he never drew
His lips from hers till overhead the lark of warning flew.

There realized in the verses of "Charmides" was the night of marbled passion with which his longings had tantalized him when writing "The Burden of Itys." The poet went on to tell how the Grecian lad thereafter cared for nothing in life since he had seen the "breasts of Pallas and the naked wonder of the Queen."

So when next his galley sailed he leaped from the lofty poop into the sea with the cry "I come." His drowned body was by some Triton-god borne back to Greece. Made beautiful by the attention of the mermaids, it was placed upon the shore. A girl, mistaking this for the form of some sleeping sea-god, lay beside him, "thirsty with love's drought," only to experience the tantalizings Shakespeare, in greater verses, described in his "Venus and Adonis." The Dryad maid, languishing beside the unresponsive body of the youth, was slain by the arrow of some jealous god. Like a flame a barbed reed flew whizzing down the glade.

  And when the little flowers of her breast
Just brake into their milky blossoming,
  This murderous paramour, this unbidden guest,
Pierced and struck deep in horrid chambering,
  And ploughed a bloody furrow with its dart,
And dug a long red road, and cleft with wingèd death her
    heart.

Sobbing her life out with a bitter cry
  On the boy's body fell the Dryad maid,
Sobbing for incomplete virginity,
  And raptures unenjoyed, and pleasures dead,

And all the pain of things unsatisfied,
*   And the bright drops of crimson youth crept down her*
*   Throbbing side.*

.   .   .   .   .

Even with this the poet's imaginings were not ended. By
the intervention of Venus, Desire is allowed to cross the icy
ford of Charon. Charmides and the Dryad maid have their
moment of fulfilment in melancholy Acheron.

The loves of stony marble, the arrow emptying the blood
of pierced beauty, passion in the melancholy country of the
dead, these are not the imaginings of normal-minded, youthful poets. The tainted vision persisted and in "The Sphinx,"
finest wrought of this Wilde's verses, there was a new conception of fantastic couplings inspired by some songless, "tongue-
less ghost of sin." Conceived in his Oxford days ("some twenty
summers" is the tally for his age) but not completed until
some years later (probably 1883) this piece, an erotic apos-
trophe, is delivered in lines charged with sensual abandon-
ment.

Again the theme is simply presented. In a dim corner of his
room his fancy places a beautiful silent Sphinx, somnolent,
statuesque, half-woman, half-animal. He invites her, fantastic
Sphinx, to sing of all her memories. Who, he asks, were her
lovers—"Which was the vessel of your lust, what Leman
had you, every day?"

Did giant Lizards come and crouch before you on the reedy
*   banks?*
*   Did Gryphons with great metal flanks leap on you in*
*   your trampled couch?*

Or had you shameful secret quests and did you harry to
*   your home*

Some Nereid coiled in amber foam with curious rock
*   crystal breasts?*

Had she climbed to meet the swarthy Ethiop whose body
was of polished jet, or had she gone climbing into the vault
and made the Pyramid her lupanar? Perhaps she had loved the
God of flies, or Pasht. Or had great Ammon been her bedfellow, her chamber the steaming Nile where she watched
his passion come and go? The language becomes more exotic
as the verse proceeds.

On pearl and porphyry pedestalled he was too bright to
*   look upon;*
*   For on his ivory breast there shone the wondrous*
*   ocean-emerald.*

Ammon's monument was broken into pieces, the God scattered here and there. The Sphinx should seek his fragments—

Go, seek them where they lie alone and from their broken
*   pieces make*
*   Thy bruisèd bedfellow! And wake mad passions in the*
*   senseless stone.*

She should charm his dull ear with Syrian hymns, weave purple for his shrunken hips, and purple for his barren loins. Or,
there were other lovers if she was grown sick of dead divini-
ties. Let her go across the plain, follow some spoor, seize by
the mane a lion and bid him be her paramour.

Couch by his side upon the grass and set your white
*   teeth in his throat*
And when you hear his dying note lash your long flanks
*   of polished brass,*

*And take a tiger for your mate, whose amber sides are
    flecked with black,
And ride upon his gilded back in triumph through the
    Theban gate.*

*And toy with him in amorous jests, and when he turns
    and snarls and gnaws,
O smite him with your jasper claws! and bruise him with
    your agate breasts!*

A revulsion seizes the poet brought on by his own imaginings and the poisonous melodies to which he has been inspired. He bids the Sphinx "Away!" Why had the ghost of
sin crept through his curtains? And he asks:

*Are there not others more accursed, whiter with leprosies
    than I?
Are Abana and Pharpar dry that you come here to slake
    your thirst?*

*Get hence, you loathsome mystery! Hideous animal, get
    hence!
You wake in me each bestial sense, you make me what
    I would not be*

*You make my creed a barren sham, you wake foul dreams
    of sensual life. . . .*

The critic points out that this poem is in the meter of Tennyson's "In Memoriam." He finds it saturated with classic lore.
It is, surely, saturated with more than that. The man who wrote
these poems as his early contributions to literature was carrying into life a burden of strange promptings, mysterious,
tainted desires.

These poems, so revealing of the nature of their author,

have a parallel in Swinburne's earlier work. The verses of the two poets disclose a kinship in eroticism. To what extent Wilde was influenced by the older man it is not possible to say. He was still a schoolboy when the publication of "Atalanta" and "Poems & Ballads" opened the fleshly school of poetry. Victorian susceptibilities, so tender that even Tennyson could disturb them, were outraged by Swinburne's verses, in which sex and sadism, the "latent relations of pain and pleasure," were not disguised. The protests over the "uncleanness" and "carnality" of these poems were not soon forgotten.

Swinburne, who had left Oxford under a cloud, without taking a degree, was, in Wilde's day, an occasional visitor to the university. Sometimes his flowing head of hair was to be seen at the side of Walter Pater. Sometimes his shrill voice, rising as harsh as a peacock's scream, was to be heard issuing from Jowett's rooms. Swinburne was an obvious model for an Oxford poet in the seventies. In his poetry, as in Wilde's, strange tendencies were disclosed. Lives such as those, cast in no common mold, would clearly impose stresses and strains that do not burden the man of easy normality. Swinburne in his later years was to be shepherded into respectability. In his exile there was to be no such assistance for Oscar Wilde.

5. ADVENTURES OF
AN AESTHETE

*There is only one thing in the world worse than being
talked about, and that is not being talked about.*

For ten years after going down from Oxford
Oscar Wilde was variously engaged in try-
ing to find his proper place in the world. He set himself up as
Professor of Aesthetics; made tours as a lecturer in the aesthete
in America and England; was a man of fashion in London and
a man of letters in Paris; published his volume of poems, elegant
and slim; tried his apprentice hand at a couple of plays that were
of no particular merit; courted one woman romantically rather
than with serious intentions; finally married another, and set up
home with every prospect of domestic bliss.

The self-appointed professorship in aesthetics was a position
of small dignity but rather limited in profit. In these times big
business knows how to make use of young university men with
charm of manner and established social position, for whom
there are many openings. These were not available to Mr.
Wilde, setting out to make his name in the world, a young man
very much in a hurry. Disdaining the toil and tedium of slow
endeavor he made a grab for fame. Noise without achievement
produced notoriety. It was better than neglect.

At Oxford he had experimented in dressing up. His Prince
Rupert at Mrs. Morrell's ball had been acclaimed. It had given
him ideas. Now he presented himself to the public as the young
eccentric, with the long locks of the poet and the costume of

the aesthete. The costume attracted notice. People began to talk, as they were intended to do, of the strange sight to be seen in Piccadilly, the young man in a velvet coat, knee breeches, loose shirt with turned-down collar, flaunting a tie of an unusual shade. The picture was completed with the famous lily, or sunflower, contemplated with a rapt expression of intense admiration. Something better (or worse) than this would be needed today to startle the Piccadilly gossips or attract the peripatetic photographer. In Queen Victoria's time it sufficed. The eccentric was gratefully accepted by the writers for the comic papers.

Wilde became a subject for the satirist within a few months of his descent upon London and continued to be a target for the next fifteen years. "Punch" introduced his poems as "Swinburne and water"—"The cover is consummate, the paper is distinctly precious, the binding beautiful, and the type is utterly too." Nevertheless the verses, aesthetically offered in white vellum and gold, found favor with the public. The publisher, David Bogue, financed by the author, issued a first printing of 250 copies, artistically printed on Dutch hand-made paper, handsomely bound in parchment. The first edition sold out and so did its successor. Author and publisher were gratified to find that public demand required four printings in four weeks. "Punch" could lampoon the author,

> *Aesthete of aesthetes*
> *What's in a name?*
> *The poet is Wilde*
> *But his poetry's tame.*

The author was gratified with the solid satisfaction of copies sold. And, anyway, his poetry was scarcely as tepid as poor Mr. Punch's puns.

The literary investigators have probed into Wilde's aesthetic origins. The roots are traced back to the Pre-Raphaelites and John Ruskin, the French Impressionists and Walter Pater, with some shoots linking with Morris and Burne-Jones. Aesthetically the results of the inquiry are satisfying, but they are not very rewarding so far as concerns Oscar Wilde. His aestheticism did not go much more than costume deep. It was enough. He qualified for admission to Mr. Gilbert's gallery of oddities.

Walter Pater had originally been chosen as the original for Aesthete-in-Chief in the Gilbert and Sullivan opera "Patience." Mr. Pater's aesthetic pretensions were faraway more considerable than Mr. Wilde's, but as a personality he was outclassed. The rather dreary, rather commonplace, rather insignificant don could not hold a sunflower to the flamboyant Wilde. So Bunthorne took the stage, to personify Wilde as the ultra-poetical, superaesthetical, and to sing

If you're anxious for to shine in the high aesthetic line
as a man of culture rare,
You must get up all the germs of the transcendental terms,
and plant them everywhere.
You must lie upon the daisies, and discourse in novel phrases
of your complicated state of mind,
The meaning doesn't matter if it's only idle chatter of a tran-
scendental kind.

In his first period in London Wilde lived away from the center of fashion in furnished rooms in Salisbury Street off the Strand. He had a limited income, and no immediate prospects. He had the entrée to London society but not the means to support himself as a man of fashion. From his acquaintances at Magdalen he had the introduction to the right people. He was on terms of intimacy with the Duke of Newcastle. His friend Hunter Blair was considered to be a "sufficient passport to what

the French used to call Le High Life." He was helped by some
of the great ladies of London, notably the beautiful Constance,
Duchess of Westminster, sister of another friend, Ronald
Sutherland-Gower. But there were no funds to support the
role of man of fashion.

Under the pressure of financial need and ambition he set to
work on a play. Not even the most fervent Wilde enthusiast
ranks "Vera" among his masterpieces. This four-act melodrama
was set in Russia. The best thing about it was the description
he wrote to introduce the piece to Marie Prescott, the talented
American actress.

"I have tried to express within the limits of art the Titan cry
of the peoples for liberty which in Europe today is threatening
thrones and making governments unstable from Spain to Russia
and from north to southern seas. But it is a play not of politics
but of passion. It deals with no theories of government but with
men and women simply; the modern Nihilistic Russia, with all
the terror of its tyranny and the marvel of its martyrdoms, is
merely the fiery and fervent background in front of which the
persons of my dream live and love. With this feeling was the
play written and with this aim should the play be acted."

Bernard Shaw as an experienced and accomplished dramatist
was able to set his plays in countries and centuries about which
his knowledge was limited. It was beyond the capacity of the
apprentice pen of Oscar Wilde. "Vera" as a drama failed to be
dramatic. Its Russian background is shown to be riddled with
absurdities. The lowliest Oxonian would have been better
informed than to have had trains running in the year of grace
1800 in Russia, or anywhere else in the wide world. "Vera"
narrowly escaped production at the Adelphi Theater, but the
performance was canceled at the last moment. Mr. Punch
chronicled the cancellation in his insufferable puns:

The production of Mr. Oscar Wilde's play Vera is deferred. Naturally no one would expect a veerer to be at all certain; it must be like a pretendedly infallible forecast, so weather-cocky. Vera is about Nihilism; this looks as if there were nothing in it.

There was more of this, but for the sake of Mr. Punch's reputation, I forbear to quote further. Wilde's first essay in playwriting had not advanced his fame nor relieved his needs. At the moment of disappointment, aestheticism and Mr. Gilbert gave him his opportunity. He embarked on Christmas Eve of the year 1881 for New York to undertake a lecture tour in America. Before following him across the Atlantic in the "Arizona," his aesthetic adventure in pursuit of beauty in the person of the ravishing Miss Lily Langtry must first be related.

Oscar Wilde marked the spring of his first year in London by falling romantically in love with Lily Langtry. It was a summer idyll.

Lily Langtry—even after the passage of a lifetime of years the name still stands for beauty. The queens of the cinema come and go, have their little day and fade away. Her fame lingers on, the beauty who charmed a prince. As she passed they stood on chairs in the Row to glimpse her in her loveliness. It was to her that Oscar offered his homage and his verses.

Today young men dream dreams of pin-up girls. In Victoria's reign they offered their homage to the Professional Beauties. Of their status Max, the incomparable, wrote "what the term 'professional beauty' signified, how any lady gained a right to it we do not and may never know. It is certain that there were many ladies of tone upon whom it was bestowed. They received special attention from the Prince of Wales, and hostesses would move heaven and earth to have them in their rooms. Their photographs were on sale in the window of every shop. Crowds assembled every morning to see them start for Rotten Row."

Of these illustrious fair, Max cites four examples—Lady Lonsdale (afterwards Lady de Grey), Mrs. Wheeler "who always appeared in black," Mrs. Cornwallis West, and Mrs. Langtry "cétté Cléopâtre de son siècle."

Emilie Charlotte were her names, daughter of Le Breton, Dean of Jersey. As a girl she was married to Mr. Langtry, an elderly widower from Belfast. Her beauty was not fated to be lost in the apartments of Mr. Langtry's home and soon London began to talk of her ravishing loveliness. The drawings of Frank Miles made her the beauty of the hour. It was at his studio they first met—the beauty and the wit. Oscar was moved to immediate adoration. She was more beautiful even than Venus de Milo. He must salute her. He could not wait for tardy inspiration to produce his poem. Already on his tablets there was a verse of greeting to a "fair slim boy." A deft alteration and it would suit the new occasion, and so he made his first offering to her, "Madonna Mia":

> *A lily girl, not made for this world's pain,*
> *With brown, soft hair close braided by her ears,*
> *And longing eyes half-veiled by slumberous tears.*

She might be Langtry's wife, but he saw pale cheeks where love had left no stain, red underlip, drawn in indeed, for fear of love. He worshiped his Madonna with becoming reverence.

> *Even to kiss her feet I am not bold,*
> *Being o'er shadowed by the wings of awe,*
> *Like Dante, when he stood with Beatrice.*

They went about together, through the summer months of that year of 1879. He was fresh from his triumphs at Oxford. She heard of them from others, and the winning of the Newdigate, and was the more impressed because he had not vaunted of these things himself. She pronounced him modest and ingenuous. She overlooked the mannerisms and eccentricities in the young fellow bubbling over with temperament and enthusiasms. How easy to pardon him when his greatest enthusiasm was for her. He hymned her in "The New Helen."

> *Lily of love, pure and inviolate!*
> *Tower of ivory! Red rose of fire!*
> *Thou hast come down our darkness to illume.*

He hymned her with becoming diffidence as one so bowed and broken on love's troubled wheel that he had lost all hope. Through six stanzas he questioned her about her past to discover where she had been lingering since the sons of gods fought for her around the walls of Troy. He had the heart to sing but not the hope of love, for he knew she would not tarry, but would leave him to a loveless life. He bade her extend her stay:

> *Oh Helen! Helen! Helen! yet a while,*
> *Yet for a little while, O, tarry here*
> *Till the dawn cometh and the shadows flee!*
> *For in the gladsome sunlight of thy smile*
> *Of heaven or hell I have no thought or fear,*
> *Seeing I know no other God but thee.*

Any woman might tarry for a space to listen to such an invocation delivered in one of the most alluring voices she had ever heard, and one that hymned the white glory of her loveliness. She had marked him walking around the streets outside her home for hours at a time composing a declaration of his love. She would tell, in after years, how, exhausted, he curled himself up to sleep on her doorstep so that Mr. Langtry returning home unusually late put an end to the poet's dreams by tripping over him. Her husband—much given, it seems, to fishing —was not concerned about Mrs. Langtry's aesthetic lover, so she tarried with him through the months of that summer season.

You can glimpse them from her reminiscences and his verses going about decorously together. One day he brought Ruskin to meet her, showing such humility in the presence of the master critic, that she scarcely dared to lift her eyes to look at him. He escorted her to the British Museum to hear lectures on Greek art, so improving to her mind, and her presence so disturbing to the minds of the students, who gathered at the door to receive her with cheers. Together, she and Oscar pored over the collection of coins and pottery of antiquity searching, she says, to match the likeness of Sarah Bernhardt's symmetrically Latin features. Her memory perhaps played her false and the search was for old likenesses on vase or intaglia, of the New Helen whom men called, after Millais who painted her, the Jersey Lily.

Posies as well as poems gave expression to his adoration. Inspiration could not provide a poem for each meeting, but Covent Garden could always offer a flower. Lacking the means for more magnificent bouquets, he would buy a single gorgeous amaryllis and stroll down Piccadilly bearing the solitary bloom before him. To the public gaze it was the aesthetic posturing and so it was she, as she claims, who innocently conferred on him the title of "Apostle of the Lily."

There were moments of closer intimacy than these public occasions, moments by an ivied seat where they sat and he listened enchanted by her warbled words of rippling laughter, and by her hair, a tangled sunbeam of gold. He was privileged to tie it for her. Then he looked into her eyes, green and gray—

> *But lit into amethyst*
> *When I stooped and kissed.*

The summer shower sent her scurrying off on feet that were wonderful, even luminous as he remembered them, feet with wings that bore her off so swiftly that never could he catch her with his lumbering strides. There was lilac outside her room and its blooms beat on the window as the warm June rain fell outside. Afterwards he could imagine the scene so well as he sat with her in her room, she in the glory of her amber-colored gown, a satin bow on either shoulder. And that was as far as memory went, for next her hands, with veins of blue, were waving him good-bye and she was telling him he was only wasting his life. He ran off through the garden gate and this love affair was over. He reproached her in his verse.

> . . . *hadst thou liked me less and loved me more*
> *Through all these summer days of joy and rain*
> *I had not now been summer's heritor*
> *Or stood a lackey in the House of Pain.*

He was left to nurse a barren memory of unkissed kisses, to mourn a passionate past that was fled. He was glad to have loved her and reflected that if his heart must break

> *Dear love for your sake*
> *It will break in music, I know*
> *Poets' hearts break so.*

Two other ladies, actresses both, received the homage of Wilde's verse. One of them was Sarah Bernhardt to whom the sonnet "Phèdre" was addressed. The other was the beautiful Ellen Terry to whom he dedicated "Portia," and "Queen Henrietta Maria," sonnets both of them. The French tragedienne he saluted for her brains, the English actress for her beauty. No woman whom Veronese had looked upon was half so fair as she.

> *O Portia! take my heart: it is thy due!*
> *I think I will not quarrel with the Bond.*

The second piece pleased the lady more than "Portia," as indeed it surely might—

> *O hair of gold! O crimson lips! O face*
> *Made for the luring and the love of man!*
> *With thee I do forget the toil and stress,*
> *The loveless road that knows no resting place.*

The loveliness of woman did not quite make of him an inspired poet, but he was ready to become her impassioned lover.

Oscar Wilde's first visit to America lasted throughout the year 1882. He traveled the length and breadth of the United States, from New York to Texas, from California to New Haven. He went north to Canada. He addressed the Mormons of Salt Lake City and the miners of Leadville. He was taken into custody for breach of contract, he was rooked by the poker players of New York. He did not make a fortune, to be sure, but he enjoyed himself. And he went on the record in praise of American girls—"Charming little oases in the vast desert of practical commonsense."

That he should, at that stage, have undertaken a lecture tour at all was the reversal of accepted practice. British authors who lecture in America have usually the backing of a reputation based on solid achievement. When Charles Dickens appeared before American audiences the characters of his creation were already household words on that side of the Atlantic, as familiar as they were at home. Wilde was no celebrity even in London. In America his name was unknown. Only the association between Wilde the aesthete and Bunthorne of "Patience" had made the tour possible. The satire of the comedy was not as well appreciated in the United States, where the aesthete was a rare variety of homo sapiens. If a specimen could be exhibited in America it would add point to Gilbert's wit. Accordingly,

D'Oyly Carte's business manager in New York, Col. W. F. Morse, sent a cablegram of inquiry to Mr. Oscar Wilde in London: "Will you consider offer for fifty readings." Wilde cabled back: "Yes, if offer good." It is asserted that whatever purpose Col. Morse had in making the offer Wilde in accepting had one only—not the advancement of D'Oyly Carte's opera, but the advancement of Mr. Wilde. His career might be begun just as effectively in New York as in London and a visit there might result in the production of "Vera" on Broadway.

His arrival in the United States was signalized by two jests —to the Customs men that he had nothing to declare except his genius; and to the questioning reporters that he had been impressed only by the tameness of the Atlantic. The reporters were impressed by Mr. Wilde's hair that fell down to his shoulders, by his un-English complexion that resembled putty, and by the muscularity of his fist—not a delicate hand, fit only to caress a lily, but one ready to be used if necessary in an argument of force.

In the newspapers there were some chilling references to the new arrival, but they were soon forgotten in the warmth of greeting from the hostesses of New York and the American beauties. Many of them wore aesthetic robes in honor of the guest. Dining-tables displayed exquisite lilies and splendid sun-flowers amidst banks of roses. Whereas the hostess on one occasion was seated at dinner in a chair of normal dimensions, the poet was installed in a high back chair, large and ornate. The two prettiest women of the company were seated to his right and left. One was in a costume of pale green satin, the other in a dazzling affair of yellow topaz. Mr. Wilde, it was noted, "allowed his glance to roam from one to other of his fair followers with increasing pleasure in his smile of approval." It was on this occasion that he offered his celebrated compliment to

American beauty: "America reminds me of one of Edgar Allan Poe's exquisite poems because it is full of belles."

"Behold," cried one, "the tribute of the belles," seizing some roses and proffering them to the poet. The others followed her example and roses rained on him from every side—truly a touching display of aestheticism.

He made his début as lecturer seven days after landing. Chickering Hall was filled to capacity by an audience attracted by the person of the aesthete rather than the principles of aestheticism. He introduced himself quite simply—"You have listened to the charming music of Mr. Sullivan and the clever satire of Mr. Gilbert for three hundred nights and I am sure, having given so much time to satire, it is not asking too much to ask you to listen to the truth for one evening." Thereafter in sentences that struck one hearer as "long and melodious," a vocabulary as wide as Swinburne's and well nigh as musical, he discoursed on beauty. The lecture was enriched with noble thoughts, for Ruskin and Pater were the sources upon which he drew for his inspiration. It was a success, but not for aesthetic reasons. Audiences were attracted by the man's personality, his wit, his charm, his voice, his elegance and his difference —above all his difference, for in those days America was not well acquainted with the Oxford manner. And if America was pleased, so was he. No itinerant lecturer had been so well received since Charles Dickens toured the States.

New York was a good beginning and there was promise of better things. Said a gushing young lady at a reception: "Oh! Mr. Wilde, you have been adored in New York but in Boston you will be worshiped." It was not as simple as that. The Harvard students planned to take a rise out of the lecturer, walking in in procession, each with a large lily for a buttonhole and bearing a sunflower. He turned the tables on them.

"I see about me," he said, "signs of an aesthetic movement. As I look about me I am impelled for the first time to breathe a fervent prayer: Save me from my disciples." The masquerade misfired. Again, at New Haven, the students tried to guy him, two hundred of them marching through the streets flaunting ties of unimaginable reds and bearing sunflowers. Led by a magnificent negro in aesthetic costume they took possession of the gallery, but they did not disconcert the lecturer.

In San Francisco there was a variation. Since the lecturer was not to be disconcerted he should be exposed to the ordeal by drink. What was there here to fear for a young man who had been brought up in the Bohemia of Sir William Wilde's home in Merrion Square? The game, the American chronicler relates, began. As the night wore on the Americans slumped, one by one, in their cups beneath the table. Still Oscar took all drinks as fast as they came, and still his voice, unhurried and unceasing, went on. Out-drunk and out-talked, San Francisco was sleeping among the table legs when Wilde looked at the gray dawn in the windows, arose, put on his greatcoat and sauntered off to his rooms. Word of the feat spread through the city. Here was a three-bottle man indeed.

From Leadville, toughest of mining towns, where it was policy for every man to be armed with a revolver, he was warned that the miners would be sure to shoot him or his traveling manager. Whatever they did to his traveling manager, replied Wilde indomitably, they would not intimidate him. He read them passages from the autobiography of Benvenuto Cellini. They were delighted. Why had he not brought Cellini along with him? When he explained that only the man's death had prevented it, they asked "Who shot him?" When he described Whistler's nocturnes in blue and gold they swore that such things should not be. Some of the younger men pulled out their revolvers and left hurriedly to see if the painter were "prowling about the saloons" or "wrestling a hash" at a café.

Wilde's tour enabled him to meet Walt Whitman. The patriarchal figure, now in his sixties, received him in a room of the cottage in which he had made his home since he had suffered a paralytic stroke. Wilde was entertained with elderberry wine. Whitman, he thought, was grand, original, unique. "I have come to you," he said, "as to one with whom I have been acquainted almost from the cradle." Walt challenged his guest's views on the beautiful. "Why, Oscar," he said, "it always seems to me that the fellow who makes a dead set at beauty by itself is in a bad way. My idea is that beauty is a result, not an abstraction." Nevertheless Walt was flattered by the homage Oscar had paid him. "Have you," he wrote to a friend in London, "met Oscar Wilde? He is a fine, large, handsome youngster and has had the good sense to take a fancy to me."

While in Philadelphia Wilde arranged for the publication of a book of poems by his friend James Rennell Rodd. Rodd had followed Wilde's example at Oxford by winning the Newdigate, two years later, with a poem on Walter Raleigh. In 1881 he published in London a collection of lyrics, "Songs of the South," of which he sent a presentation copy to Wilde. Under Wilde's direction the verses were issued in Philadelphia under the new title "Rose Leaf and Apple Leaf," in an elegantly produced volume. The print occupied only one side of a thin, transparent sheet of hand-made parchment, originally intended for paper currency, that had been lying for years in an old warehouse. The pages were inter-leaved with pale apple-green, the delicate tint showing through the printed page. An appreciative foreward "Envoi" was furnished by Wilde as an introduction to the verses. Rennell Rodd was delighted with the dress in which his work had been attired—"charming, I have seen no edition de luxe in England to compare with it." But the dedication startled and angered him. Inserted by Wilde without his consent or knowledge it read:

To Oscar Wilde, "Heart's Brother"
These few songs and many songs to come.

Rodd wrote in protest to the publishers. "It has annoyed me intensely. . . . The dedication is too effusive. I have written to Mr. Wilde on this score, but if he does not write to you, I must ask you as a personal favor to see to it. I want to have it removed from all copies that go out in future." "Heart's Brother" had a curious ring about it. Perhaps the self-dedicator considered he had earned the right to use it by the choice phrase of praise in which he had recommended his friend's verses—"majesty of melody," "pale flower of an exquisite moment," "fiery wonder of imagination." The words of the dedication were restrained by comparison with the encomiums that introduced the poems.

It was Mr. Wilde's first published piece in prose and this too, like his own poems, was derivative. He used the occasion to discharge some of the best things he had acquired from Ruskin and Pater. The style was his own, not so richly ornate as it was to become, but even in this initial essay, recognizably, unmistakably Oscar Wilde.

From the United States he went north to Quebec, Montreal and Toronto. The Niagara Falls disappointed him as much as the Atlantic—"Every American bride is taken there and the sight of this stupendous waterfall must be one of the earliest, if not one of the keenest disappointments of American married life."

When Lily Langtry landed in New York in the autumn (1882) Oscar Wilde was there to meet her with an offering of lilies, and the tribute "I would rather have discovered Mrs. Langtry than have made the discovery of America." When she made her New York début in a Tom Taylor play, he was invited to do a notice of the piece for the "New York Herald." Again he paid homage to her loveliness—"Pure Greek it is, with the grave low forehead, the exquisitely arched brow, the noble chiseling of the mouth, shaped as if it were the mouth-piece of an instrument of music, the supreme and splendid curve of the cheek, the augustly pillared throat that bears it all."

A few weeks before the American adventure was ended, Wilde met Marie Prescott and her husband at breakfast at Delmonico's. They were interested in "Vera." It was agreed that the piece should be put on in the following year. To conclude the history of "Vera"—Wilde made a second and brief visit to America in the summer of 1883, arriving in time to supervise the last rehearsals of the play that was given a first performance at Union Square Theatre on August 20. It met with the reception it merited and was withdrawn within a week. "Little better than a fizzle," "long drawn dramatic rot," "sickening rant"—the critics were crudely frank.

Oscar Wilde returned to England in January 1883. He had a draft agreement for the writing of a five-act tragedy for Mary Anderson. There were also the profits of the lecture tour, nothing like a fortune, but sufficient to enable him to contemplate a stay in Paris. In experience he had gained vastly. The man who could charm the hostesses of New York, silence the masqueraders, overawe the miners of Leadville, clearly had the force of personality. He had developed his sense of business. It is also claimed that contact with the Americans had resulted in a quickening of his character. The old languors vanished. So too did the eccentricities of Mr. Wilde the aesthete.

In those years of the early Eighties Oscar Wilde was on friendly terms with the painter, Whistler. It was an association that ended in a quarrel; when wit meets wit a conflict must be expected, and particularly so with personalities who thought so highly of themselves as these two. Wit, in the person of James McNeill Whistler, had a sting in the tail. He chose for his emblem the butterfly. It should have been nothing so fragile. The wasp, quite evidently, would have been more appropriate.

In the Eighties Whistler was a man with a considerable body of work to his credit. Wilde could show only a few verses. His association with the painter enlarged the stock-in-trade of ideas essential to the exponent of aestheticism. That indeed was the cause of the rumpus between them—passing off the other man's ideas as his own. Not that Whistler could claim copyright in what he had acquired in his early days in Paris. But Whistler was a painter of genius who spoke on art from knowledge: Wilde was only a professor of the aesthete, with his name still to make.

When first they met all was well. With his instinct for associating himself with the eminent amongst whom he intended his place to be, Wilde had sought out Whistler. The painter liked to have companions about him as he worked and this young man down from Oxford was entertaining company, who offered homage to genius most engagingly. Soon he was a frequenter of the studio and he and Whistler were to be seen about together. Whistler was well selected as a celebrity to whom an aesthete should attach himself. Ruskin had talked art: Whistler was art.

Since his student days amongst the Bohemians of Paris, Whistler had established himself in London. The jaunty little man out of Massachusetts had become a familiar figure with his yellow tie, his wasp waist, his wandlike stick. He impressed one observer as an Hungarian bandmaster aping Mephistopheles. His monocle was as well known as his nocturnes. Only a year or so before, while Wilde was still at Oxford, Whistler had challenged the great Ruskin in the courts and had worsted him.

With a farthing damages and costs to pay it had been a pyrrhic victory, but even though it had broken Whistler in pocket, it had ended Ruskin's term as Slade Professor and the nation's arbiter in art. They were still talking of the brilliance of Whistler's repartees in the witness-box—indeed there are echoes of them still.

Ruskin had called it Cockney impudence for Whistler to charge two hundred guineas for flinging a pot of paint in the public's face. Whistler sued for libel. In the box he faced the Attorney-General and scored off him with ease. How long had he taken to knock off one of his nocturnes? Possibly a couple of days. Two hundred guineas for the labor of two days? Oh, no—for the knowledge of a lifetime. Young Mr. Wilde, with a talent, himself, for repartee, would have noted the wit's replies with admiration. Perhaps he pictured himself in Whistler's place, flashing in brilliancy before a spellbound court.

So it came about that Oscar Wilde was much in Whistler's company, often to be seen dining with him at the Café Royal. At this stage of the acquaintance, Wilde was the junior convive, taking pleasure in offering compliments to the "fine old Virginian gentleman."

Back in England from his American travels, Wilde resumed the role of itinerant lecturer. In the summer season he was billed at the resorts, Margate, Ramsgate, Southport, and in the autumn in London and the cities where men work. He made 65 appearances on the lecture platform speaking on his impressions of America, and also, as became a professor of aesthetes, on "The Value of Art in Modern Life." This discourse was first offered to students of the Royal Academy at their club in Golden Square, Westminster. For his subject matter Wilde drew lavishly on two authorities, Ruskin and Whistler, incongruously presented in the same mélange. Whistler never forgave him. To have his ideas offered to the world as Mr. Wilde's own and to have those ideas passed off in an address that also recommended the opinions of his old opponent Ruskin—it was insufferable.

Whistler's displeasure was conveyed in the jests that he was to collect in his scrap-book that is called "The Gentle Art of Making Enemies." Wilde the plagiarist was neatly pricked. "I wish I had said that, Whistler." "You will, Oscar, you will." And again: "Oscar went forth as my St. John, but, forgetting that humility should be his chief characteristic, and unable to withstand the unaccustomed respect with which his utterances were received, he not only trifled with my shoe, but bolted with the latchet."

When Wilde was married there was the Whistler greeting on his wedding day: "Fear I may not be able to reach you in time for ceremony. Don't wait."

When Whistler himself appeared on the lecture platform to deliver at first hand his views on art, Wilde was there to hear and to report. In his "Ten O'clock" lecture at Prince's Hall, Whistler summed up his long reflections on the art for art's sake gospel he had first heard preached in Paris in his student days. Art for art's sake; art concerned with seeking perfection not with teaching or moralizing. There were a few tilts at the parasites of art—the self-appointed experts, the appointed preachers, a reference to Ruskin, and the dilettante, plainly enough Wilde—"The voice of the aesthete is heard in the land and catastrophe is upon us."

In the next day's issue of the "Pall Mall Gazette" (February 21, 1885) Wilde reported Whistler in his own fashion, the patronizing note well sustained, and with a jest or two of his own to level the score. "Mr. Whistler," he began, "made his first public appearance as a lecturer on Art and spoke for more than an hour with really marvelous eloquence on the absolute uselessness of lectures of all kinds. . . . He stood there a min-

iature Mephistopheles mocking the majority." In a phrase
Wilde the reporter conveyed that he ranked himself on the artistic level of Whistler the lecturer—"Of course, with regard
to beautiful surroundings, I entirely differ from Mr. Whistler."
In another phrase he conveyed his own sense of superiority as
poet over painter—"For there are not many arts, but one art,
namely: poem, picture, and Parthenon, sonnet and statue—all
are in their essence the same, and he who knows one knows all.
But the poet is the supreme artist and the real musician besides,
and is lord over all life and all arts." The report ended with a
final tilt. The lecture had been a masterpiece of jests and of
beauty—"passages delivered with an earnestness which seemed
to amaze those who looked on Mr. Whistler as a master of persi-
flage only, and had not known him, as we do, as a master of
painting also. For that he is indeed one of the greatest masters of
painting in my opinion. And I may add that in this opinion Mr.
Whistler himself entirely concurs."

It was deft and it was fun. It was not to the relish of the
painter who had further to suffer the knowledge that in some
quarters, which did not know better, the opinion was held that
it was from Wilde himself that the Ten O'clock lecturer had
derived his ideas. There was an exchange of acid pleasantries between the wits. Wilde, with less fun and more malice, pointed
a shaft: "Mr. Whistler always spelt art and we believe still
spells it with a capital 'I.' . . . His brilliant wit, caustic satire,
and his amusing epigrams, or perhaps we should say epitaphs
on his contemporaries, made his views on art as delightful as
they are misleading and as fascinating as they were unsound."

Whistler lashed out at the "all pervading plagiarist," who
should be made to pick oakum, as he had hitherto picked brains
and pockets. Wilde was an ignoramus—"What has our Oscar
in common with art? Except that he dines at our table and picks
from our platter the plums for the pudding he peddles in the

Provinces. Oscar, the amiable, irresponsible, esurient Oscar—with no more sense of a picture than the fit of a coat, has the courage of the opinions—of others."

Some time later there was a rejoinder from Oscar in the "World"—"Alas, this is very sad! With our James 'vulgarity begins at home' and should be allowed to stay there."

These things may be read in "The Gentle Art of Making Enemies," that rather disappointing collection of witticisms. They appear with examples of Whistler's "Our 'Arry" type of jesting. Wilde held his own in the exchanges, but he was at once too indolent and too amiable to be a controversialist. "It is," he pronounced, "only the intellectually lost who ever argue."

6. THE FIRST FRIENDSHIP

*The people who have adored me have always insisted
on living on long after I had ceased to care for them.*

DURING his visit to Paris in 1883 Oscar Wilde
met Robert Sherard and so began the first of
the major friendships of his life. It was notable among those
that Wilde was to form. It was based on feelings deeper than
mere friends usually kindle, a romantic attachment, and it was
nothing beyond that. Had not Sherard been a person completely normal in his make-up it might have developed as
Wilde's later friendships developed.

It persisted for some months on terms of close affection and
then on Wilde's side there was a cooling off. He fell in love with
the woman he was to marry and his feelings for Sherard were
never the same afterwards. There was no decline in Sherard's
affection. He remained steadfast in his loyalty to the end, a
man always to be depended on in time of trouble. But he was
hurt to find he was taking a lower place in Wilde's affections,
hurt and baffled over the cause of it. Sherard had no clue to
the mysteries of the friendship in which he had been involved.

Robert Harborough Sherard, a young man of twenty-two at
the time of his first encounter with Wilde, had literary ambitions, as befitted Wordsworth's grandson. He had gone down
from Oxford without taking his degree and had crossed to
France to graduate as a man of letters, with little money for his
support. Most young men would have lived in Paris with the
Bohemians. Not so Sherard, in his Puritanism. He found a
cottage for himself in a remote part of Plassy where he lived a

73

solitary existence. The news of the arrival in Paris of the aesthete from London reached him in his retreat. He was not pleased with what he heard, and felt a repulsion for the mannered Irishman who was pushing himself forward amongst the French men of letters. Wilde had come to Paris with no more solid achievement behind him than his slim volume of poems which he used as a visiting card where he thought it might promote worth-while acquaintanceships. Sherard was annoyed by the reports of Wilde's push and poses. He too had a notion to play the man of letters and he felt a hostility towards Wilde born of "a petty spirit of trade jealousy."

There came an opportunity to meet Wilde at dinner. Sherard's first impulse was to refuse the invitation but in the end he sent a telegram of acceptance. He joined the party. Events followed the course that was often to mark first acquaintanceship with Wilde. Before the evening was over his antagonism had melted before the other's charm. In the drawing room Sherard was in so disgruntled a mood as to be unmannerly. Through dinner he was boorishly silent, while Oscar talked in a fashion that was so infuriatingly affected. He was discoursing of the Louvre and of the delight given to him by the Venus de Milo.

It was all too ecstatic for Robert. "I have never," he exclaimed, "been to the Louvre. When that name is mentioned I always think of the Grands Magasins du Louvre, where I can get the cheapest ties in Paris."

"I like that," said Wilde, "that is very fine."

When the ineptitude of your churlishness is applauded what can you do? The melting process has begun. And then you find further that your ineptitude is not merely accepted but applauded.

"When," said Oscar afterwards, "you bluntly disclaimed all artistic interests, I discovered that you had scientifically

thought out a pose that interested me." An invitation to lunch
followed, a meeting the following day and the captivation was
complete.

Sherard found Wilde living in what he reckoned to be the
writer's true quarter in Paris—a hotel on the Quai Voltaire,
amidst the haunts of booksellers and bookhunters on the left
bank. His suite looked out on the Seine and the Louvre and
Sherard spoke of the fine view. Wilde waved it away.

"Immaterial," he said, "except to the innkeeper who charges
for it on the bill. A gentleman never looks out of the window."

The visitor found the author giving his celebrated impersona-
tion of Balzac. There was a white dressing-gown fashioned after
the monkish cowl in which the Frenchman used to work.
There was the replica of the famous ivory cane which Balzac
carried when he went wooing. About the room were the books
required for creating the part—lives and studies of Balzac.

Sherard came to lunch and stayed for dinner; dinner with a
resplendent host who came curled to the feast, fresh from an
hour with his hairdresser. It was not the sort of thing to which
the austerely living Sherard was accustomed. There was some
lingering churlishness as dinner began. It passed.

Dinner over, they made a tour of the cafés of the Latin Quarter. After that they walked the Paris streets till the early hours,
talking of books, just books, for they were both young men
with ambitions to be authors. Wilde discoursed on Swinburne
and Pater, his twin idols. He recited favorite bits from Car-
lyle's "French Revolution." They stood before Notre Dame
and Oscar discoursed so solemnly for the occasion that his
companion thought his conscience must be working very
strongly within him. They paused before the dismantled palace
of the Tuileries and he discoursed again. "There is not," he
said, "one little blackened stone there which is not to me

a chapter in the Bible of democracy." There is no record of how this solemn thought was received.

It was two o'clock before they brought themselves to part. They agreed they were to be good friends. They fixed a meeting for the morrow.

It was the first walk of many about the city of Paris. It was the first of many days of enchantment. Each delighted in the discovery of a friend, or, stated a shade more accurately, one delighted in the discovery of a friend and the other of a friend and an undisguised admirer. In Sherard the memory of those days stood out across the years, with the sorrows they were to bring, so that twenty years later he could write—"In the sequence and during the six weeks which preceded my departure for London my whole time was almost spent in his company. It was for me a new and joyous life, an unending feast of the soul. Each day my admiration for my friend grew almost more enthusiastic. By nature, heredity and environment disposed to melancholy (as I was), viewing mankind and life as Calvin may have viewed them, this joyous Celt showed me the gladness of things, suggested the possibility of great and buoyant happiness in the world. With his exuberant vitality he scattered the black butterflies that enclouded my spiritual vision. It was perhaps because we were so dissimilar that we were from the very first so attracted one to the other. I may say that he professed for me the same friendship and in some degree also the same admiration that I most truly felt for him."

It might almost have been Alfred Douglas writing. There was the same feeling of affectionate adoration and enchantment. One played Jonathan to Wilde's David—the other did not, but must have come perilously near to it. So the idyll continued untainted. Sherard the Puritan was impressed by the other man's purity of life, his decency of language, his innocence of thought. Men who in each other's company exchanged the tales

men usually exchange were silenced into decency by the reproof of this man. Looking back, afterwards, taking into account the reputation of one who was denounced as a corrupter
of youth, Sherard marveled. The friend with whom he spent
those days in intimacy was one who would have made a gentleman, at least outwardly, of a man of bad morals and of un-
clean tongue.

Discovering for himself unsuspected happiness in life, Sherard concluded naturally enough that these were the happiest
days that his friend was to live, unclouded by worries, free from
material cares. Encouraged by the sweet balm of the young
man's adoration, Wilde was able to overcome his natural inertia
and was undertaking the drudgery of composition, putting
black on white. During those weeks of companionship he completed two pieces—a play in blank verse "The Duchess of
Padua" and the poem "The Sphinx" which had been for some
time on the fire.

There were privileges and responsibilities in being Oscar's
intimate friend. It was Sherard's privilege to assist when the
muse left gaps in the verse. It was his triumph, like the collab-
orator in a crossword puzzle, to find the answer to the clue "a
trisyllabic rhyme for catafalque" or "a rhyme in 'ar' for a
lagging verse." The reader who heedlessly scans the lines of
"The Sphinx"—

> *Or did huge Apis from his car leap down and lay before*
> *your feet*
> *Big blossoms of the honey-sweet and honey-coloured*
> *nenuphar*

can have no notion of the pride with which Sherard contributed the final word "nenuphar." The poet made him feel by
his thanks as though he had achieved great things in literature.
But there were responsibilities, too, none perhaps heavier than

discovering unsuspected felicities in "The Duchess of Padua."
Imagine walking abroad beside an author who could delight
himself in reciting his favorite lines from that the least successful of his plays and hearing

Am I not Duchess here in Padua?

repeated time and again, for the sound of the words fell so
sweetly on the author's ear. Alfred Douglas, when his turn
came, was bored by these little offices expected of the author's
mate, but the more obliging Sherard took pride in rendering
the services, offering them with appropriate incense. He could
share in the arduous labors of revision when a morning was
spent taking out a comma from a verse and the afternoon in
putting the comma back.

The reward came when Oscar devoted an entire day to finding a rarity to present to his friend, a life of Gerard de Nerval,
an author whom literary folk in England talked about but of
whom few knew anything. "For," said Oscar, "de Nerval
has become a classic and classics are what everybody talks about
but never reads." The book was found at last and, though his
purse was nearly empty, Wilde paid the high price asked so
that the gift could be made.

"With this little book," he explained, "you will be able to
write an article that will be welcomed, which may help your
reputation." By such gestures do men endear themselves to their
disciples.

Gerard de Nerval was the interest of the moment, the poet
who like Chatterton, Poe and Baudelaire came to a tragic end.
The two friends walked Paris late into the night trying to re-
trace the tragic footsteps leading to an evil house where, early
one morning, de Nerval had been found hanging dead from an
iron railing. As they looked at the spot one of them thought
uneasily about the future, feeling a wonder mixed with fear

whether "like Gerard our sightless souls might not stray to
some red hell like his." Such stirrings might bring disquiet to
the man of Calvinistic moods but not, surely, to Oscar, living
with too great satisfaction in the delights of the present to be
troubled by forebodings of the future.

They were an ill-assorted pair the Calvinist and the hedonist.
Sherard was conscious of some incongruity. But while the
rigor of his Calvinism was sweetened by his friend, his austerity of outlook had no effect on Wilde. Sherard looked almost
with envy on the intense joy in life of the friend to whose
nature asceticism was impossible. He experienced vicariously
the pleasures of the table, the delight in wearing good clothes,
the sense of bounding gratitude for all the good things of
existence. He thought it was proper that Oscar should have all
he wanted in enjoyment, conceded even the other man's right
to turn away from anything that to such refined susceptibilities
had the appearance of ugliness.

Oscar could not meet the poet with the satyr's face—"it was
too dreadful." Oscar could not tolerate the sight of a poor old
Englishman who had a skin disfigurement—"the sight of him
made me ill." This nicety was accepted as natural for a man
of such exquisite refinement. Indeed, when he considered
Wilde's aversion for the ill-favored, Sherard could scarcely
understand how his own appearance could be tolerated. There
was no necessity for concern.

"You are wonderful, Robert," his friend assured him. "Your's
is the head of a Roman Emperor of the decadence—the head of
an emperor who reigned only for a day—a head found stamped
on a coin."

Wilde's own head had recently been remodeled to the design
of another Roman, the Emperor Nero. The flowing locks of the
aesthete had gone. Instead the hair was cut close to the head,
with a tightly curled fringe that descended low on the fore-

head. The model for this coiffure was found in the Louvre. A hairdresser was taken along to see the example on the spot. "Afterwards," said Wilde, "I found that the bust represented Nero, one of the worst behaved men in the world and yet a man of strong artistic passion. I thought it just suited my case."

The days passed pleasantly but they brought greater satisfaction to Sherard than to his friend. Wilde was well enough received in Paris. He had introduced himself in the right circles with the slim, elegant volume of verses. But Paris was not ready to capitulate before the Irishman who talked with wit in French that was good enough. He met most of those he reckoned to be worth the while meeting. There were moments when he caught the attention of his hearers, but he was not permitted to shine. Was there not something a trifle presumptuous about the young visitor from London? Was he not a shade too eager for others to listen to his brilliancies rather than to exchange pleasantry for pleasantry in a contest of wit? Soliloquy, after all, is not conversation as conceived in a French drawing room.

Alphonse Daudet listened and found him artificial. Victor Hugo—Wilde discoursed with fluency in his house, but the great man, drowsy with the incense he himself had received, was sleeping an old man's sleep beside the fire. There were meetings with Degas, Pissarro, Sargent and Coqueline. With Paul Bourget he reached a closer acquaintance, or at least the Frenchman was prepared for the other man to talk. De Goncourt listened to the tales of the American tour, finding material for his diary.

"May 5, 1883—Dined with Oscar Wilde. This poet, who tells the most improbable stories, gives an amusing picture of a town in Texas with its population of convicts. He tells us of the hall of the Casino which, as it is the biggest room in the place, is used as the Assize Court and here they hang the criminals on the stage after the performance. He told us that he had

seen there a man who had been hanged to the scenery up-
rights while the audience fired their revolvers at him from their
seats."

It was some consolation to be welcomed by Sarah Bernhardt,
who showed not merely liking but admiration for the visitor.
She was appearing in one of Sardou's plays at the Vaudeville
when Wilde, attended by Sherard, called on her. Behind the
curtains in her dressing room she was preparing for her part
and she put out her head to give him a welcoming smile. Sherard was gratified to note that the French admirers present were
piqued at the cordiality of her greeting. A few days afterwards
they called on her at her home, Wilde presenting to her a mass
of wallflowers he had bought from a hawker. The limitations
of his purse dictated the choice, but Sarah received the wallflowers with delight no less than had it been a sumptuous
bouquet. He had offered her, too, the homage of his poetry
and, beyond that, comradeship of a kind that she was not
invited to share with the men she was accustomed to meet. Sherard records the tribute she paid without a hint that it was a
commentary on the nature of the man of whom she spoke.
"What attracted me to Oscar Wilde," she said, "was that he
showed me from the very first that his many kindnesses were
not rendered to me for the sake of establishing a claim on my
favor, as is the case with nearly every man who comes near
me. I found a comrade, not a suitor and a deep and real friendship was possible. It is rarely so between a woman and a man."
The Bernhardt was not the only woman who was to be offered
comradeship undisturbed by courtship from Oscar Wilde.

One day at the Hôtel Voltaire there came a telegram from
Mary Anderson. It announced the rejection of the play he had
written for her, "The Duchess of Padua," his five-act tragedy.
It was the end of his immediate hopes. Sherard admired his
stoicism at the reverse. "This, Robert, is rather tedious," was all

he had to say, and he sat tearing off little paper pellets from the telegraph form, and putting them into his mouth. It was one of his unconscious mannerisms.

Robert, loyal admiring Robert, was a sustaining presence during the disappointments of the stay in Paris. The time came when the friends had to part. Sherard, to his infinite regret, found himself compelled to return to England as a first step to a fresh life in the East. He had planned the adventure before the new friendship had been formed. When the chance offered, he resented the offer of an opening that previously he had sought. He left for London in a bitter mood, railing against the circumstances that were separating him from his friend. So strong was his regret that he decided to throw the chance away. He could not bring himself to break off a communionship that was investing life with a new and warm interest.

Funds were short. Wilde was still in Paris. So Sherard went north to Wordsworth's country to meet the spring in a cottage in Westmorland. It was not long before he received a telegram from Wilde, back in London, asking to be allowed to share the simple life. It must have been joy to receive the request and sadness not to bid him welcome, but Robert could not bring himself to invite the lover of the good things of life to share the narrow things at his home. He replied that for all the daffodils and violets Oscar would find the rough living of the north intolerable. Several letters passed to and fro, letters that were a constant delight to read in Westmorland, letters that Wilde in London welcomed in language that was only a shade less restrained than that which he was to use to Alfred Douglas.

There was a longish interval before the two men met again. It is likely enough that being out of funds himself Sherard did not like to rejoin his friend, but put him off with excuses so that Wilde may have considered himself rebuffed. Whatever the reason for it, a rift developed. When Sherard returned to Lon-

The parents—Jane Francesca and her husband, Sir William Wilde.

(from Horace Wyndham's "Speranza")

*When the aesthete went lectur-
ing he appeared in this resplendent costume complete with cane
and gloves.* (From Boris Brasol's "Oscar Wilde," by courtesy of Williams & Norgate)

*The quaint, bowler-hatted figure is Os-
car Wilde as he was known to his contemporaries at Oxford in the eighteen-
seventies.*

don it was not to rejoin Wilde. They met by chance a couple
of months later, passengers on the same train.

Sherard was invited to become Wilde's guest in rooms in
Charles Street (later Carlos Street), but the careless rapture of
Paris was not to be recreated. There "life had been invested
with a new meaning." Now it was "a pleasant life." Preoccupa-
tion with money may have had a chilling effect. Sherard was not
much above penury. Wilde was driven to undertake another
lecture tour to supplement his resources. When an engagement
had turned out profitably he would return to pull notes from
the pocket of his fur coat, and press them on the other—"As
much mine as yours." Sherard, with his proper notions, could
not have found it easy to live on benefactions. The hopes he
had rested on his own first publication, a three-decker novel,
were no better grounded than Wilde's in his five-act tragedy
in blank verse. His thoughts turned to Paris where one could
starve in less discomfort than watching the carriages drive by
in Mayfair.

Then came the day when Wilde announced his intention to
marry. "He woke me in bed early one morning to give me the
news," Sherard relates. "I said, 'I am very sorry to hear it,' and
turned over to resume my slumbers. He said, 'What a brute you
are, Robert' and that was the end of the conversation." It was
the end, too, of Robert's role as favorite friend.

Throughout the years to come Sherard was to appear from
time to time in the subordinate place of loyal follower. Wilde
moved on and forgot. Sherard changed less in his affection.
Through the pages of the record of the unhappy friendship—
"a friendship that went nigh to wreck my life"—he appears
rather baffled by the rebuffs he was to receive. Having changed
so little in his own affection he failed to realize that the other
had changed so much. Always he preserved in the intimate
picture album of his mind the portrait of the Oscar Wilde

he knew in Paris, the young man filled with joyous enthusiasms, whose conversation was an exhilarating wine, whose presence was stimulating and exalting, a man of generous instincts, of such refinement that sensualist as he might be nothing coarse or gross was possible for him. When time's changes brought out another Oscar Wilde, Sherard still saw his Paris portrait as the real man, attributing the changes to temporary aberrations brought about by drink, madness or vicious company. Loyalty could scarcely make a man more blind. Nor was it mere impressions that lingered from the past. The affection he had felt struck deep and it remained. When the catastrophe came Sherard felt the shame more keenly than the man who stood in the Old Bailey dock. "I had gone down with him," he said, "my best years had been lost."

Wilde inspired greater affection amongst his chosen friends than he could feel himself for those friends. Robert Ross was inspired to friendship's feelings that survived till his dust was mingled in the tomb with his master's. Alfred Douglas passed from the extremity of affection to hate, and yet was never free from the spell of the enchanter of his youth. These two knew the nature of the bond that linked them with Wilde. It was Sherard's fate to experience the bond without realization of the nature of its origin. It seems that in this case Oscar Wilde, too, was ignorant. We may say of them what Somerset Maugham has written of two of his characters: "Neither suspected that in the pleasure they took in each other's company there was anything more than the casual friendship of two persons thrown together by the circumstances of life."

7. MARRIAGE

How marriage ruins a man! It's as demoralizing as ciga-
rettes and far more expensive.

IN 1884, being then thirty years of age, Oscar
Wilde married a girl from his native city of
Dublin. They set up home in London at Tite Street, Chelsea.
Two sons were born, Cyril (1885) who was to be killed while
serving in the World War I, and Vyvyan (1886) who sixty
years later was to direct the publication in its completeness of
his father's last work in prose. During the early years of his
marriage Wilde supplemented his income by writing fugitive
pieces of literary journalism and for two years (1887–9) he
edited a woman's magazine. Therein he anticipated another
author, Arnold Bennett, who was for some years editor of the
weekly paper "Woman."

For a time the current of Wilde's career flowed smoothly. It
seems as if this was a deliberate pause, the caesura of his life. The
forces that had produced the early years of striving were spent.
There must be an interval for the refreshing of life's impetus
that was to push him forward through the hectic, glittering
years of achievement. Of this there was no sign for the world
to note. The world, the little world that had been aware of his
existence and had noted the ripples of his aesthetic posturings,
might have concluded that life was subduing the man Wilde.
He had set off, a young man in a flurry, but with no strength
to sustain him; he was now left subdued by domesticity and the
burden of a family.

It was while he was lecturing in Dublin that Wilde became

acquainted with the woman he was to marry. Constance was the daughter of an Irish lawyer, Horace Lloyd, Q.C., who had been dead for some years. His widow remarrying, Constance went to live with her grandfather who had a fortune to leave. He had made the grand-daughter his heiress. This provided the basis for Frank Harris's taunt that Oscar was marrying the money rather than the woman. With the same breath Harris chided Oscar for not waiting until he could have netted a woman with more money and an assured position, and so placed himself above want and care for ever. It is quite an achievement to have run both these ideas in the same sentence.

In fact, it is clear enough, Oscar chose Constance for the ages-old reason that has served through the generations of men. He was in love with her and she with him.

Constance Lloyd, then in her twenty-sixth year, had pretti-ness and charm. She was gentle, retiring in disposition, of a sweet and submissive nature. She had a mass of ruddy-brown hair, high coloring, large, dark, lustrous eyes. A woman—women see their own sex more realistically than do men—re-calling her to mind twenty years afterwards, wrote: "A vision of her sweet face and graceful personality seems to arise from the vistas of the past. It was a face whose loveliness was derived more from the expression and exquisite coloring than from any claim to the regular lines that constitute beauty." A thor-oughly womanly woman is the summing up of her character.

There is no room for doubting that Wilde was passionately in love. When she agreed to become engaged to him he wrote off to announce his good fortune to Lily Langtry, and to pic-ture the loveliness of Constance. The Lloyd family were pleased with the match. Constance's brother Otho sent Wilde a letter of congratulation. "I am pleased indeed, and for my own part I welcome you as a new brother. Constance also is greatly to be congratulated to have got your love."

Oscar chafed at the necessities of his work that kept him away from Dublin. She too was saddened by the partings but they schooled each other to support the burden of separation. They telegraphed to each other twice a day. He offered lilies to his little Artemis when he was in Dublin and when he was away they exchanged letters that had all the phrases to gladden a lover's heart. He thought it necessary to confess to her about his past as an honest lover should do. And she, in proper fashion of a confiding woman, waved his past aside, it was no concern of hers.

He offered her his heart, he sent her lilies as the token of his loving. He gave her the book of his poems and he wrote for her the poem of his loving, the simplest, sincerest of the verses from his pen.

> *I can write no stately proem*
> *As a prelude to my lay,*
> *From a poet to a poem*
> *I would dare to say.*
>
> *If of these fallen petals*
> *One to you seems fair,*
> *Love will waft it till it settles*
> *On your hair.*
>
> *And when wind and winter harden*
> *All the loveless land,*
> *It will whisper of the garden,*
> *You will understand.*

The romantic courtship ended in an aesthetic wedding. Grandfather Lloyd was ill so the ceremony that took place on May 29, 1884, at St. James's, Paddington, was designed to be almost private in character. None the less the church was crowded and the assembled congregation were rewarded by the sight of a bridal procession arranged to the décor of the bridegroom. He, for the occasion, surrendered the leading role, self-effacing to the degree that he was said to have borne himself with calm dignity. So attention was not directed away from the bride.

She was a study in cream, cowslip cream and green. Her veil was of saffron-colored Indian silk gauze, worn in Marie Stuart fashion. Myrtle leaves gleamed in her frizzed hair, there were clusters of myrtle leaves to ornament her dress, and green, rather than white, was dominant in the bouquet. The two leading bridesmaids were quaintly gowned in silk the color of a ripe gooseberry, set off with large sashes of pale yellow. They wore Gainsborough hats of red silk, amber necklaces, and yellow gloves, and yellow roses clustered at the throat. The four elder bridesmaids had skirts of red Surah silk, high hats crowned with cream-colored feathers, and amber necklaces. Yellow roses were at their throats, and they bore lilies in their hands.

Not every groom is concerned about the dress that adorns his bride. Male thoughts on such occasions do not run so much on dress. He is content to leave the paraphernalia of these preliminary trappings to her, the charming autocrat of the occasion, her busy mind taken up with fashion in all its detail. Her's is the planning, his to be admiringly acquiescent. On that occasion roles were reversed, such was the yielding nature of the bride. If she could submit to him in this, what could be the limit of her devotion?

They went off to Paris for their honeymoon. Here, usually, the blinds are discreetly drawn. It was not so with Oscar. In the pride of his new fulfilment he had to show himself to Robert Sherard, who was admitted to the bridal ante-chamber. It was full of flowers and youth and laughter. He was presented to the bride. She was supremely happy. He walked out into

the street with the groom. Oscar confided that marriage was
indeed wonderful. Sherard was embarrassed by the intimacy
of the praise of the delights. They had not gone many yards
before Oscar stopped at a flower-stall where he chose the
loveliest blossoms to send, with a message of love, to the bride
he had just quitted.

The three of them drove, later, in a fiacre through the Paris
streets.

Sherard asked leave to throw away the stick he was carrying.
"Would you mind, Oscar?" he asked. Oscar did mind, it might
cause a scene; but why should he wish to do so?

"It's a swordstick," Sherard explained, "and I don't know
how it is, but for the last minute I have had a wild desire to
pull out the blade and run it through you. I think it's because
you look too happy."

At this Mrs. Wilde took the stick from his hand. "I will keep
it," she said, and as a memento of the days of radiance she
treasured it for years afterwards.

All opened merrily as the marriage bell. Oscar gave himself
up to the new role of family man. They set up home in Tite
Street, Chelsea, where some of the rooms had been decorated
by Whistler. Quite recently a blue tablet was put up to mark
the house now numbered 34, but in those days number 16.

The affectionate husband, the fond father, it is Oscar Wilde
in a role not generally suspected of him. There are a few
glimpses of him with his children, a Sherard vignette of father
Oscar, at his wife's At Home, fondling with a fat finger one of
his baby sons. You find him, later, lamenting that he was unable
to keep an engagement at Cambridge with Oscar Browning
because one of his children was ill. In a letter to another friend,
he recorded his satisfaction at the birth of one of his children.
The proud father, the fond husband, the advocate of matri-
mony, it is an unusual facet of Oscar Wilde.

As head of a family he had family cares. His wife's dowry had enabled him to set up house, but itinerant lecturing and free-lance journalism were not to be depended upon for the family's support. One day there would be the Lloyd fortune, but that day was deferred. The grandfather who had been too ill to attend the wedding "blossomed out into fresh life" as Oscar put it, "after he had joined our hands and given us his blessing." So Oscar, for the first and only time, joined the ranks of the wage-earners. It is a sign of his adaptability that, having known no restraints on freedom's hours about town, he could submit to the requirements of office routine.

His job was to edit a woman's magazine, the "Woman's World," a post offered to him by the firm of Cassell. His salary was £300 a year which, taking into account the fall in the value of the pound and the rise in taxation, is equivalent to nearly a thousand today. It was not affluence but it was a contribution, even after paying for carnations and cab fares, that supplemented his wife's income sufficiently for the family to be maintained.

For two years Wilde occupied himself as editor and as a free-lance literary journalist. Like any suburban householder he traveled to and fro, by underground train, kept office hours, did the duties required of an editor and for a time he was content. In the first days of novelty he was proud of his editorship, enjoyed the opportunities for patronage. He was an efficient, exacting editor. His list of contributors included such names as Olive Schreiner of the "Story of an African Farm," Oscar Browning, Marie Corelli, Arthur Symons, and Ouida.

The editor himself contributed a column of literary notes which enabled him to welcome the early verse of W. B. Yeats ("full of promise") and to reprove Professor Saintsbury for his bad grammar. Of one poorish novel he wrote: "The plot is the property of Mrs. Henry Wood; we think it should be sent back to her by the next post." He was able to praise his mother's "Ancient Legends" as revealing the innermost heart of the Celt. Lady Wilde, who since her husband's death had installed her salon in London, contributed to the magazine. Constance wrote a couple of pieces on muffs, historically considered, and on children's dresses.

With the passing of time the monotony of office life, even an editor's office, began to weigh upon him. At first he had been prompt in his arrival in the morning, but as the months passed he became later and later. When chided for leaving early he answered in the classic words of Charles Lamb: "But then I always arrive late."

When the two years were ended his contract was not renewed. It was not so much that he had failed as editor, but that his name had not proved to be the pulling power the proprietors had hoped. He was released from the office routine. No longer had he to give his thoughts to frills, fripperies and fashions, fancy dress for children, shorthand for girls, field work for women. But the necessities of life forced themselves on his attention. Cash was short at times in Tite Street. There were days when a friendly neighbor furnished the means for buying the children a pair of shoes. There were visits to the pawnshop. The gold medal was on occasion placed in pawn and there were difficulties when the ticket was mislaid. The encounter with the tax collector belongs to those days.

One day, as Richard le Gallienne tells the tale, as Oscar stood outside his door, a little man came up saying he had called about the taxes. "Taxes!" exclaimed Wilde, looking down from his lordly height. "Why should I pay taxes?"

"But Sir," said the little man. "You are the householder are you not? You live here, you sleep here?"

"Ah yes," replied Wilde, with utter solemnity, "but then, you see—I sleep so badly."

It must, in those earlier years, have been a happy home to live in. The fond husband, the proud father and the adoring wife. But, as time passed, though his fondness for Constance remained —it was to remain till the end—there was a cooling off in his ardor. It was not merely the fading of love's ecstasy from which only the rarest love is fortunate enough to escape, but the transformation of the rhapsodizing lover into the Wilde of the later phase, who tired not only of his wife but of all women. Was it gradual in its onset? Did it, in the first place, spring from the intellectual disparities between this husband and wife? Even in their happy, early years, the shrewd observer felt doubts about the couple, so unevenly matched in their mental equipment, the wife, so simple and domestic, mated with a mind so searching and so perverse.

You can picture her, a figure almost pathetic at one of her own At Homes. She sat decked out according to her husband's aesthetic conceptions. A costume in the Greek mode adorned her, cowslip yellow and apple green. Bands of yellow ribbon set off her hair. It needed an assured exhibitionist to live up to the attire that Oscar had designed, but she could not sustain the role. Self-conscious and shy, she gave the onlookers the appearance of a young actress suffering from stage-fright. Oscar would go up to her with words of encouragement: "You are looking lovely, Constance—not a bit too tired with all these people?" Then Oscar would begin to discourse to the assembly, and Constance could sink into the background, eclipsed by the flow of her husband's brilliancies. As he spoke, her face could be seen to take on a rapt expression of love and pride.

Not far from Tite Street Lady Wilde was presiding at her literary salon. The small home she shared with her son Willie did not provide the setting of the Merrion Square mansion, but she ignored the handicap of space. Her ample presence caused other women in the crowded room to dwindle into insignificance. Her entry was likened to a ship with all sails set and billowing in the breeze, sweeping into harbor. Speranza might have been a queen graciously giving audience. Was her son disappointed that his wife, retiring and gentle, could not queen it over the assemblies in Tite Street? Or was he simply bored by her natural goodness and simplicity?

A prophet may be without honor in his own country, but a wit does expect to be appreciated at his own table, and Constance was not gifted in appreciation of this kind. Le Gallienne, looking at them with his shrewd eyes, could only marvel how she, so sweet and good, could have been mated with her outrageously intellectual husband, to whose wit little was sacred. Her chief interest after her children was missionaries and her bosom friend one of the pillars of Church work.

"Missionaries, my dear," he recalls Wilde saying at dinner, "don't you realize that missionaries are the divinely provided food for destitute and under-fed cannibals? Whenever they are on the brink of starvation, Heaven in its infinite mercy sends them a nice plump missionary." To which Mrs. Wilde could only exclaim—"Oh dear, you cannot surely be in earnest. You can only be joking."

There is no mistaking the character of Constance. She is sketched by several of the chroniclers and the portrait is recognizably the same. A pleasant woman, not distinguished in looks or character—gentle, lovely, charming, are the usual terms. Of no particular qualities or beauty says Frank Harris, but Harris' preference was for the flamboyant in woman and I do not reckon his phrase to be dissent from the other opinions. This gentle woman, when the need arose, could exercise little authority over her husband. She was all submission. The blundering instinct of sex that dictated his choice led him to a wife who was dependent in her woman's weakness. The essential need of his nature was not to give but to receive support.

A wife of stronger character would have sought to enforce her will on his and might have forced the happy continuance of the marriage. Constance in her weakness submitted to her own displacement. Before the marriage was four years old Wilde's preoccupations had ranged outside his home. It was his own experiences that he captured in the epigram: "Marriage is a sort of forcing house—it brings strange sins to fruit and sometimes strange renunciations."

8. CHANGE OF NATURE

These are terrible temptations that it requires strength—
strength and courage—to yield to.

THE emergence of Robert Ross in the Oscar
Wilde history is veiled in obscurity. His importance in the drama is not to be over-estimated. His acts in
the latter years are well known, attested by ample documents.
But of his emergence and of what happened in those earlier
years little has been recorded. Ross was there in the background, an influence, but as a presence scarcely discernible.
The molehills in the meadows are plain for all to see, but who
sets eyes on the little gentleman in black velvet? Ross was the
most self-effacing of Wilde's friends and favorites, so retiring
that the story has been told without so much as a mention of
the part he played in the years when Wilde turned to the unnatural from the natural ways of men.

It was at Oxford in 1886 that Ross was first introduced to
Wilde. Robbie was then seventeen, Wilde being about fourteen
years his senior. The shadowy influence does not emerge as an
actual creature of flesh and blood till a later date when we meet
the little, round figure of a man. A little man—always there is
the diminutive epithet, which even Oscar used in rather patronizing fashion. Alfred Douglas, who knew him well and liked
him too at first, speaks of Ross as having been a nervous, affectionate, sentimental and emotional man. To this it should be
added that his father having died when he was a child, Ross
had been brought up by his mother. It is not, surely, without
some significance that this trio, Wilde himself, Ross, and Doug-

las, were devoted sons. Douglas, hating his father, adored his mother. Wilde's devotion to his mother reached the degree of "sheer veneration."

Robert Baldwin Ross, Canadian by descent, was the grandson, on his mother's side, of the Hon. Robert Baldwin, first Prime Minister of Upper Canada. His father, John Ross, Q.C., Attorney-General, died when Robbie was two years of age, leaving directions that his three sons, of whom Robert was the youngest, were to be educated in England. His mother sent him to King's College, Cambridge, where he was severely ragged by his fellows, and ducked in the college fountain. Robbie left Cambridge within a year, with the intention of following a literary career. He wrote for the "Saturday Review" and for Henley in the "Scots Observer." Later he was to win the friendship of Edmund Gosse, and to get on good terms with the leading figures of his day in literature and art, to conduct an art gallery of his own, and to become a recognized authority in matters of art. He was one of those who without being able to achieve distinction in their own right, are able to contribute to achievements in others. The first of the many who were to derive encouragement from self-effacing Robbie was Oscar Wilde.

The years of his close association with Ross were those when a new tone was to be detected in Wilde's writing. The Fairy Tales were pure and innocent as a child's verses, but there was a sinister streak in some of the other pieces, an intellectual toying with strange sins, hints of perverse tendencies. These manifestations were attended by a change in the nature of the man, and since all took place during the Ross period it is easy enough to reach the conclusion that Ross was the cause, to see in Ross the corrupting influence, the tempter in the garden beautiful that brought about the fall. As the known facts are few, one can as one's fancy suggests move about the weights in the scales that weigh moral responsibility. One weighing is unlikely to be more determinate and conclusive than the next. Wilde himself would have rejected such efforts with disdain. He did not concede that one man can take responsibility for another's failures.

Sherard once questioned him about intervening to save a man from suicide—if he were to see a man throw himself into the river would he try to deter him? "I should consider it an act of gross impertinence to do so," Wilde replied. "His suicide would be a definitely thought-out act, the definite result of a scientific process, with which I should have no right whatever to interfere."

The facts concerning the change in Wilde can be briefly stated. He first began the course of conduct that led to his downfall in the year 1886 when he "began to experiment." The practices became a habit in 1889. This testimony is given by his biographer Ransome and is supposed to have the authority of Robert Ross himself, who provided Ransome with much of his material. To this is added the statement of Frank Harris that Ross boasted that he was the first boy Oscar had and that Ross, not Alfred Douglas, was "Oscar's real mistress." Harris was so gifted in prevarication that nothing he says can be accepted without corroboration, but here the circumstances seem to support him. Even the innocent-minded Sherard came to have his suspicions about Ross.

What produced the change in Wilde's nature? It was a psychological reversal as complete as that physical change which may transform the father of two children into a comely woman. In the times when there was no uncertainty about the moral lapses of men, his aberrations could be summarily dismissed as the degraded experiments of a man who deliberately transgressed, perversely pursuing iniquity for the relish of new and forbidden experiences. The explanation would now be dismissed as too facile. It was nothing so superficial as the voluptuary's momentary pursuit of evil experience for the perverse satisfaction of novelty.

The change in him was complete, fundamental, irreversible. Was he to be held responsible for it? Or was he the passive subject who had to submit to the workings of his own character? The answer comes in an uncertain voice. Study of the mysteries of the abnormal has not yet penetrated far enough into the complexity of human make-up for the revealing of its ultimate secrets. The final verdict on the conduct of Oscar Wilde has yet to be registered. Pathology has been invoked to challenge the verdict of the criminal courts. What was termed perversion has been renamed abnormal and the abnormal has been seen as another but unusual manifestation of the normal. What, it is asked, is the norm? In a world in which women turn out to be men, in which a man who has begotten children is transformed into a woman, the old rigid conceptions of 100 per cent normality are vanishing like Newton's concepts before the new relativity. If nature blunders sometimes over the bodily attributes of sex, is there any reason to suppose that there may not be a mix-up in the subtler, less-defined differentiations between the sexes, in the mental, the emotional and the psychological?

It has been asserted that the reason Wilde first turned from his wife was that he was suffering from the recurrence of disease contracted during a chance amour while he was at the university. The disease, it is further claimed, was the cause of his death. That Wilde had in fact contracted the disease is disputed. The main authority on the point is Sherard who about the year 1935, being then in his seventies, made the following statement to Boris Brasol, one of the most painstaking of biographers:

Oscar Wilde while at Oxford had contracted syphilis for the cure of which mercury injections were administered. It was probably due to these treatments that his teeth subsequently grew black and became diseased. Before proposing to Miss Constance Lloyd, he went to see a London doctor who assured him that he had been completely cured and that there was no pathological obstacle to his marriage. However, at some later time he discovered that the disease which had been dormant had broken out in his system. Naturally from that time on he was actually forced to give up physical relations with Constance. It was then that one of his friends initiated him into homosexual practices.[1]

Once the probabilities of this account are considered, it must seem difficult to understand that the husband who was concerned about his wife was a man with so little solicitude for the welfare of his intimate friends for whom the risks of association were presumably the same. One of these, Alfred Douglas, had ampler opportunity than Sherard for ascertaining the truth. In his "Summing Up" Douglas wrote: "Sherard's explanation of what first caused a cooling of the relations between Oscar and his wife, a sweet, gentle and exceedingly pretty girl, is one which I cannot accept. Sherard makes statements about a malady which he declared Wilde had contracted but I fail to find he gives any proof or evidence of this. I am in no position to disprove what he says but frankly I do not believe it."

Sherard himself recanted, in the last of his books devoted to Wilde. Blandly, without a hint that he had been a party to spreading the original report, he wrote:

During all the years I knew him I never once saw him ill or in pain. . . . Ransome attributes to him a certain disease and added that it was the final cause of his death. In his later edition he omits the indiscretion. I can only say that during the seventeen years I never saw in Wilde the slightest sign of a malady which has a very distinct way of announcing its existence, a disease which certainly

[1] Brasol attempted to obtain first-hand information of the cause of death but every endeavor to discover the medical records was fruitless.

does not hide its fatal light under any bushel whatever. The fact is the man had a wonderful constitution just as he had a wonderful brain.

Two men made the statement, both changed their view about its truth. There remains little evidence to support what on the face of it seems to be an unlikely proposition. What may possibly have occurred is that Wilde, being asked on some occasion to explain the reason he was deserting his wife, invented the shocking story to explain the otherwise inexplicable.

The years of Wilde's change of nature and of his intimacy with Robbie Ross were those of the first period of achievement and the writing of his prose works. It had been Pater's advice to him that he should turn from poetry to prose—prose was so much more difficult. Wilde knew about the difficulties of composition. In verse or prose it made no difference, he resented having to devote to toil hours snatched from the more rewarding application to pleasure and the society of his friends.

"Writing," he sighed, "so bores me!" And to be sure writing could be only a minor affair in the life of a man of fashion. Nevertheless the spur of necessity pricked him into industry and he labored at his prose. Gone were the days of lyrical ardor, "Days when one loved the exquisite intricacy and musical repetitions of the ballade and villanelle, days when one solemnly sought to discover the proper temper in which a triolet should be written." Slowly he came to realize what a wonderful self-conscious art English prose writing could be made to be. But though he abandoned verse he continued to write by ear. The sound and musical pattern of his periods gave the rhetorical quality to his prose. There is scarcely a page without a passage rolling out in the rhythm of spoken English. Such indeed was the origin of so much of it.

These were the author's years of industry. He was a regular and frequent contributor to the "Pall Mall Gazette" then in its golden days. He also contributed to the "Dramatic Review" and to the "Court and Society Review." He wrote for "Black-woods'," the "Fortnightly" and the "Nineteenth Century." There were occasional pieces elsewhere and his writings for, in addition to editing, the "Woman's World."

By now he had learned how to turn his particular talents to account. Conversational impromptus became the epigrams of the essayist. The inventions that delighted the drawing room and the dinner party needed only to be written down and extended to form an article. Wilde was never the complete critic giving well-considered, solidly based judgments, but his flashes were as enlightening of their subject as another man's column of prose. Take a few at random:

GEORGE MEREDITH—His style is chaos illuminated by brilliant flashes of intellect. As a writer he has mastered everything but language; as a novelist he can do everything except tell a story; as an artist he is everything except articulate.

RUDYARD KIPLING—As one turns the pages of "Plain Tales from the Hills" one feels as if one were seated under a palm tree reading life by superb flashes of vulgarity. . . . From the point of view of literature Mr. Kipling is a genius who drops his aspirates. From the point of view of life he is a reporter who knows vulgarity better than anyone has ever known it. . . . He is our first authority on the second-rate and has seen marvellous things through keyholes, and his backgrounds are real works of art.

HENRY JAMES—He writes fiction as if it were a painful duty and wastes upon mean motives and imperceptible "points of view" his real literary style, his felicitous phrases, his swift and caustic satire.

MR. JAMES PAYN—Is an adept in the art of concealing what is not worth finding. He hunts down the obvious with the enthusiasm of a short-sighted detective. As one turns over the pages the suspense of the author becomes unbearable.

Wilde has been reproached for the ornateness of his prose, but he is more readable than many who are considered to be his superior as stylists. His purples are frequent and lurid, but there is a relish about his rhetoric so that it almost compels one to read it out aloud. Who can resist giving sound to the rhythms of a piece like this on English drama?

At first, in the hands of the monks, dramatic art was abstract, decorative and mythological. Then she enlisted life in her service and using some of life's external forms she created an entirely new race of beings, whose sorrows were more terrible than any sorrow man has ever felt, whose joys were keener than lovers' joys, who had the rage of the Titans and the calm of the Gods who had monstrous and marvellous sins, monstrous and marvellous virtues. To them she gave language different from that of actual use, a language full of resonant music and sweet rhythm made stately by solemn cadence, or made delicate by fanciful rhyme, jewelled with wonderful words and enriched with lofty diction. She clothed her children in strange raiment, and gave them masks, and at her word the antique world rose from its marble tomb. A new Caesar stalked through the streets of ruined Rome, and, with purple sails and fluteled oars, another Cleopatra passed up the river to Antioch. Old myth and legend and dream took shape and substance. History was rewritten and there was hardly one of the dramatists who did not recognize that the object of art is not simple truth but complex beauty.

Purple passage, epigram and paradox—the writings of Wilde the author began to familiarize a wider, but no less appreciative public, with the felicities that had earned him fame in the circles of society frequented by the wit and conversationalist, Mr. Oscar Wilde. He was living down his former eccentricities and laying solid foundations for the renown he had tried to achieve by the processes of notoriety. And, even as he was establishing his reputation, he began to let fall hints, suggestions faint at first, of notoriety of another kind.

First in point of time (1889) was the so-called "Study in green" which under the title of "Pen, Pencil and Poison" is a biographical study of Wainewright, poet, painter, "forger of no mean capabilities and secret poisoner without rival in this or any other age." It is an essay written with a curious moral detachment. The normal Victorian approach required some expression of reprobation against Wainewright's crimes. Wilde discussed the artist in the man without feeling called upon to censure the criminal—"the fact of a man being a poisoner is nothing against his prose." But it was possible to conceive that Wilde was not merely condoning the crime because Wainewright had the proper approach to art, but that he had found some satisfaction in the perfection of Wainewright's approach to crime. What was paraded was the identity, short of crime, that Wilde conceived himself to share aesthetically with this forger-poisoner. Murder gave the added zest of interest.

The fantasy, "The Portrait of Mr. W. H.," was published later in that same year. It gave the first hint of Wilde's interest in the condition of homo-sexuality. In the Eighties the subject of boy-love was not one that an author could choose as a topic for public discussion without causing eyebrows to be lifted. Authors had speculated before about the identity of the mysterious Mr. W. H. to whom the printer had dedicated Shakespeare's Sonnets as their "onlie begetter," and it had been argued that the initials stood for Will Hughes. In the form of a piece of fiction, Wilde presented an essay in Shakespearean scholarship, in which he submitted ingeniously and elegantly, that Will Hughes was a young actor for whom Shakespeare had conceived a passion and for whom he had created several of his most celebrated female roles, notably Rosalind, Juliet, Desdemona and Portia. As a scholar's argument it might have passed. But in his fantasy Wilde clothed his character of W. H. with the presentments of flesh and blood and human passion.

Whether or no the Bard was in love with Willie Hughes is arguable, but clearly Wilde had fallen for the youth of his imagining. Whether Shakespeare had, or had not an interest in youth, there was not much room for doubt about the tendencies of the author of the "Portrait." Even in a society that has become as familiar as our own with evidences of abnormality, the undisguised interest in boy-love would be the cause for comment. To have proclaimed it in the state of opinion when Queen Victoria was celebrating her Jubilee was provocative folly for anyone whose reputation was less well established than the Archbishop of Canterbury's.

In the comparative obscurity of "Blackwoods'," the essay on Mr. W. H. did not attract general attention. Wilde's next piece raised a storm. The novel "The Picture of Dorian Gray" was written as a serial for "Lippincotts' Magazine," the sum of £200 being paid for the rights. The first instalment appeared in June 1890. In March of the following year it was published as a book by Ward Lock, the author having added six chapters to bring the serial to the necessary length.

The story is a simple one about a dual personality, a variation on the Jekyll and Hyde theme, set against a voluptuous background. Dorian Gray, the young exquisite, has his portrait painted and it is contrived that while the handsome hero shall preserve the appearance of eternal youth, the portrait shall be saddled with the ravages of the years and the excesses of a voluptuary. After chapters in which the pleasures of luxury are pictured with relish the spell is broken. Dorian Gray falls dead, a figure of senile ugliness, while the portrait shines from the wall in the radiance of original youth.

The sources of Wilde's inspiration have been painstakingly traced. His debt to the French decadents was too obvious to be missed, a touch of Balzac, another of Huysmans, a hint from Poe. Basil Ward the artist related how he had stood model for the painter of the story, named, revealingly, Basil Hallward. Wilde was a friend who used to watch Ward working in his studio, one of his sitters being a young man of such unusual good looks that he was nicknamed "the radiant youth." When the portrait was finished and the young man had gone, Wilde sighed and said "What a pity such a glorious creature should ever grow old."

Richard Aldington, whose sketch is about the most penetrating of the shorter pieces on Wilde, has found the germ of Wilde's idea in the first novel written by young Disraeli, the Victorian Prime Minister. This work had the title "Vivian Grey." Wilde named his hero Gray and his second son Vyvyan. In Dizzy's novel there is a brief account of a young man, Max Rodenstein, the glory of his house, a being beautiful beyond description in body and soul. His mother had longed for a portrait of her son who would never allow himself to be painted, for his old nurse had warned him that the moment it was done he would die. Somehow the portrait was done, and in mysterious and terrifying circumstances the young man in the picture was seen by his mother to smile at the very moment young Max died, wounded in battle by a Polish lancer. Mr. Aldington's was a rewarding discovery for his wide excursions in literature.

Today, the epigrams of "Dorian Gray" might excite comment, but scarcely its moral deficiencies. Readers of fiction have been accustomed to profligacy, sensuality and sadism on a scale that makes Wilde's characters respectable by comparison. In days when there was no general familiarity with indecency, the moralists detected an outrage. Here was poisonous work, tainted with leprous distilment, corruption, writing fit for the crime investigator, unmanly, sickening, vicious, spawned from the leprous literature of the French decadents, heavy with the mephitic odors of moral and spiritual putrefaction. Little was omitted from the catalogue of vilification. The author was advised to give up literature and take up tailoring, or something useful, if he could do no more with his pen than write for out-lawed noblemen and perverted telegraph boys.

Wilde made reply to some of his critics. There was a long exchange of artillery in the "St. James's Gazette," a skirmish in the "Daily Chronicle" and a heavier engagement in Henley's "Scots Observer," which had begun, in reference to the novel, with the query "Why go grubbing in muck-heaps?" Henley, who was then assisting in the compilation of a pornographic dictionary, was qualified to ask and answer.

Wilde, in his various replies to the critics, submitted first that his novel was good morally. It was a point taken by Walter Pater in his review in the "Bookman": "It is a vivid, though carefully considered exposure of the corruption of the soul, with a very plain moral pushed home to the effect that vice and crime make people coarse and ugly." This championship did Pater more harm than it did Wilde good. Having argued himself on the side of the morality, Wilde next claimed that art had no concern with morals. The book might be poisonous but "you cannot deny it is also perfect, and perfection is what the artists aim at."

The battle of art versus morality was fought out in an in-conclusive engagement, as inconclusive it always will be since the moralist sets himself above art with the same facility that the artist claims to be above morals. As there are always few who do not reckon themselves moralists, and there are few who can reckon themselves to be artists, the champions of morality will always have the support of the greatest numbers and the greatest noise.

Read after the passing of seventy years, attacks and re-joinders seem to be rather jaded, certainly not the equal in brilliance of the book that provoked them. Wilde himself, curiously enough, is labored and by no means an easy victor over his opponents. One of the few jests he made was his re-

quest to one critic to cease his daily attacks and leave the novel
"to the immortality it deserves." He had the satisfaction that
the controversy was publicity, but in his position it was publicity of the wrong kind. Wilde had a place in society as well
as in the world of letters. The artist might repudiate morals.
There was not the same license for the man who frequented
the drawing rooms of fashion. Nor was his private life one
to invite attention. The saints may talk about sin where the
sinner is wise to be silent. A prudent man with Mr. Wilde's
tendencies would not have courted notoriety over Dorian
Gray.

By then Wilde had been captivated by the sophistries of his
own gospel of art. It was delightful to preach art for art's sake,
to declare the superiority of the artist, aristocrat of culture,
privileged, elect, superior. The challenging phrases were in-
toxicating:

> *They are the elect to whom beautiful things mean
> only Beauty;*
> *There is no such thing as a moral or an immoral
> book. Books are well-written or badly written, that
> is all;*
> *The moral life of man forms part of the subject
> matter of the artist, but the morality of art consists in
> the perfect use of an imperfect medium.*

It was delightful to toy with the ideas, but the man who took
them as the guide for his conduct was heading for a fall. In the
coterie that formed his little world, Wilde was assuming the
mantle of the Lord of Language and beginning to lose touch
with the realities of everyday life.

The battle of the moralists has been forgotten. "The Picture
of Dorian Gray" has inched its way among the classics, its
place won by the felicity of its phrasing, the wit of its epigrams.

In the literary development of its author it is seen to mark the link between the prose pieces and the comedies. Already Wilde the playwright is nearly there. Only in form does the novel differ from the plays that lay ahead just round the corner. There is the same setting of the society drawing room, the same figures from society talking the same brilliancies of dialogue.

The personality of the creator of Dorian Gray emerges quite plainly from the pages of the story. From the dialogue one can catch an echo across the years of the talk that made Wilde the delight of any company he kept. In Lord Henry Wotton you may glimpse touches of the ideal man that he would have been, the exquisite hedonist, leading a life devoted to the elegant pursuit of beauty.

The tall graceful young man, with cool, white, flowerlike hands, speaking in a low, languid, fascinating voice, was the mouthpiece of the philosophy of Wilde's new hedonism—"Nothing can cure the soul but the senses, just as nothing can cure the senses but the soul. . . . The only way to get rid of temptation is to yield to it; resist it and your soul becomes sick with longing for the things that it has forbidden to itself, with the desire for what its monstrous laws have made monstrous and unlawful. . . . Live the wonderful life that is in you. . . . Be always searching for new sensations. Be afraid of nothing. . . . Conscience and cowardice are really the same things—conscience is the trade name of the firm, that is all." Wilde had learned what Walter Pater had had to tell.

Through the mouth of Lord Henry confession was made of the secret fancies of Wilde's youth, "You, Mr. Gray, you yourself with your rose-red youth and your rose-white boyhood, you have had the passions that made you afraid, thoughts that have filled you with terror, day dreams and sleeping dreams whose mere memory might stain your cheeks with shame."

Through Lord Henry and in words addressed to Dorian Gray, Wilde offered his panegyric of youth: "You have the most marvelous youth, and youth is the one thing worth having. You have a wonderfully beautiful face and beauty of form of genius. To me beauty is the wonder of wonders." And then Wilde betrayed his secret sorrow, mourning his own vanished youth:

Yes, Mr. Gray, the gods have been good to you. But what the gods give they quickly take away. You have only a few years in which to live really, perfectly and fully. When your youth goes, your beauty will go with it, and then you will suddenly discover that there are no triumphs left for you, or have to content yourself with those mean triumphs that the memory of your past will make more bitter than defeats. Every month as it wanes brings you nearer to something dreadful. Time is jealous of you and wars against your lilies and your roses. You will become sallow, and hollow-cheeked, and dull-eyed. . . . There is such a little time that your youth will last. We never get back our youth. The pulse of joy that beats in us at twenty becomes sluggish. Our limbs fail, our senses rot. We degenerate into hideous puppets, haunted by the memory of passions of which we were too much afraid and the exquisite temptations that we had not the courage to yield to. Youth! Youth! There is absolutely nothing in the world but youth.

In this confession Wilde set down the longings that had come to dominate his life. The impulses that led to those baffling associations which this man of intellectual refinement was to form with dreary, commonplace specimens of young manhood were here explained. He saw not the commonplace but the embodiment of splendid youth. The haunting memories of what in his youth he had resisted had taken possession of him. He had learned to stand out no longer against the impulses he had once striven to strangle. Henceforth he was dedicated to youth and the spirit of youth was now to present itself to him most alluringly incarnate.

It is possible to see an appropriateness in the fact that "The Picture of Dorian Gray" served to introduce Wilde to Alfred Douglas just before they met in the flesh, face to face. Douglas was passionately absorbed in the story which he read on its publication. By his own experience he understood, as a kindred spirit, the full meaning of the references to exquisite temptations. He could have appreciated the full implications of the scene in which the languorous Lord Henry exercised all his charm to accomplish the seduction of the innocent loveliness of the young Dorian Gray. Douglas seems to have lost no time in making the acquaintance of the author of the novel.

9. YEARS OF SUCCESS

Anybody can sympathize with the sufferings of a friend, but it requires a very fine nature to sympathize with a friend's success.

IT was not, curiously enough, Oscar Wilde who conceived the idea that established his own fame as playwright. By 1890 his wit as a talker was undisputed. His wit as a writer was proved by his essays. His skill in the fashioning of brilliant dialogue was attested by "The Portrait of Dorian Gray." Everything, you might think, was there and he had only to sit down at his desk for a comedy to come off his pen. Strangely enough he did not make that effort, discouraged, perhaps, by his previous failures as a dramatist. He had to be pushed into the job by Mr. George Alexander, of the St. James's Theatre.

As a spotter of talent in the person of Wilde, Alexander is in the debt of theater-goers. Imagine a man being able to say—It was by my discernment and encouragement that Wilde took to comedy writing and so gave us the quartet of plays including the inimitable "The Importance of Being Earnest." But by the time Alexander could have made this boast, the prudent man did not make any claims at all about that lamented author, Oscar Wilde.

Among the qualifications young Mr. Alexander would have assigned to Mr. Wilde as an author deserving encouragement, would undoubtedly have been the place he held in society. Alexander had not decided to take over the fashionable St. James's as just one theater that chanced to be available. St.

James's stood for fashion and society and so did Mr. Alexander, and it was his intention that his theater should be pre-eminently the house for fashion and society. Mr. Wilde, who was so bright an ornament of the fashionable world, might be expected to deliver a play that would meet society's requirements. Mr. Alexander was shrewd. The £100 advance that he made was a risk well judged. After some initial hesitancy, Wilde went off to draw inspiration from the beauties of Lakeland and he returned with the script of "Lady Windermere's Fan."

It is a story concerning a woman with a past, a Mrs. Erlynne. She is the mother of the beautiful Lady Windermere, a relationship known to Lord Windermere but not to his wife. Placing the wrong construction on her husband's association with Mrs. Erlynne, Lady Windermere prepares to offer herself to the seduction of her admirer, Lord Darlington, but her mother saves her from the lover's embraces. The fan plays its part in the climax of the piece. Mrs. Erlynne preserves the secret of her past and finds a titled husband before the final curtain.

The melodramatic plot was no more than the skeleton for the display of the particular offerings the author had to present—scenes from the drawing rooms of the world of fashion, decorated with the brilliancies of the epigrams he had been firing off these several years past, for many of them were epigrams that had already passed the test of delivery. It was something new in the theater and with Alexander himself in the main part it drew the Town. The first night, on February 20, 1892, ended with calls for the author, who appeared before the footlights with a half-smoked cigarette in his hand. With impromptu wit he congratulated the audience on their contribution to the success of the evening.

"Ladies and gentlemen," he said, "I have enjoyed this evening immensely. The actors have given me a charming rendering of a delightful play and your appreciation has been most in-

telligent. I congratulate you on the great success of your performance which persuades me that you think almost as highly
of the play as I do myself."

He earned himself a double reproof. For his wit he was reproved as impertinent. For his solecism over the cigarette he
was reproached for ill-manners. But there was praise for the
play—"absolutely unique as a comedy of fine life and manners," "sparkling dialogue." William Archer declared the play
to be a classic. The run lasted for twenty-three weeks, which
in the Nineties was a considerable success.

But for the intervention of the stage censor the year 1892
would also have seen the staging in London of "Salomé," the
horror play. It was actually under rehearsal by Sarah Bernhardt
when a license for it was refused under the rule forbidding the
performance on the London stage of plays with biblical subjects, and the production had to be abandoned. Wilde, in his
disgust, threatened to become a naturalized Frenchman, to the
delight of "Punch," Bernard Partridge, in one of his earlier
cartoons, representing the dramatist as a French conscript
above the caption "A Wilde idea; or more injustice to Ireland."
From William Watson came the lament:

> And wilt thou, Oscar, from us flee
> And must we, henceforth, wholly sever?
> Shall thy laborious jeux d'esprit
> Sadden our lives no more for ever?

Although Wilde announced publicly in France that his intention had been deliberately taken, he relented and remained
in England to write again another day. Had he turned Frenchman and transferred himself to Paris at that time the course of
his life would have avoided the catastrophe of 1895 and—but
what does it serve to speculate on a might-have-been? Because
of the censor's ban, the author was never privileged to see a

production of the play that was to be the eventual foundation
of his fame in Germany, and which was to provide the libretto
for Strauss's opera. The play could surely have been produced
without great offense against the rule, for it is Oscar Wilde
much more than biblical in its origin as anyone may establish
who cares to take the trouble to turn up the laconic passages in
the Gospels that tell of the fate of John the Baptist.

"Salomé" is held to be unique among the productions of
British dramatists in that it was written in the French tongue.
It was translated into English by Alfred Douglas, whose rendering was corrected by the author. Over the writing of it
several apocryphal accounts have appeared. One, to the effect
that it was written for the great Sarah, drew a disdainful denial
from Wilde—"I have never written a play for any actor or
actress, nor shall I ever do so. Such work is for the artisan in
literature—not the artist." How this is to be squared with the
acceptance of Alexander's commission for the first comedy I
do not know.

There is a highly colored account in Vincent O'Sullivan's
"Aspects of Wilde" of how the play was written. This relates
that Wilde had been turning over the theme in his mind for
some time. While staying in Paris he had entertained friends at
lunch by improvising some of the dialogue. Returning to his
lodgings in the afternoon he found a blank book lying on his
table and, sitting down, began to write. Words flowed freely
and he was still seated writing at eleven o'clock at night. He
hurried out to a café, ordered food and called for the leader
of the orchestra.

"I am," he said, "writing a play about a woman dancing in
her bare feet in the blood of a man she has craved for and slain.
I want you to play something in harmony with my thoughts."
The orchestra played such terrible music that those who were
present ceased their talk and looked at each other with blanched

Three men who influenced Oscar Wilde: John Ruskin, of the strange, haunted eyes, the art critic whose example induced Wilde to set up as a professor of aesthetics. The impish painter, James McNeil Whistler, who quarreled with both Ruskin and Wilde. (Picture Post) Walter Pater, Oxford don and literary stylist, a drawing by Sir John Rothenstein. (Reproduced by courtesy of his executors)

Mrs. Wilde—Constance Mary, daughter of Harold Lloyd, Q.C. (from Boris Brasol's "Oscar Wilde")

The three heads of Lily Langtry (Lady de Bathe) are by Frank Miles, whose many drawings founded the fame of this Victorian beauty, with whom Oscar Wilde, as a young man, fell in love.

faces. Then he went back and finished "Salomé." According, however, to Robbie Ross, the play had a much less romantic origin, having been written at Torquay.

Alfred Douglas took the final touch from the story by asserting that Wilde composed the original in English and translated it into French with the assistance of Pierre Louÿs and André Gide. "At the time," Douglas stated, "Oscar wrote this play he did not know French well enough to write a play in that language and André Gide told me later that Oscar's first draft was a mass of blunders and misspellings." This is curious because that same André Gide testifies in print that Wilde's French was good, "admirable" is the term—"He narrated, gently, slowly, he knew French admirably. . . . He had almost no accent, or, at least only such as it pleased him to maintain." Could it be that Lord Alfred's disparagements arose from his own wounded vanity at the faults Wilde found in his translation? "Schoolboy faults" was Wilde's phrase—"a translation unworthy of you as an ordinary Oxonian."

That "Salomé" is a work of art is scarcely to be disputed. Within the chosen style it is perfectly achieved, an artistic whole, without a phrase out of key. It is the work not of the man who wrote the comedies, but of the mind that produced "The Sphinx." It is a masterpiece in sadism. It gives evidence of the relationship between Wilde and the Maturin "Melmoth the Wanderer." Read by a flickering light in an empty house in midwinter, with the wind playing weird tunes in the rafters, the play grips you with the sense of mounting horror. It is a study in evilness. It is unfolded in simple language, in terse, reiterated hammer phrases. Stark scene follows stark scene, mounting to the evil climax.

At the behest of Herod, Salomé dances the dance of the seven veils on a stage spattered with blood, the flesh of the young dancer's naked feet on a stage of blood. Then she claims from

Herod her promised reward for having danced the dance at his behest, demanding to be given on a silver charger the head of the prophet Jokanaan, the head of the man she had desired but who had rejected her, the wanton girl. The reluctant Herod, unable to avoid honoring his pledged word to the young dancer who had danced at his behest, orders the prophet's execution. He is beheaded in a cistern.

According to the stage direction a huge black arm, the arm of the executioner, comes forth from the cistern, bearing on a silver shield the head of Jokanaan. Salomé seizes it. Herod hides his face in his cloak. Herodias, the girl's mother, smiles and fans herself. The Nazarenes fall on their knees and begin to pray.

Then Salomé breaks into an impassioned monologue. "Ah! Thou wouldst not suffer me to kiss thy mouth, Jokanaan. Well! I will kiss it now. I will bite it with my teeth as one bites a ripe fruit. Yes, I will kiss thy mouth, Jokanaan. I said it; did I not say it? I said it. Ah! I will kiss it now."

There is a pause and the chanted monologue is resumed with taunting of the man who had rejected the wanton. His eyes, wherefore were they shut? The tongue, the scarlet viper that spat its venom, stirred no more. The head, she could do with it as she willed, she could throw it to the dogs and to the birds of the air.

"Ah Jokanaan, Jokanaan!" the chanting voice goes on: "Thou wert the only man that I have loved. All other men are hateful to me. But thou wert beautiful. Thy body was a column of ivory set in a silver socket. It was a garden full of doves and silver lilies. There was nothing in the world as white as thy body. In the whole world there was nothing so red as thy mouth. . . . Oh! how I loved thee. I love thee yet, Jokanaan, I love only thee. I am athirst for thy beauty. I am hungry for thy body. Neither wine nor fruits can appease my desire."

Herod brings the lascivious scene to a close. The slaves put out the torches, the stars disappear. A great black cloud crosses the moon and conceals it completely. The stage becomes very dark. Herod the Tetrarch begins to climb the staircase. The chanting voice of the dancer resumes her monologue on a note of triumph. "Ah! I have kissed thy mouth, Jokanaan, I have kissed thy mouth. There was a bitter taste on thy lips, was it the taste of blood? But perchance it is the taste of love. They say that love hath a bitter taste. But what of that? I have kissed thy mouth, Jokanaan."

A moonbeam, says the stage direction, falls on Salomé covering her with light. Herod turning round and seeing Salomé orders: "Kill that woman." The soldiers rush forward and crush beneath their shields Salomé, daughter of Herodias, Princess of Judaea.

"Salomé" stands by itself in the corpus of Wilde's work. It was the product of processes different from those that inspired the comedies. The wit of those plays was thrown off by the superficial workings of the intellect. "Salomé" originated from something deeper. This play was not thought but felt. A vividness and intensity of feeling went to its making. It was written with imagination working at white heat. The words flowed from his pen on to the paper, but whatever the rapidity with which it was delivered, he had for long been engaged on conception.

"In those days," records one of his acquaintances, "his thoughts were busied only with the lustful dances of Salomé. No day went by but he was talking to me of her. Now it was a passing woman who started him dreaming of the Hebraic princess. Again, he stood for hours before the jewelers' windows, building for himself an ideal combination of gems with which to festoon the body of his idol. One evening he asked me suddenly in the midst of the street: 'Don't you think she is better entirely naked?' 'Yes,' he went on, 'absolutely naked, but strewn with jewels all ringing and tinkling in her hair, on her ankles, her wrists, her throat, enclosing her hips and heightening, with their myriad reflections, the unchastity of that unchaste, amber flesh."

"Another time his Salomé was all chastity. I recall an evening when he came from the Louvre and began to speak to me of a gentle princess who danced before Herod as if by a call from Heaven that she might finally be able to demand punishment on the lying enemy of Jehovah. 'Her quivering body,' he said, 'is tall and pale as a lily, nothing sexual is in her beauty. Veils woven by angels conceal her slenderness, her blonde hair flows like molten gold over her shoulders'. . . . Many a time he simply repeated Huysmans's words: 'She is nearly naked. In the whirl of the dance the veils are unloosed, the shawls are fallen to the ground and only jewels clothe her body. The tiniest of girdles spans her hips; between her breasts, a jewel glitters.' "

The strands of genuis in Wilde were strangely mixed. Somewhere there was a cleavage. The duality of the nature of the man, showing himself now as the pursuer of women and now as the lover of youth, was paralleled in his intellectual make-up. He had the capacity to write fanciful comedies, all gaiety and charm, and the sinister study in sadism that is called "Salomé." The two strands, supported so incongruously by the same mind, were separate and distinct. So there were the two aspects of his living—the pursuit of beauty and the exquisite, and the mingling with humanity on the lower levels of the streets.

The sinister strain that found its expression in "Salomé" and "The Sphinx" can be traced back to the juvenile poems. The cleaving of human flesh and the spectacle of crimson blood had always fascinated his mind. Twenty years before there had been the vision of the killing of St. Sebastian that had so deeply impressed him.

As the censor's interdict prevented a stage presentation, "Salomé" was offered to the public in book form, first in French and then in English. It was decided, on the suggestion of Robbie Ross, to engage the genius of Aubrey Beardsley as illustrator. It was an unfortunate choice. The two masters of the decadent were not to be aligned in the production of one harmonious whole simply by nominating one to illustrate the other. Beardsley's were not pictures that illustrated the text, they were productions of his own imaginings. There was an evil about them, but it was the evil of Beardsley's conception not of Wilde's "Salomé," an evil of sophistication. Wilde's characters are lustful in their evil; Beardsley's figures are degenerate. The artist's feelings towards Wilde are shown in the illustrations in which the dramatist's features are recognizable and satirically portrayed. Wilde did not like Beardsley and Beardsley despised Wilde.

"Salomé" on publication excited a storm of denunciation that eclipsed the reception of "Dorian Gray." Blasphemy was the general verdict. Nothing, pronounced "The Times," but "an arrangement in blood and ferocity, morbid, bizarre, repulsive and very offensive in its adaptation of scriptural phraseology to situations the reverse of sacred." The diablerie of the illustrator has been blamed for intensifying the distaste and disgust of the critics. It was the only occasion on which Wilde and Beardsley were professionally associated.

10. THE FATEFUL FRIENDSHIP

Life cheats us with shadows like a puppet-master. We ask it for pleasure. It gives it to us with bitterness and disappointment in its train.

THE most publicized friendship in the world of letters was begun when Oscar Wilde and Lord Alfred Douglas met for the first time one summer's afternoon in the year 1891. The young man of twenty, with the radiance of a boy, was the incarnation of the dreams that Wilde had dreamed when he created the Prince Charming of his novel.

The youthfulness of Douglas was no less striking than his good looks. By the calendar he was twenty, but by appearance he would have passed for sixteen. It was a quality that persisted. Even when he was twenty-seven he was refused admittance to the gambling rooms at Monte Carlo on the ground that he was under age. The apologizing guardian of the door explained: "I hope, milord, you will excuse me. I have a son of sixteen and he looks much older than you do." To youth and good looks, he added an artistic outlook, a poet's sensitiveness, and the aura of the aristocrat, with a name descended through ten centuries of Scottish history. Wilde has been accused of snobbish satisfaction over Lord Alfred's title. His opinion of it is on record: "The little title of which you were so vain—and indeed it made your name sound like the name of a flower."

There was another side of the picture. The Douglases were an unruly race, distinguished even among the Scottish nobles for their turbulence. In Lord Alfred, who was called Bosie (an affectionate diminutive of boy), there was a lack of balance that resulted from the mixing of the Douglas blood with the artistic strain on his mother's side. Wilde, according to one of the women who knew him, had the "critical, capricious feminine temperament." Of the two men it might be thought it was Bosie who was the more feminine in characteristics, with his vanity that was colossal in its proportions, his pettiness, his lack of judgment and his lack of balance.

The easy-going, good-natured Wilde found that he was associating with a termagant. Such, however, was the attraction each had for the other that their attachment survived the strains of quarrels, rows and ructions, over a period of years. To the outer world the association had the appearance of gilded infamy. The actual record of it discloses the disturbances of a particularly ill-assorted couple joined in uneasy domesticity.

Wilde had no need to use on his friend the wiles of the corrupter. Years afterwards when he had reverted to normality and, as a Roman Catholic, reprobated the practices he had forsaken, Douglas gave a frank account of his youth. As a child he was pure and innocent, the idol of his mother. He was sent to Winchester—"it was a sink of iniquity"—and his innocence did not long survive; he left school a "finished young blackguard, ripe for any kind of wickedness." On this the family chronicler makes comment: "Was Winchester College so bad as he makes out? . . . Perhaps Bosie found what he was looking for; he and iniquity made excellent bedfellows."

On leaving Winchester he was sent on a Continental tour with a tutor and extended his experience in association with the divorced wife of an English earl, he being then a young man of eighteen. "The affair," he relates, "proceeded on classic lines except that there was no outraged husband. It culminated in a terrible moment when my tutor (cousin of the lady), very indiscreetly as I thought then and still maintain, knocked at the door of the lady's bedroom one night and demanded in stern tones the restitution of his ravished ewe-lamb." The ewe-lamb, reduced to tears and dressed in one of the lady's much be-ribboned night-gowns, was duly handed over after a painful scene, to the accompaniment of loud barks from the lady's pet dog. Thereafter the poor lady was blamed by whole juries of matrons for her wickedness in "seducing an innocent boy."

Bosie's education was continued at Magdalen, Oxford, where, again to quote the chronicler: "He did not recover his lost innocence. At that time the cult of boy-love was extremely fashionable among the more aesthetic undergraduates. Of this set Bosie was soon the unquestioned leader." He showed his mixed make-up by indulging sporting, convivial, intellectual and artistic interests. He played games, went on the river, and was fond of cross-country running. He read poetry, with a preference for Shakespeare, and began to write verse. He had a passion for music, and scarcely missed an evening's service in college chapel, reckoning the choir to be the finest in the world. His Oxford Magazine the "Spirit Lamp" contained a number of good things, among them an essay on "The Incomparable beauty of Modern Dress." It was the first appearance in print of the incomparable himself—Max Beerbohm.

One of Bosie's greatest friends was the old Wykehamist and fellow-poet, Lionel Johnson, who introduced him to Wilde. Lionel was a little man who, with a fine record of scholarship, gave promise of being a poet of distinction, but who took alcohol in quantities his small frame could not withstand, and died at an early age, having fractured his skull by falling. It was the regret of his later years that he had been instrumental in bringing together his dearest friend and Oscar Wilde, to whom he addressed his celebrated sonnet that begins "I hate you with a necessary hate." There was no portent of the future when he called for Douglas one afternoon in 1891 and took him along to Tite Street.

The meeting that was to govern the future of their lives is laconically described by Bosie: "What really happened at that interview was just the ordinary interchange of courtesies. Wilde was very agreeable and talked a great deal. I was very much impressed and before I left Wilde had asked me to lunch or dinner at his Club and I had accepted the invitation." Each in fact had made an impression on the other. Bosie, says the family chronicler, fell a willing victim to Wilde's wit and charm, while Wilde fell in love with Bosie's beauty and was flattered by his own evident fascination for the young Adonis.

It was some months after the first meeting before the friendship developed. Wilde dated the real beginning of their attachment from the appeal for help he received one spring day in 1892. Bosie was in trouble. His association with boys was being exploited by a blackmailer. Wilde immediately responded to the appeal, went to Oxford and arranged matters. A lawyer paid £100 to hush up the scandal and Wilde seems to have taken some of the blame upon himself. The blackmailing incident led to a quickening of the friendship. The next entry in the record, Wilde's celebrated letter that was afterwards to be used in evidence at the Old Bailey, shows that a new stage had been reached in their relationship:

It was addressed to "My Own Boy" and bore the subscription "Always with undying love." It lyricised the sweetness Oscar found in his own boy's lips,—red, rose-leaf lips that had been made no less for the music of song than for madness of kisses. Oscar was moved to declare in a phrase better in sound than sense that Bosie's soul, his slim gilt soul, walked between passion and poetry. Bosie doubtless was sufficiently satisfied with the ardor of the feelings expressed, not to ponder over the

strange nature of corporeal souls, that have the quality of slim-
ness and the capacity for walking. To complete the expression
of his delight Oscar found a comparison between his Alfred
and Hyacinthus whom Apollo loved so madly. This love-letter
from the playwright to his minion that was to be given the
publicity of recital at the Old Bailey, was regarded by its author as a sort of "prose sonnet." It was translated into French
and appeared in the "Spirit Lamp," the aesthetic magazine of
which Douglas was editor. The first verse of this literary curi-
osity, described as "a letter written in prose poetry by Mr.
Oscar Wilde to a friend and translated [1] into rhymed poetry
by a poet of no importance," read as follows:

> *Hyacinthe! ô mon coeur, jeune dieu doux et blond!*
> *Tes yeux sont la lumière de la mer! ta bouche*
> *Le sang rouge du soir où mon soleil se couche.*
> *Je t'aime, enfant câlin, cher aux bras d'Apollon.*

Wilde's letter had been written in acknowledgment of a sonnet that Douglas had sent to him, possibly the piece, written
about that time, called "Amoris Vincula" which spoke of the
ties of love, triple links, more binding than bars. Bosie was subject to moods of despondency in which he had no joy to live.
He realized the frailty of the little boat he called his happiness.
There is a sonnet of the year 1891 in which, in an unusual moment of self-analysis, he described himself as one who found
the security of his happiness to be easily disturbed—

> *. . . one note*
> *Of harsh discord, one word of bitterness,*
> *And a fierce overwhelming wilderness*
> *Of angry waters chokes my gasping throat.*

[1] The translation was the work of Pierre Louÿs, son-in-law of a French
academician.

The friendship with Wilde was not very old before the inevitable discord was produced. Wilde was dismayed at the first revelation of what rage could do when it seized upon his friend, what a transformation could be wrought. After the first bitter scene Douglas made off to Salisbury. Having got the better of his evil temper he wrote in youthful contrition to Oscar who replied in another letter of prose poetry.

Bosie was the dearest of all boys, a divine thing, the divine thing Oscar wanted, a thing of beauty and grace. But these were endearments that took some of the sting out of the accompanying reproaches. There was the other Bosie, the young man who made scenes, and so spoiled the loveliness of life. The lips that previously had displayed the allurements of kissing had been transformed into curved lips that uttered hideous things. The new incarnation of Hyacinth was still Greek and gracious, but he had been distorted by the passion of rage. Nevertheless, though his feelings had been lacerated by the first experience of a Douglas in a temper, Oscar was still pining for his wonder boy.

On this occasion the prose sonnet was not selected for translation by the "poet of no importance." Douglas received many more love-letters from his Oscar but most of them he destroyed. They were, he claimed, better stuff than these. It may be so. These too have about them a distinction of their own, examples of what can result when a master of English chooses to write in the style of the penny novelette.

In his retreat at Salisbury Douglas wrote another sonnet. "Poor stuff" was the footnote he attached to it when he printed it years afterwards in his collected poems. Whatever its quality as poetry, the sonnet shows, almost as an entry in a diary, the state of mind of its author. He had gone to Salisbury "tired of passion and the love that brings satiety's unrest." He had thought that in Sarum Close he would, adopting Wilde's phrase, be soothed "in this calm twilight of gray Gothic things." He had found the relief he had expected—love had laughed and mocked him and he cried out—

> *But thou, my love, my flower, my jewel, set*
> *In a fair setting, help me, or I die*
> *To bear Love's burden.*

The first quarrel did no more than quicken the affection between the two men. At Bosie's request Wilde wrote a sonnet, "The New Remorse," for publication in the "Spirit Lamp." That winter Wilde was engaged on his second comedy, but his progress was slow; he could not write, things were "all wrong" with him.

With Douglas, also, things had gone ill. There was more trouble over his association with boys and at the request of the authorities of the university he left Oxford without taking a degree.

Now began the most fantastic period of Wilde's life. He was writing at his best. The success of his first plays and the popularity they brought, furnished the necessary stimulus for him to continue. His royalties were yielding him an income of several hundreds a year. He devoted his money and his time to the dubious pleasure of entertaining Alfred Douglas.

The friendship yielded for Wilde the extremes of affection and aversion, of delight and utter despair. Days when the radiance of friendship touched unimaginable heights were succeeded by quarrels that rent his spirit and sent him flying from the young man who, by his rages, flayed him beyond bearing. Quarrels reached the pitch that made him resolve to cut the tormentor from his life, but each time he yielded to the importunities of the other and to the promptings of his own feelings. That time after time he suffered himself to be reconciled attests the strength of the attraction. Not he alone, but Douglas

also felt the pull of the chains of affection that bound them,
knew what it was to grow sick with longing for a voice un-
heard. And he, too, found after one of his outbursts, that

What seemed a sword to cleave its chain
Was but a link to rivet it again.

For Douglas Wilde provided gifts and entertainment with
the lavishness of an indulgent father. He shared in the indulgences of the life his money provided and was himself corrupted by the reckless profusion of pleasures, extravagances
that outstripped taste and temperance. With the indifference
of a prodigal son, Douglas took what was offered and sought for
more. His sense of the value of money was less than Wilde's.
When Wilde suggested that money was being extravagantly
wasted, Douglas replied that it was an exaggeration and it was
in bad taste to refer to it anyway. It was natural that the two
men should not think of money in the same terms. Douglas
came of a family that reckoned in terms of a thousand where
Wilde had been accustomed to think in tens. Even in his most
prosperous years Wilde's income did not reach £5000. Douglas's father had inherited property with a rent roll of at least
£20,000 annually. This did not meet his needs and he squandered a fortune of about half a million pounds.

After his Oxford disgrace Bosie sought refuge with Wilde
who, with his family, was then staying at Goring in a cottage
beside the Thames. The visit began well. Bosie wrote a couple
of poems. Wilde was engaged on his new play, but found it
more pleasant to idle away the hours in a canoe on the river.
The summer idyll was shattered by a Douglas tempest. It was
the blackest rage that had distorted him and Wilde told him
they must part. Leaving an offensive letter behind him Douglas
made off. Within three days he was telegraphing from London,
begging to be allowed to return. He was forgiven.

Next there was trouble over "Salomé" when Wilde pointed out errors in Douglas's translations. That was more than Bosie's vanity could accept, and he expressed himself in a series of violent letters. Again Wilde thought it best to part, but a friend intervened. Was Wilde not expecting too much? Would not Douglas be hurt, even humiliated, if his translation were returned like a schoolboy's exercise? No matter what he wrote or did, the friend represented, Bosie was absolutely and entirely devoted. Wilde was ready to find an excuse to relent.

Wilde's second comedy, "A Woman of No Importance," was produced in the Spring of 1893. As with the first, the play concerns a woman with a past, a Mrs. Arbuthnot, the woman of the title. Her indiscretion had resulted in a son. The situations of the piece are melodramatic and Victorian, the son, now a young man, being caused much distress by the sins of the father and of his mother too. There is a scene in which the mother cries, "Child of my shame, be still the child of my shame." It was a strangely old-fashioned setting for the display of Wilde's new-fashioned dialogue.

The plot was different from the first, but the epigrams were from the same mint. It was put into rehearsal by Beerbohm Tree at his newly built theater, the Haymarket. Son of a German grain merchant, Julius Beerbohm, and brother of the incomparable Max, Beerbohm Tree was fairly launched on his career as actor-manager, following in the footsteps of the great Irving. During rehearsals of the new play Tree was handed a copy of the letter Wilde had written praising the red rose-leaf lips of Alfred Douglas. Considering it to be dangerous, Tree showed it to Wilde who airily brushed it aside. But that was only the beginning of his troubles.

That Douglas should have allowed the letter to fall into other hands was a major contribution to the ultimate catastrophe. The letter became an instrument of blackmailers and of the lawyers who were to cross-examine Wilde at the Old Bailey, which results flowed from Bosie's carelessness. He had left it in the pocket of an old suit he gave to his valet, Wood.

Not long after Tree's warning, Wilde was menaced by blackmailers. The first opened the attack by stating that he had a letter he thought Wilde ought to have.

"I suppose," said Wilde, "you mean the beautiful letter of mine to Lord Alfred Douglas. If you had not been so foolish as to send a copy to Mr. Beerbohm Tree I should have been glad to have paid you a large sum for it as I think it is one of the best I ever wrote."

The man, Allen by name, commented: "A curious construction could be put upon that letter."

"No doubt," Wilde replied. "Art is rarely intelligible to the criminal classes."

"A man has offered me £60 for it," said Allen.

"You should take the offer," advised Wilde. " £60 is a great price. I myself never received such a large sum for any prose work of that length. But I am glad to find there is anyone in England who is willing to pay so large a sum for a letter of mine."

Wilde then rose to show Allen to the door. The man changed his tune, said he had not a penny in the world. Wilde gave him half a sovereign and ushered him out.

A little later there was another caller. This time a youth called Cliburn appeared. "I have come to you," he explained, "with a letter of Allen's."

"I can't be bothered about the letter any more," said Wilde. "Let him do what he likes with it."

At this Cliburn produced a piece of paper and said, "Allen has asked me to give it back to you."

"Why does he give it back?" asked Wilde.

"He says you were kind to him and that it is no use trying to 'rent' [blackmail] you as you only laugh at us."

The paper was dirty and Wilde said: "I think it is unpardonable that better care should not have been taken with a manuscript of mine."

Cliburn apologized—the letter had passed through many hands. Dismissing him with half a sovereign Wilde said reprovingly: "I am afraid you are leading a desperately wicked life." Some years later both Allen and Cliburn were sent to prison for another attempt at blackmail.

The second comedy ran at the Haymarket for seventeen weeks. As Wilde's fame mounted his reputation began to decline. He took on the appearance of a man coarsened by a life of sensual ease. Robert Sherard, meeting him again after an interval, was surprised to note the change that had overtaken him. His face had lost its spiritual beauty and he was oozing with material prosperity. His conversation was no longer so agreeable. Sherard detected a new, sharper note of arrogance and was in no doubt about the source of it and the "evil influence" that was corrupting him.

Too much good living and too much adulation had affected Wilde morally and physically. He was suffering from a swollen head. Like another Oxford man who had a first-rate intellectual equipment he exaggerated the value of cleverness. Margot Asquith's verdict on Lord Birkenhead is applicable to the Wilde of this period: "There is nothing more deceptive—and I might add unfortunate—than to make a cult of cleverness. It will always win the applause of a flattering circle of narrow, cultivated people; but those who possess it are inclined to believe that they are men of genius and in consequence allow themselves the latitude which they think is their due."

During the summer of that year (1893) the troubled friendship was broken off. Douglas, like a neurotic woman, seemed to have an emotional need for incessantly recurring scenes for the discharge of some of the venom of his nature. Wilde was disillusioned. The radiance was fading from the friendship. The Prince Charming, he found, was covetous of luxury, unscrupulous, and ungracious, given to outbursts of fury.

This was no realization of the life Wilde had created for Dorian Gray. That was a phantom, an illusion that had no roots in reality. The froth and folly of the life he shared with Bosie grew wearisome. After a scene more than usually revolting, Wilde could tolerate it no longer. Offering some pretext to his family he set out for Paris, leaving a false address behind lest Bosie should follow. Seated in the train he thought that his life had gone into an utterly wrong state when he, a man of worldwide reputation, was forced to run away from England to escape from a friend who was ruining him as an artist and degrading his life. The usual telegrams of remorse and entreaty followed. This time they were disregarded.

Not Wilde only, but Lady Queensberry was concerned about Alfred's future. Several times she had talked to Wilde about him, and the two chief faults in his character, his vanity and, as she termed it, his "being all wrong about money." When first she spoke to him Wilde laughed in disbelief, but within a month Bosie had demonstrated to him that the fond mother knew her own son. Wilde found that there were incessant demands for money. He was expected to pay for all his friend's pleasures whether they were together or not. It got him into his money difficulties and to make the extravagances insufferably tedious was the fact that the money was spent on little more than the pleasures of the table.

The mother grew anxious over the stories that reached her of Alfred's extravagant way of life. She sent Wilde frequent notes asking him not to give Bosie money, and not to take him out to dinner so frequently. Each note from her that came to Tite Street was marked "Private" on the envelope and each said, "On no account let Alfred know I have written to you." Why did she not speak herself to her son? She did not care to do so because it roused the fury of his temper and he was "the one of my children who has inherited the fatal Douglas temperament."

It was finally agreed that Alfred should be packed off to Egypt to stay with Lord and Lady Cromer. Lady Queensberry asked Wilde not to meet Alfred while he was abroad. He replied that he had not the slightest intention of meeting Bosie who, he urged, should be kept abroad for two or three years for his own sake as well as for her son's.

In Cairo, Douglas met a trio of young men who were to make a name for themselves as novelists—E. F. Benson, son of the Archbishop of Canterbury; Robert Hichens who was to write best sellers, including "The Garden of Allah"; and Reggie Turner, a relative of the Lawsons, owners of the "Daily Telegraph," author of a number of novels, who never succeeded in capturing with his pen the lightness and brightness of his tongue.

Bosie saw a lot of Hichens and talked a lot to him about his friend Oscar. Making clever use of Bosie's indiscretions Hichens wrote a story called "The Green Carnation," a clever satire on Wilde, who, with Douglas, was pictured so realistically that there was no mistaking the identity in real life of the Esmé Amarinth of the book. Although the novel contained no direct suggestion of improprieties, it hinted at strange sins.

It was material for gossips in London, wounding material that had originated from Bosie's indiscretions in Egypt. In his autobiography he made complaint against Hichens—"He wrote his book, 'The Green Carnation,' entirely on the strength of and as the result of association with me, for he had not at that time met Oscar Wilde." The leakages to Hichens about Wilde's hidden life must have been unlimited for so faithful a picture to have been drawn by the young novelist. It was one of Bosie's peculiar manifestations of the responsibilities of friendship.

Despite a romantic meeting with Lord Kitchener, Douglas became bored with life in Egypt. Through Lord Cromer, he was offered an honorary post in the Diplomatic Service as attaché to the British Ambassador to Turkey. He did not take up the appointment. He was next heard of in Athens. Wilde, one day, was surprised to receive from Lady Queensberry a letter stating that Alfred, whose address she gave, was anxious to have a letter. Wilde says that he advised Lady Queensberry to prevent her son from returning; with Bosie he did not then communicate. Approach through his mother having failed, Bosie appealed to Mrs. Wilde to use her influence to induce Oscar to write. Still Wilde was adamant.

Bosie wired that he was on his way to Paris. Wilde retreated to London. Bosie sent off a long letter of appeal ending with a threat of suicide. This was not to be lightly disregarded in view of his emotional instability and his ancestry. Wilde relented, crossed to Paris and there was an emotional reunion. Tears fell like rain from Bosie's cheeks as he sat throughout most of the evening holding Wilde's hand in his own like a gentle and penitent child. Two days later they returned to London to be seen at dinner at the Café Royal by Lord Queensberry. The sight set Queensberry off on the rampage.[1]

After the months of estrangement Wilde and Douglas resumed their old association. For some time, for a longer time than before, peace was preserved. Bosie was engaged in a violent and abusive dispute with his father which gave him an outlet

[1] This account of Douglas's stay in Egypt follows Wilde's version in his De Profundis letter. Douglas denied that Wilde never wrote to him.

for the discharge of his rancor. The old life was resumed and the former extravagances. Wilde, despite the success of two plays, was short of money. There were times when he was, menaced by writs, utterly despondent. He was invited to go to Paris but he could not afford to accept the invitation.

While his private life was troubled, Wilde appeared to the world as a man at the height of success. Since first he came to London he had had his place in the world of fashion. His social graces had widened the circle of his acquaintance. His friendship with Alfred Douglas extended it still further. "Lady Windermere's Fan" had established him in the theater, and given him the solid basis of achievement. His fame began to catch up with his ambition. His reputation extended across the Channel. In Paris they were beginning to count him among the European celebrities. The tall man in a frock coat of magnificence was a familiar figure in the salons and fashionable restaurants. In London his epigrams passed from speaker to speaker. Society welcomed the rare human phenomenon—celebrity with good manners.

There are accounts in a score of reminiscences of those times that attest the charm of the man, lavish maker of mirth, whose talk dazzled and intoxicated listeners. It was likened to a sunlit fountain, it had the hue of a rainbow upon it. His joyousness of life was exhilarating. The first sight of him might repel a new acquaintance, for in middle age he was fat, his hand flabby, and there was an over-elaboration about his costume. But as he talked, it is the evidence of a dozen witnesses, dislike vanished, dispelled by the enchantment of his spells. Let Frank Harris testify on this point. I chose Harris because, out of the 300 pages of his so-called Life of Wilde, there are so few statements that can be accepted as anything but inventions of his fertile imagination. But his personal impressions of the man can be received:

"His talk soon made me forget his repellent physical peculi-

arities, indeed I soon lost sight of them so completely that I have
wondered since how I could have been so disagreeably affected
by them at first sight. There was an extraordinary physical
vivacity and geniality in the man, an extraordinary charm in his
gaiety, and lightning-quick intelligence. His enthusiasms, too,
were infectious. Every mental question interested him, especially if it had anything to do with art or literature. His whole
face lit up as he spoke and one saw nothing but his soulful
eyes, heard nothing but his musical tenor voice; he was, indeed,
what the French call a *charmeur*."

As evidence of what Wilde could achieve Harris cites the
story told by Ernest Beckett of the encounter with the sporting
squires. As the author of the *mot* on their sport, "The unspeakable in pursuit of the uneatable," Wilde is no gracious memory
for the hunting man.

Mr. Beckett had a party of Yorkshire squires, chiefly fox-
hunters and lovers of outdoor life when he heard that Oscar
Wilde was in the neighboring town. Immediately he asked him
to lunch at the Grange, chuckling to himself at the thought of
the novelty of the experiment. Next day "Mr. Oscar Wilde"
was announced and as he came into the room the sportsmen
forthwith began hiding themselves behind newspapers or moving together in groups to avoid seeing or being introduced to
the notorious writer. Oscar shook hands with his host as if he
had noticed nothing and began to talk. In five minutes all the
papers were down and everyone had gathered round him to
listen and laugh. At the end of the meal one Yorkshireman after
the other begged the host to follow the lunch with a dinner
and invite them to meet the wonder again.

Wilde delighted in talking—or perhaps the word should be
discoursing. As a runner displays his speed, or a strong man his
strength, he exercised and displayed his wit. Talk, not writing,
was his natural form of self-expression. He paid his own tribute

to his gifts in the phrase: "A man who can dominate a London dinner-table can dominate the world." It was more than a phrase—it was a belief. With the success achieved in the theater he came to entertain perilous notions of his own superiority. He had come to think, as he was later to confess, that he could do anything he chose. And while he was savoring the heady wine of success, he was advancing towards the catastrophe that was to shatter in ruins the life he looked upon as being so "wonderful."

Behind the façade of the house beautiful there were sordid scenes. The friendship with the handsome Douglas was paraded for the world to see. Unseen was the hidden life and the odd characters, grooms, valets, book-makers' clerks. There was the house with the veiled windows and rooms heavy with incense, maintained by the ex-public schoolboy who having squandered a fortune of £40,000 was engaging in the wretched business of go-between. The exquisite was finding diversion in the squalid, and sometimes the squalid was disclosed to public view. There were queer guests to be seen in Mr. Wilde's company at Kettners, the Florence, the Solferino, the St. James's, even at the Savoy. The tongues of the gossips were set a'twittering. There had been that curious essay about Shakespeare, that incredible novel of Dorian Gray, and now these youths, such undesirable company for a man of fashion to be keeping. With the publication of "The Green Carnation" there was more food for gossip. And the incensed Lord Queensberry was set on touching off the grievous scandal.

11. THE SCARLET MARQUIS

It is perfectly monstrous the way people go about nowadays saying things behind one's back that are absolutely and entirely true.

THE climax to the third act of the drama of Oscar Wilde was contrived with a skill in stagecraft as great as he had himself displayed in his plays. The fashionable playwright taken at the height of his glittering success; the young friend, poet of promise, descended from one of the most ancient houses of Scottish nobility; and the Marquis of Queensberry, head of the house of Douglas, which claims to be the most ancient in Scotland, tracing its line back through ten centuries of history.

It is a sorry thing that men of such distinction should have been caught in the spotlight, exposed in their weaknesses and their shame. When it was over, and the dust of conflict had cleared away, each was seen to have been fouled in reputation by the smirching processes in which they had involved themselves. One will pity them, or revile them, according to his view of a man's responsibility for his own affairs. It is uncharitable to scorn or to ridicule them, to find in them figures of fun as they struggled in the nets in which their fates had involved them.

There must be some sense of regret that shame fell on an illustrious house and that, all to no purpose, there was the wrecking of the careers of the young poet of promise and the playwright of distinction and achievement. Out of the wreckage humanity gained nothing on the credit side, barring a prison lament and a ballad of jail. On the debit side there was the loss in comedies unwritten and some poems never sung.

What instrument of a perverse, destructive fate brought greater ruin upon his house than this Douglas? When as a boy of thirteen John Sholto Douglas succeeded as eighth holder to the Queensberry Marquisate, the world lay before him in brilliant prospect. He was heir to large estates and a fortune estimated at three-quarters of a million pounds. He married a cultured and beautiful girl, descendant through the Earls of Eglinton of a line nearly as ancient in England as that of Douglas in Scotland. But with the ancestral castle and estates Queensberry inherited the "mad, bad blood" of the Douglases. He squandered his wealth, he turned away from his wife, and he passed his last years in bitter quarrels with his children. When his heir came to take leave of his dying father, Queensberry spat at him from his deathbed.

No son has written of his father as Alfred Douglas wrote of this Queensberry. Unmanly brute, crazy lunatic, persecutor of his wife, bully of his children—the phrases were the reproaches against a Douglas father uttered by a Douglas son.

Alfred was the devoted child of a fond mother who came to look upon himself as her champion against his father. "My father," he relates, "was a madman, and his mania was to persecute my mother, an angel and a saint. He had bullied and persecuted and outraged my mother for years (long even before she divorced him in 1887). The final straw that broke the back of my mother's angelic patience was that my father wanted to bring his mistress to my mother's house and proposed that they should all three live together under one roof." After the divorce the Marquis married a girl of nineteen, to be divorced by her in a short space of time.

As to the children, Alfred Douglas claims that by twenty

years' neglect and ill-treatment, Queensberry had forfeited
all claim to a father's authority.

With his eldest son and heir, Lord Drumlanrig, Lord Queensberry involved himself in the first of his furious disputes. It
arose from political affairs. Queensberry wrote abusive letters
to Queen Victoria, to the Prime Minister, Mr. Gladstone, and
to the Foreign Secretary, Lord Rosebery. He went to the
length of threatening to horse-whip Rosebery, following him
for that purpose to Hamburg, where, horse-whip in hand, he
patroled outside Rosebery's hotel. The Prince of Wales had
to intervene. By his authority and tact the ranting Marquis
was induced to return home.

Lord Queensberry was next involved with his two younger
sons—with Lord Alfred because of his association with Oscar
Wilde, and with Percy, Lord Douglas of Hawick, for taking
Alfred's part. The father was roused to a new pitch of fury,
showered abuse on both his sons, wrote insultingly to their
mother, and even sent abusive letters and postcards to Percy's
young wife, a girl he had never met. With such a father and
such a son as Alfred, inheritors both of the imperious Douglas
nature and the rancorous Douglas temper, there would be no
restraints on actions that anger might suggest. Wilde, in his
saner moments, saw himself involved as the cat's-paw between
them in their violent hatred of each other. The exquisite in life
was implicated as third party in a back-yard quarrel between
the turbulent son and the Marquis.

Almost at the outset of the friendship Douglas had been
ordered by his father to give up Wilde. But Bosie being of age,
saw no reason to be guided by a parent who had neglected him
for years. Queensberry was not to be put off, the controversy,
as Bosie puts it, became acrimonious and the withholding of
the son's allowance was threatened. Then the Marquis met

Wilde and his animosity was charmed away. The incident of the Yorkshire squires was repeated.

It was over the lunch table at the Café Royal. The Marquis sat down in a sulky fashion. Within a couple of courses he was laughing and listening eagerly to Wilde's talk. In the end Bosie, feeling left out of things, walked out leaving the other two discussing Christianity over their liqueurs. Thereafter Queensberry relented, telling his son that Wilde was a charming fellow, man of genius, "perfectly all right."

Within six months the old animosity was revived. Gossip reached Queensberry's ear and he saw the two friends together. "With my own eyes," he wrote to his son, "I saw you in the most loathsome and disgusting relationship as expressed by your manner and expression. Never in all my experience have I ever seen such a sight as your terrible features. If I thought the thing was true I should be quite justified in shooting him at sight." The Marquis signed himself "Your disgusted, so-called father."

Alfred replied with the terse telegram: "What a funny little man you are."

The father wrote back to "the impertinent young jackanapes" threatening him with a thrashing and the cutting off of financial supplies. He would make a public scandal to expose Wilde. He would tour the London hotels and restaurants to inform the proprietors that if he caught his son and Wilde together he would thrash them there and then, and, what was more, wreck the premises. He set a detective to follow Wilde and he made his complaints known to Alfred's brother Percy and to their mother. Brother and mother both backed Alfred, bringing the Marquis to a state of heightened frenzy.

By now fashionable London was gossiping about Oscar Wilde and the "boy" he went about with. A man of twenty-five, Douglas still had the appearance of a youth of seventeen.

A prudent man would have withdrawn a little from the public gaze instead of flaunting himself with Queensberry's son. There were times when Wilde might have been tempted into prudence, but to this Douglas would not have consented. Wilde might disdain public opinion; Alfred Douglas found a perverse satisfaction in flouting it. He shared with his father an aristocratic boldness and took pleasure in courting notoriety. There is the story told by André Gide to show how impossible it would have been for Wilde to preserve any sort of discretion concerning his association with Bosie. Much of Gide's writings about Wilde are the impressions of an imaginative novelist, not the record of sober fact, but here there is the touch of reality:

"Bosie does nothing but make scenes." Gide reports Wilde as saying: "He's terrible—isn't he terrible? In London a little while ago we stayed at the Savoy: we used to take our meals there and had a marvelous little suite of rooms with a view over the Thames. We spent a great deal of money and everyone was furious with us because they thought we were enjoying ourselves and London hates people who enjoy themselves. We used to take our meals in the hotel restaurant; it was a big place and a great many people I knew used to go there; but even a greater number who knew me and whom I didn't know—because a play of mine was being acted just at the time; it was very successful and there were articles about me and portraits of me in all the papers.

"So in order to be quiet with Bosie I chose a table at the further end of the restaurant a long way from the main entrance, but quite close to a little door which led to the inside of the hotel. And when he saw me come in by this little door Bosie who was waiting for me made a scene—oh! a terrible, frightful scene. 'I won't have you come in by the side door,' he said, 'I won't tolerate it. I insist on your coming in by the main entrance with me; I want everyone in the restaurant to see us; I want everyone to say, "There goes Oscar Wilde and his minion." ' Oh! isn't he terrible?"

Irony is inherent in the nature of things. Nature, in Wilde's oft-repeated phrase, imitates art. In irony, nature with unstudied ease can surpass art in its effects. Mark the irony in the drama as Wilde moved towards his catastrophe. A blundering and half-demented father was threatening to expose him to the world for his friendship with his son, while Wilde himself, distracted by the turbulence of the son, was seeking to extricate himself from the terrible strain of a companionship that was, he feared, sterilizing him as an artist. At the outset of the acquaintance the father was warning the son to break off with Wilde while, coincidentally, the mother, a fond mother, was warning Wilde of the faults in the character of the son. While the father was denouncing the "white-livered son," the mother was lamenting to Wilde that the son was the one of her children who had inherited the fatal Douglas temperament. There was the fantastic jig half-way across Europe—Bosie hurrying to Paris in search of Wilde, Wilde flying to London to escape Bosie. There were entreaties, threats of suicide and Wilde relented. The sight of the reunited friends at the Café Royal inspired Queensberry to renewed attacks.

The publication of Hichens' "The Green Carnation" and the gossip it caused added to the Marquis's fury over Alfred's conduct. Having failed to impress his sons or his ex-wife, he wrote in outrageous terms to her father: "Your daughter must be mad by the way she is behaving. . . . I have made out a case against Oscar Wilde. . . . If I was quite certain of the thing I would shoot the fellow on sight."

The idea appealed to his son who retorted: "If you try to assault me I shall defend myself with a loaded revolver which

I always carry, and if I shoot you, or he shoots you, we shall be completely justified as we shall be acting in self-defense against a dangerous rough, and I think if you were dead many people would not miss you."

To confirm that he meant what he said Douglas staged a scene at the Berkeley Hotel. Seated with Wilde at a table in the public restaurant of the hotel, he suddenly produced his revolver and fired it off at the ceiling. He excused himself on the pretext that he did not know that it was loaded. His father reiterated his threats of a thrashing—"you reptile—you are no son of mine and I never thought you were." The letter of the date August 24th, 1894, is one for which it would be difficult to find a parallel in the entire range of parental correspondence. Addressed to "You Miserable Creature," it stated:

What could be keener pain than to have a son as yourself fathered on one. . . . If you are my son it is only confirming proof to me, if I needed any, how right I was to face every horror and misery I have done rather than run the risk of bringing more creatures into the world like yourself, and that was the entire and only reason of my breaking with your mother as my wife, so intensely was I dissatisfied with her as the mother of you children, and particularly yourself, whom, even when quite a baby, I cried over you the bitterest tears man ever shed, that I had brought such a creature into the world and unwittingly had committed such a crime.

If you are not my son, and in this Christian country with these hypocrites, 'tis a wise father who knows his own child and no wonder on the principles they inter-marry on, but to be fore-warned is forearmed. No wonder you have fallen a prey to this horrible brute, I am only sorry for you as a human creature. You must gang your ain gait. Well, it would be rather a satisfaction to me, because the crime then is not to me. As you see I am philo-sophical and take comfort from anything: but really I am sorry for you. You must be demented; there is a madness on your mother's side and indeed few families in this Christian country are without it, if you look into them.

Wilde, by now, had been brought to the point of considering legal action to silence the Marquis. Bosie encouraged the
idea that it might be possible to have his father imprisoned—
seven years' penal servitude was the prospect of his filial hopes.
In May 1894 Wilde took solicitors' advice, consulting for this
purpose Humphreys, Son & Kershaw, a well-known firm recommended to him by Robbie Ross. Action might then have
been taken but Douglas's cousin, George Wyndham, M.P.,
intervened to stop a family scandal becoming public property.
Mr. Humphreys was instructed to demand an apology from
the Marquis, who flatly declined to offer one. Instead he called
in person on Mr. Wilde at his house in Tite Street.

Queensberry was at one time lightweight amateur boxing
champion. He was accompanied for intimidation purposes, by
a bodyguard of one. He started off the interview in the library
in intimidating fashion by commanding Wilde to sit down. He
was "waving his hands in the air in epileptic fury." What followed is related in Wilde's own narrative:

I said to him, "I do not allow anyone to talk to me like that in
my house or anywhere else. I suppose you have come to apologize
for the statement you made about my wife and myself [that Mrs.
Wilde was petitioning for divorce] in letters you wrote to your
son. I should have the right any day I chose to prosecute you for
writing such a letter."

He said, "The letter was privileged as it was written to my son."

I said, "How dare you say such things to me about your son and
me?"

He said, "You were both kicked out of the Savoy Hotel at a
moment's notice for your disgusting conduct."

I said, "That is a lie."

He said, "You have taken furnished rooms for him in Piccadilly."

I said, "Somebody has been telling you an absurd set of lies
about your son and me. I have not done anything of the kind."

He said, "I hear you were thoroughly blackmailed for a disgusting letter you wrote to my son."

I said, "The letter was a beautiful letter and I never write except for publication." Then I asked "Lord Queensberry, do you seriously accuse your son and me of improper conduct?"

He said, "I do not say that you are it but you look it. You look it and you pose as it which is just as bad. If I catch you and my son together in any public restaurant I will thrash you."

I said, "I do not know what the Queensberry Rules are, but the Oscar Wilde rule is to shoot at sight."

I then told Lord Queensberry to leave my house. He said he would not do so. I told him I would have him put out by the police. He said, "It is a disgusting scandal."

I said, "If it be so you are the author of the scandal and no one else."

I then went into the hall and pointed him out to my servant. I said, "This is the Marquis of Queensberry, the most infamous brute in London. You are never to allow him to enter my house again."

Queensberry, with bodyguard in tow, then left the house, but not before he had delivered himself of a torrent of abuse with threats of action to come. By this time the Marquis and his son were equally resolved in their determination that one should break the other, and both disguised their rancor behind the pretense of a nobly inspired purpose. A mere glance at Lord Queensberry's letters is sufficient to dispose of the suggestion that he had any sincere regard for Alfred's welfare. The letter he wrote, between the trials, to his daughter-in-law, Lord Percy's wife, will suffice. Forwarding to her a letter Alfred had sent him, he wrote:

I enclose letter from the gilt soul whose rose-leaf lips are made for the madness of kissing—see Oscar Wilde's letter—so that you may see the sort of lot you have got amongst and are supporting. Look out for your own children, there is such a thing as heredity as is well known they throw back to the Montgomery grandpere. I don't read these letters myself, just the first few lines seeing who it is from, and don't distress yourself. His letters [Alfred's] can be used for shutting him up in an asylum should he return, but death will surely end all this long before, but your friend O.W. is responsible for having reduced this wretch to this state.

While this domestic fracas was proceeding around him, Wilde wrote his last two comedies. The third, "An Ideal Husband," had like its predecessors a melodramatic plot, concerning a designing woman and a Cabinet Minister, the disclosure of a State secret and an attempt at blackmail. It is a fair assumption that the author's experience of blackmail in actual life, suggested blackmail as the theme for the piece.

This play did not come so trippingly from the pen. It was at last completed for production at the Haymarket, with Lewis Waller and Julia Neilson in the leading parts. The critics were agreed that the plot of the play was inferior to its predecessors. There was no difference, it was conceded, in the quality of the talk.

Almost as soon as this play had left the stocks the playwright went into production again, being in need of funds to meet the mounting bills of his extravagances. The labor of composition was this time discharged at the South Coast resort of Worthing, a fact commemorated by the name of one of the characters. Writing proceeded quickly despite difficulties with Bosie and the attractions of a youth whose acquaintance Wilde had formed on the Worthing beach.

The fourth and last of the comedies was the finest of the series—"The Importance of Being Earnest." On almost every other matter concerning Wilde opinions differ, but on this play opinion is unanimous and acclamation universal. Strictly speaking it is not a comedy and it is of too delicate a fabric to be termed farce. It is a fairy tale that might have been invented by Gilbert, ornamented with Wilde settings and epigrams, a piece of sheer, innocent, sparkling fun. It introduced to the world the device of Bunburyism and the character of Lady Bracknell.

In after times Wilde was to accuse Alfred Douglas of having made incessant demands on his time, thus making it difficult for him to undertake his literary work. There was no thought of this when he set out with his family for Worthing. Before leaving London he sent a pressing invitation to Bosie to join him by the sea. Douglas paid one short visit to Worthing and after leaving sent a poem with which his friend was charmed. The playwright was able to report with satisfaction on the progress of his work. His stay at Worthing extended beyond the limits of Bosie's patience. He was bored with his own company in London, he could not tolerate being alone, without diversion, for any length of time, and by letter and telegram, he suggested that they should share a few days away together. Wilde was delighted at the prospect.

Bosie traveled down from London. He arrived at Worthing with a companion whom Wilde refused to admit in the house. The companion having "returned to the duties of his profession," Wilde and Douglas went off together to Brighton where they stayed at the Grand. The visit was ruined by a visitation of influenza. First Bosie was a victim and was nursed by Wilde. Then Wilde went down with 'flu and found himself neglected by Bosie, who went off on his pleasures. When taxed with selfishness, he flew into a passion.

The quarrel was one that stood out for sheer ugliness even amongst their ugly bickerings. The description of it that he wrote in prison conveys Wilde's sense of horror at the outrage to which he was submitted, a sick man with a fever exposed to the battering of Bosie's abuse. He related how, as he lay on his bed, Douglas, in hysterical rage, made for him, as if he were going to attack him as he lay ill. Overcome with a sense of horror Wilde jumped from the bed and fled. The doctor found him in a state of nervous prostration.

A taunting letter from Bosie followed, a letter that mocked

him with common jests over his illness. "When you are not on your pedestal you are not interesting. The next time you are ill I will go away at once." Wilde was revolted. No longer must his life be polluted by association with a man of such a nature. He decided to request Sir George Lewis (founder of the noted firm of solicitors) to notify Lord Queensberry that never again would there be any association with his son.

By one of the twists of fate it chanced that tragedy in the House of Douglas should at that moment divert Wilde from his purpose. To those superstitiously inclined the title of Viscount Drumlanrig, that is borne by the heir to the Queensberry Marquisate, seemed to be under a curse, so many of the holders had met with an untimely end. Even as Wilde was preparing his instructions for the solicitors, he read in the newspapers that Lord Alfred's brother had been discovered dead. Lord Drumlanrig had been found shot, with his gun lying beside him, in circumstances that did not rule out suicide.

Wilde could not add to the distress of his friend who had suffered so tragic a loss. Instead of writing to the solicitors, he sent a telegram of sympathy to Bosie. Shortly afterwards the young man returned, his eyes dim with tears, seeking consolation in his sorrow. Thus again the friendship was renewed. The career of Oscar Wilde moved to its appointed catastrophe. After the reconciliation the old feelings were renewed.

The year 1895 opened well for Wilde. His third comedy "An Ideal Husband" was put on at the Haymarket. The Prince of Wales, who was present at the première (January 3), was delighted with the piece. When there was talk of cutting some of the dialogue the Prince forbade it to be done. "Do not take out a single word," he ordered. For the dramatist it was a most acceptable command.

Not long afterwards "The Importance of Being Earnest" went into rehearsal at the St. James's. Wilde's gratification was

marred by the disturbances in his private life. He was pressed
by creditors, disturbed by the provocations of Alfred Douglas
and pursued by the menacing Queensberry. He was puffed
up with pride and in an unbalanced state of mind. At rehearsals
he conducted himself so intolerably that Alexander told him to
leave the theater and not to return until the first night. A few
days before the run he was asked by a reporter whether he
thought the new play was going to be a success.

"My dear fellow," Wilde expostulated, "you have got it
wrong. The play *is* a success. The only question is whether the
first night audience will be one."

The audience had to make their way to the theater, on the
evening of February 14, through streets deep in snow. Valen-
tine's Day had been marked by the worst snowstorm London
had experienced for years past. A bitter wind whipped the
snow into drifts. Nevertheless a distinguished company
gathered at the theater such as was not often seen away from
Covent Garden at the season's height. Outside the theater a
crowd of sightseers braved the wintry night to cheer celebrities
as they drove up. None was more loudly greeted than the playwright as he helped his pretty wife from their carriage. To all
appearance he was at the zenith of a carefree, glittering career.

When the company had disappeared within, the Marquis of
Queensberry appeared burdened with his bunch of carrots and
other vegetables with which to demonstrate inside the house
against that "brute" Wilde. But he was refused admittance.
Fortunately for Wilde he had talked too much beforehand
when in his cups. Lady Queensberry was warned by a friend
and the warning was passed on to Wilde, who informed the
police.

The audience that night at the St. James's were even more
"successful" than the author could have hoped. The comedy
was rapturously received. In the morning the critics joined in

the acclaim, welcoming the new piece as a work of genius.
Wilde could forget the Scarlet Marquis and his carrots as he
read the lavish praise. It was balm for his soul. For his enemy
it was an added bitterness. He had been balked of his prey and
the applause that Wilde received inflamed the rancor of his
jealousy and hatred.

Four days later (February 18) Queensberry presented himself at Wilde's club, the Albemarle. To the hall porter he
presented his visiting card on which he had written the words
"To Oscar Wilde posing as a somdomite." With procedure
appropriate to the occasion, the porter placed the card, with its
misspelled inscription, in an envelope, noting on it the date and
time. Ten days later on entering the club, Wilde was handed
the envelope. He took out the card and read Lord Queensberry's challenge.

12. CROWNING FOLLY

One should never make one's début with a scandal; one should reserve that to give an interest to one's old age.

IT was early in the evening when Lord Queensberry's card was handed to Wilde. Before midnight he had decided to accept the challenge. He would take the Marquis into court and prosecute him for criminal libel. Scarcely could he have reached a worse decision. But he was a man of letters, a lord of language, not a man of affairs. His judgment was not of the best and he had no advisers to guide him—just Robbie Ross, young and inexperienced, Bosie Douglas, an elemental force, and the sycophantic hangers-on of his literary entourage.

The simplest thing to have done was to sit tight, ignore the card and leave the next move to the Marquis. It is what you would have expected of Wilde, with his easy-going, indolent nature. More prudently, he could have left London for a space, withdrawn across the Channel on the excuse of poor health, or for the prosecution of his affairs in Paris. After a decent interval he could have returned to London with a new play completed to clinch his place in the theater. By then Queensberry might have calmed down a bit—even Queensberry could not indefinitely have contained the frenzy of the wrath that was consuming him.

Folly, not prudence, directed Oscar Wilde. Accepting the challenge, he placed himself obligingly at Queensberry's disposal. He claimed later that, under the double distraction of assaults on either hand from father and son, he lost his head and staggered blindly like an ox to the shambles. Judgment certainly he lacked. But decide he did, making up his mind without loss of time. It had all the appearances of decisiveness and none of a man irresolute, exhausted, succumbing unwillingly to pressure.

The decision that he had reached was determined by the character of the man and the exalted state of mind he had attained. All the circumstances of his life, stretching way back to his school days, had contributed to his belief in himself, his magnificent, outrageous conceit. He had the intellectual man's contempt for the ill-educated, half-demented Queensberry, but had Queensberry been a person of the utmost distinction, he, in his megalomania, would have had no hesitation in taking him on. In that state of exaltation he would have taken on the devil himself.

Everything in his life had encouraged him in the opinion that he was a superior person. The eminent physician his father, the distinguished Speranza his mother had nourished his childhood conceit. His easy successes at school and university, the brilliance of his Oxford record, his position in the world of fashion, the brilliancy of his fame in the theater—all had contributed to his sense of ascendancy.

Even after his fall, when a new sense of humility had affected him, he was still hypnotized by the record of his own eminence. He thought of himself, even then, as one to whom the gods had given almost everything—genius, a distinguished name, high social position, brilliancy, intellectual daring. In his early manhood he had reached the opinion that he stood in "symbolic relations to the art and culture of his age." He had made art a philosophy and philosophy an art. He had altered the minds of men. There was nothing he had said or done which had not made people wonder. He conceived himself as having evolved some new beauty in whatever he touched—drama, novel, poem in prose, poem in rhyme, subtle or fantastic dialogue. He had awakened the imagination of the century so that it had created myth and legend around him.

How was it to be imagined that a being with this sum of achievement to his credit could be intimidated by a man so much his inferior as the déclassé Marquis? These ideas about himself had formed a background to his mind for so long a period of his development that they had supplanted judgment. Already, in one encounter with the Marquis he had come off best. It was a portent. He had faced the blackmailers and worsted them. Was there anything he could not do?

The human mind is partial and selective in its operations. It tends to seize hold of the facts that support an acceptable conclusion, and the rest, facts unpalatable, it will suppress, not by conscious direction but by some automatic process of elision. In his mood of exaltation Wilde passed over the dangers of his position—his secret life, the youths, the house with curtained windows, the blackmailers. He was most vulnerable to attack. He ignored the fact. His memories of the past, of the lawsuit upon which his own parents had so injudiciously embarked, might have leaped across the years to give him warning. The circumstances were exactly paralleled. His father had been challenged in the manner in which he was threatened now. Sir William's reputation had been assailed at the point where he had been most vulnerable. He had allowed himself to be forced into foolhardy legal action to save his name and had ruined himself by so doing. Was the son to succumb in the same crevice that had been fatal to the father?

What purpose, in any case, was to be served by taking his opponent into court? Queensberry's purpose was clear—to hound the "brute Wilde" out of society. Legal action by Wilde would almost inevitably contribute to that end. Even were he to win the verdict he must emerge with his reputation so besmirched that his place in the world of fashion would be untenable.

Not, it seems, until the law had been set in motion did the weaknesses of Wilde's position enter into his consideration. Then the sense of doom came over him and by then it was too late. On the fateful evening of Thursday, February 28, he decided on a criminal prosecution of Queensberry. His mind was made up between leaving his club and sitting down in his hotel to write to Alfred Douglas and Robbie Ross to inform them of the latest "hideous" development. Ross visited him that same evening. Douglas joined him the following day.

What was said between the two friends that night in the Avondale Hotel, Piccadilly, is not on the record. The advice Ross gave is not known. Douglas's part in events is also uncertain. Later, both he and Wilde sought to place the responsibility on each other. Wilde represents himself as having been induced to act against his better judgment: Douglas asserts that not until after action had been launched did he know Wilde had begun proceedings. Both accounts appear to be false. Wilde, on the testimony of his letter to Ross, did not need to be coerced at that stage. Douglas, on the evidence of the funds he supplied to finance the proceedings, was completely aware of what was decided on.

What is fact is that on the morning of March 1 Wilde went to the offices of Humphreys, Son & Kershaw to consult Ross's legal adviser, Mr. C. D. Humphreys. Wilde explained his purpose in a statement that concealed as much truth as it contained. The man who goes to law without taking his solicitor fully into his confidence is already well advanced towards losing his case. Wilde did not explain that Queensberry's accusation was false only in the word "posing," and that far from merely posing he had been in fact engaging in the practices of which he was accused. So from the very outset he was committed to the course of deception and perjury he was to sustain.

Question was immediately raised about financing the costs of a prosecution. Douglas arranged to pay a sum of £360 to the solicitors. Bosie, on the evidence of Wilde, stated that he would be delighted to pay all that was necessary in costs: his father had been an incubus to them all: they had often discussed the possibility of getting him put into a lunatic asylum so as to keep him out of the way: if Wilde would come forward to have him shut up he would be regarded by the family as their champion and their benefactor.

The solicitor accepted instructions to proceed against Lord Queensberry for criminal libel. It was a prosecution to be founded on perjury. Wilde has been generally reproved for his imprudence in launching it. He has, curiously enough, escaped censure for appealing to the law for protection against Queensberry and against the truth. It was the most outrageous of his poses, this masquerade as an outraged innocent. The prosecution was a hypocritical sham. The only thing to be said in defense of it was that it was undertaken to oblige a friend. It was coming near to a conspiracy with Bosie to defeat the ends of justice. The moralists who have been busy enough over other aspects of this man's life, have been silent over this. Wilde knew better. It was, he declared, the "one disgraceful, unpardonable and to all time contemptible action" of his life.

On the afternoon of Saturday, March 2, 1896, Oscar Wilde appeared at Marlborough Street Police Court to prosecute the 8th Marquis of Queensberry on a charge of criminal libel. He drove to the police court in carriage and pair, and emerged the well-turned-out figure of a man about town. Lord Alfred Douglas and his brother Percy were present in court, which was crowded with perfumed youth. As Alfred Douglas was, as might be said, an exhibit in the case, the magistrate ordered him to leave the court.

The proceedings were brief, but twice Wilde incurred reproof from the bench. Asked if he was by profession a dramatist and author, he replied, "I believe I am well known in that capacity," which drew from the magistrate the curt instruction, "Only answer the questions, please." When the depositions had to be signed he asked for one passage to be read over to him a second time. "If you would just attend," said that magistrate testily, "this would not have happened." As he affixed his signature to the depositions it was noted that the hand that took the quill pen was wearing a glove.

Queensberry was committed to take his trial at the Old Bailey. Precluded, at that stage, from saying anything in his own defense, he contrived to make it known that he had acted as he did "to save my son and I abide by what I wrote."

In the month between Queensberry's committal and the trial, Wilde, guided by Bosie and the spirit of irresponsibility, hurried off with his friend to the South of France and the attractions of Monte Carlo. From these diversions he came posting back to play his role at the Old Bailey.

While Wilde and Douglas turned their backs on London and the law, the Marquis set energetically to work to build up his case. To encourage himself he fired off a broadside against his two sons—"this good for nothing, white-livered son of mine" and his "disgusting brother"—as he described them in a letter to their mother. "You must all be mad," he declared, "and if you choose to make inquiries you will find that the whole town has been reeking of this hideous scandal of Oscar Wilde for the last three years. If I were to shoot this hideous monster in the street I should be quite justified for he has almost ruined my so-called son. . . . Bosie is a perfect fool, if he is not worse. He always was double-faced and sly. . . . How can you account for the loathsome appearance of this Alfred? I am not going to try and analyze what his hideous relations with this man are. It is well known there is a gang of about twenty of them. One was caught red-handed and imprisoned in Paris a few months ago. What I say and have already told them both is that it is as bad to pose as such a thing and to give every occasion to talk, as they are doing, as being actually criminal. I myself saw them together in such hideous relationship as I have never heard or seen between two men—God save the word 'man.' "

Queensberry had at that time little support to put before a jury in justification of his charge. Up to the time of his committal for trial the only evidence in his possession were the two letters that, through the carelessness of Lord Alfred, had come into the hands of the blackmailers. The youth Allen had handed them over to a solicitor named Abrahams, who, under threat of publication, had tried to induce Wilde to buy them back. "I hope they will be published," was Wilde's disdainful reply. From Abrahams they had passed to Queensberry, who some time previously had taken legal advice on them, to be informed that they alone would not be sufficient to support a charge against Wilde. The Marquis, thereafter, had engaged a detective to follow Wilde. Now a second detective was engaged.

The task of the investigator was lightened by the intervention of a small-part actor, Charles Brookfield, who had been appearing as the valet in "An Ideal Husband." He came forward to supply the names of some of the men with whom Wilde had been associating.

Envy was the motive that made Brookfield play the informer. Son of a lady of the Court, he came down from Cambridge about the time Wilde left Oxford with much the same intentions for a career. He was a good talker, entertaining companion and wit, whom some preferred to Wilde. He too had tried his hand at playwrighting, but while Wilde achieved fame Brookfield was humiliated by lack of success. He conceived himself ill done-by. He burlesqued Wilde in a piece called "Poets and Puppets," but the ridicule was laughed off by Oscar, who offered him a part in one of his own plays. Brookfield took the role of valet so that he would not have to learn many of the author's lines. Jealousy had fermented in his mind into an obsession, and he went about stirring up opposition to his enemy. Some time afterwards he was appointed Examiner of Plays, selected, perhaps, because he had contributed to the ruin of the wittiest playwright of his time. The information he gave against Wilde was supplemented by another person moved by professional envy—a woman who resented the competition of the male prostitutes patronized by Wilde and his associates. The woman supplied the address of the house in the shadows. There the detectives found names and addresses that gave them access to the gutter world of Wilde's secret life.

These revelations put the Marquis in a strong position. He diverted himself by launching a further onslaught on his sons, addressed this time to Alfred—"You miserable misguided creature—I do not write either to argue or remonstrate with you, as I know it is useless, neither need you have any fear of me, for you are too insignificant, ridiculous and physically wretched, though I could beat you with one arm tied behind my back. I would finish such as you in five minutes, but your good-for-nothing, kicked out, run-away, turn-up brother is a different matter. He, too, is a wretched creature but has some pretensions to be a man." There followed an offer to "take on" Percy for any sum he liked ("Some of these sporting coves like Oscar Wilde may wish to back him") in a fight to the finish. The welter of abuse was continued in letters to other members of the family—to Percy's wife, to Percy's wife's father, to Percy's solicitor. In the letter to the solicitor, he made apology for the violence of his language—"In the trouble I am in it is beyond human endurance that I should have further trouble brought upon me by these good-for-nothing sons." There was also the assurance that he was endeavoring to avoid incriminating Alfred who—"goes and throws himself on our swords that mean to hack the other fellow to pieces, and which we can do without touching Alfred."

Back from Monte Carlo, Wilde was faced with the unpalatable fact that the secret of his hidden life had been pierced by Queensberry. Legal procedure required that the Marquis should give particulars of the facts on which he relied for his defense. Already he had submitted one outline. This was now amended and extended. The facts set out on this plea of justification showed that it was not going to be a matter merely of "posing" by Wilde. Set down in black and white were the names of ten associates, with times and places of the offenses alleged. There was little the detectives had not unearthed. Even the companion Wilde took on a visit to Paris was named, together with the hotel they stayed at.

The plea of justification asserted that in view of the practices and offenses alleged, and of publications calculated to subvert morality and encourage unnatural vice, John Sholto Douglas, Marquis of Queensberry, made his claim that it was "in the public interest that the libel on the said Oscar Fingal O'Flahertie Wills Wilde should have been published to the exposure of the true character and habits of the said Wilde, and to the prevention of the further debauching of the liege subjects of our Lady the Queen." The dates, ranging over the years 1892–93–94, were given with months and days. The investigators had been thorough and successful in their task.

Truly Wilde was going to impale himself on the sword of

his adversary if he persisted with this prosecution. He, with Douglas, attended at the offices of the solicitor to go over the plea of justification. Had he ever imagined that his secrets would remain undisclosed, there was no longer any pretext for self-deception.

The mood of exaltation in which Queensberry's challenge had been accepted had passed. The clouds of illusion had been wafted away and he had a sight of the realities of his situation. He had walked into the pit his enemy had dug for him. He began to lose his nerve. Some of his friends advised him to drop the prosecution and leave the country. He began to waver. Douglas was there to put some stiffening into him. Wilde would have liked to talk things over. Bosie always cut him short. Wilde thought his friend was too bored even to pretend to be sympathetic. It was not that—Bosie had enough knowledge of his friend's nature to know that if he were to keep him to the sticking point he must not be allowed to indulge his doubts.

It was during these days of his dejection that Wilde took counsel of Frank Harris, whom he had known for years. Harris was one of the leading figures in literary journalism in London of the Nineties. After adventuring as a rolling stone in his earlier years, he had married wealth, set up house in Park Lane, and had acquired a literary pulpit for himself as Editor of the "Fortnightly," in which two of Wilde's critical essays had appeared. He was a man with a zest for life and for letters, a lively talker with a booming voice, a profound knowledge of Shakespeare and an ambition to outshine Casanova. In his life of Wilde—not the least imaginative of his works of fiction—he related how he gave excellent advice to his friend at lunch one day at the Café Royal. His account is, on this occasion, borne out both by Bernard Shaw and by Alfred Douglas. Harris and Shaw were lingering in talk over the luncheon table when Wilde joined them. Shaw rose to leave but Wilde, with his usual courtesy, invited him to remain. Harris then delivered his advice very much, on the testimony of his own account, as a judge addressing a jury.

"First of all," he said, "we start with the certainty that you are going to lose the case against Queensberry; you must drop it at once, but you cannot then stay in England. Queensberry would attack you again and again. You should go abroad and as ace of trumps take your wife with you. [Alas, poor Constance!] Now for the excuse: I would sit down and write such a letter as you alone can write to 'The Times.' You should set forth how you have been insulted by the Marquis of Queensberry and how you went naturally to the courts for a remedy, but you found out very soon this was a mistake. No jury would give a verdict against Lord Alfred's father, however mistaken he might be. The only thing for you to do is to go abroad and leave the whole ring with its gloves and ropes, its sponges and its pails to Lord Queensberry. You are a maker of beautiful things, you should say, and not a fighter, whereas the Marquis takes joy only in fighting. You refuse to fight with a father in such circumstances."

Harris turned for support to Shaw who agreed; a jury would hardly give a verdict against a father trying to protect his son.

"Oscar," recounted Harris, "seemed much moved. To my astonishment Douglas got up at once and cried out, with his little white, nervous distorted face, 'Such advice shows you are no friend of Oscar's.' 'What do you mean?' I asked in wonderment; but he turned and left the room on the spot. To my astonishment Oscar also got up. 'It is not friendly of you, Frank,' he said weakly. 'It really is not friendly.' I stared at him. . . . He went through the door and disappeared. Like a flash I saw part at least of the truth. It was not Oscar who had ever misled Douglas but Lord Alfred who was 'driving' Oscar whither he would."

Left to himself Harris was at a loss to imagine what Douglas proposed to himself by hounding Oscar on to attack his father. He could not rid himself of the appearance of that white, bitter face. Suddenly, he was struck by a sort of likeness, a similarity of expression and of temper between Alfred Douglas and his unhappy father. "I could not get it out of my head—that little face blenched with rage and the wild hating eyes; the shrill voice, too, was Queensberry's."

Bernard Shaw's account of the lunch-table meeting was in substantial agreement. "I myself was present when on the eve of the Queensberry trial Harris prophesied to Wilde with marvelous precision exactly what immediately afterwards happened to him, and warned him to leave the country. Wilde, though under no illusions as to the folly of the quite unselfish suit-at-law he had been persuaded to begin, miscalculated the force of the social vengeance he was unloosing on himself. When Harris foretold him the truth, Wilde denounced him as a faint-hearted friend and left the room in anger."

Alfred Douglas himself agreed with the substantial accuracy of Harris's account. "When I met you and Shaw at the Café Royal," Douglas wrote to Frank Harris, "I had screwed Oscar up to the 'sticking-place' and I had all my family behind me. I had paid out of my pocket all the expenses of the case. When, therefore, you and Shaw gave your advice based on one-sided knowledge of the facts, I resented it and was terribly afraid Oscar would weaken and throw up the sponge. I knew he was an awful coward. I did not tell you our case for fear that I might not convince you and that you and Shaw might, even after hearing it, argue Wilde out of the state of mind I had got him into. My one object was to get him out of the café as soon as possible. Hence my rudeness. I was quite rude, I admit."

Douglas was in charge of the prosecution and in charge of the prosecutor as well. His plan of attack was that the prosecution should be opened with an onslaught on Queensberry's character. He looked forward to the opportunity of testifying in the witness-box that his father was "an inhuman brute, who had bullied and outraged my mother for years before she divorced him, that he had neglected and ill-treated his children and forfeited all claim to a father's authority." He supplied the solicitors with a proof of the evidence he was prepared to give and throughout the rest of his life he was to complain that solicitors and counsel had let him down. He does not seem to have been warned that conduct of the case as he contemplated it was not a legal possibility. The judge would have stopped it at the outset. Solicitors and counsel could have told Douglas this at the time. They considered, perhaps, that the young man was making a nuisance of himself and that the best way to rid themselves of him was to ignore him. Why should they have concerned themselves with these irrelevancies anyway? If Mr. Wilde was innocent of Queensberry's charge then he would win the verdict. They were not aware of the realities known to Wilde and Douglas.

Having deceived his solicitor Wilde had to lie to his counsel. Humphreys briefed Sir Edward Clarke, Q.C., then at the height of the fame that still shines in the memory of the Bar. A great advocate, more successful in defense than as a prosecutor, he was one of those to whom you apply the phrase that rings old-fashioned in these times—he was the soul of honor. Before he would agree to take the brief in this, the most unpleasant case in his career, he required assurances that there was no truth in the allegation the Marquis had made. This Wilde gave him "on his honor as a gentleman." It was a lie Sir Edward was never able to forget.

A night or two before the trial Wilde, accompanied by his wife and by Douglas, was present in a box at the St James's to see his comedy "The Importance of Being Earnest." It was the last time he was to be the spectator of one of his own pieces, the last time he was to enter a London theater. George Alexander remonstrated with him: it was in bad taste for him to be seen theater-going at such a time. "Then," Wilde said, "it is bad taste in the audience to attend—and I would consider it bad taste if they went to see anybody else's play."

When told it would be better for him to go abroad rather than to the Old Bailey, he commented: "I have just been abroad and come home again. One can't keep going abroad unless one is a missionary or, what comes to the same thing, a commercial traveler."

Chance working through a French journalist employed in London gave a new twist to the scandal of the case that had a bearing on Wilde's ultimate fate. By a confusion of names the journalist was summoned to serve on the Grand Jury which, under the old procedure, had to give preliminary consideration to an indictment and return a true bill before an accused person could be put on his trial at the assizes. The journalist did not decline the opportunity to take part in so celebrated a case, and thus he came to hear the name mentioned of Lord Rosebery, who had not long succeeded the aged Gladstone as Prime Minister. In his ranting letters Queensberry had accused Rosebery of having a bad influence on his oldest son. He was writing in a political sense, but the Frenchman, mistaking the meaning, thought that Rosebery's morals were at fault. Proceedings before a Grand Jury could not be reported in the English press but there was no bar abroad. So, the journalist telegraphed a report to his newspaper that the Prime Minister of England was implicated in the Wilde scandal, a report that was quickly spread in the continental press. By this means it became the talk of London Clubs, to the vast annoyance of Ministers of the Crown.

13. THE ACCUSER

Questions are never indiscreet: answers sometimes are.

ON the morning of April 3, 1895, Oscar Wilde drove in a carriage and pair to the Old Bailey. Here to all appearances was no man facing an ordeal on which his reputation and his place in society depended, but one undertaking a public duty with satisfaction to himself. He entered a court that was crowded to capacity.

The little Marquis had been the first of the principals to arrive. He came in alone and stood, hat in hand, in front of the dock. He spoke to none and no one spoke to him as he stood waiting. The unfriendly chronicler noted that there was nothing aristocratic about his appearance.

Wilde, a fine figure of a man, joined his counsel and sat with them in animated conversation. The Marquis was directed to his place in the dock, the judge took his seat on the bench and the hearing was begun.

The best men at the Bar were engaged. With Sir Edward Clarke were Charles Mathews, later to be Director of Public Prosecutions, and young Travers Humphreys, then at the beginning of the career which was to take him to the bench. Sir Travers Humphreys is the last survivor of those who fought the Wilde case. Lord Queensberry's defense was in the hands of Edward Carson, Q.C., M.P., who led Charles Gill, senior Treasury counsel at the Central Criminal Court, and Arthur Gill. A third Q.C. held a watching brief for the two Douglas brothers.

"Barebones" Carson, a plodding schoolmate of Wilde's at

Trinity, was beginning to make up the leeway that had separated him at Dublin University from his brilliant contemporary. His tall, stooping figure and dour countenance were familiar in the Courts and at the House of Commons, although the high-lights of his career as champion of Ulster, Minister of the Crown and Lord Justice of Appeal, were years ahead. Already he had made his reputation as a formidable cross-examiner. Wilde, when told that this was to be his legal opponent, remarked that no doubt he would carry out his duties with all the added bitterness of an old friend. This was an injustice to Carson, who had at first declined to accept the brief and was only prevailed upon to accept after Lord Halsbury, the Tory ex-Lord Chancellor, had told him that the main thing was to arrive at justice—"and it is you who can do it best." Carson was not an Old Bailey advocate. He was brought in as the best man to smash Wilde in cross-examination.

The duel between the two men—the florid, brilliant Irishman and the cadaverous, painstaking Ulsterman—is a legal classic. The records of evidence do not contain brighter scintillations than Wilde's display of repartee. Carson hung on to him doggedly like a hound on the scent, not to be turned from the trail. In the end he prevailed—or should it not be said that truth prevailed?

The preliminaries of the case were soon disposed of. Wilde's case was summarized to the jury by Sir Edward Clarke. The porter of the Albemarle Club proved publication of the libel. Wilde replying to his own counsel gave the evidence necessary for the jury to understand his case. Then came the cross-examination.

In the witness-box the prosecutor was seen to his best advantage. He wore a light-fitting frock coat, his hair was banked on the top of his head. His manner was confident as he stood toying with a pair of gloves as he waited for the opening questions. The Marquis turned to bestow on him a glance of withering contempt. As the evidence proceeded there came from the dock subdued but angry mutterings.

The Old Bailey was enthralled by the duel of wits in which Wilde and Carson became engaged. It is not possible here to do more than outline the proceedings that may be read in full in the account of the famous trial so admirably edited by Montgomery Hyde.

Carson began by exposing Wilde's petty posing over his age and his reluctance to admit that he had passed his fortieth birthday. Various published writings were then inquired into. Carson's purpose being to establish that Wilde was an indecent author. Was not such and such a passage immoral? It was worse —it was badly written. Was it blasphemous? It violated every canon of artistic beauty. Were his "Phrases and Philosophies for the use of Young" good for the young to read? Anything was good that stimulated thought in any age.

Counsel: Whether moral or immoral?

Witness: There is no such thing as morality or immorality in thought. There is immoral emotion.

No matter, then, how immoral it might be, a well-written book would be a good book? Agreed.

Then a well-written book, putting forward perverted moral views, may be a good book?—No work of art ever put forward views: views belonged to people who were not artists.

Passages were quoted from "The Portrait of Dorian Gray," of one young man saying to another, "I adore you madly." Had the witness ever adored a young man madly? No, not madly: he preferred the word love, that was a higher form.

Counsel: Never mind about that, let us keep down to the level we are at now.

Witness: I have never given adoration to anybody except myself.

One young man in the novel was made to say of another, "I was jealous of everyone to whom you spoke." Had the witness ever been jealous of a young man? Never in his life. He did not agree with the description of the character "Dorian Gray" as a man of very corrupt influence. "As a matter of fact I do not think that one person influences another, nor do I think there is a bad influence in the world." Was not flattering a young man and making love to him likely to corrupt him? No, it was not.

There were questions on Wilde's letter to "My Own Boy" in which he wrote of Alfred Douglas, "It is a marvel that those red rose-leaf lips of yours should have been made no less for music of song than for madness of kisses." Why should a man of his age address a man nearly twenty years younger as "My Own Boy"? Because Wilde had always been fond of him. Adored him? "No, but I have always liked him. I think it is a beautiful letter. It is a poem. I was not writing an ordinary letter. You might as well cross-examine me as to whether 'King Lear' or a sonnet of Shakespeare was proper."

Apart from art, Mr. Wilde?—I cannot answer apart from art.

Suppose a man who was not an artist had written this letter, would you say it was a proper letter?—A man who was not an artist could not have written that letter.

Counsel, quoting: "Your slim gilt soul walks between poetry and passion." Is that a beautiful phrase?—Not as you read it, Mr. Carson, you read it very badly.

Carson: I do not profess to be an artist. When I hear you give evidence I am glad I am not.

Sir Edward Clarke, intervening: I don't think my friend should talk like that. (To witness) Pray do not criticize my friend's reading again!

Was the letter, asked Carson, an exceptional letter. Witness considered it was unique. Had he often written letters in the

same style? He did not repeat himself in style. Counsel read
another of Wilde's letters to his "Dearest of all boys," telling
him not to make scenes, with his curved lips saying hideous
things. "You are the divine thing I want, the thing of grace
and beauty." Was that an ordinary letter? "Everything," expostulated Wilde, "everything I write is extraordinary. I do
not pose as being ordinary. Great heavens!"

From writings and posing, Counsel turned to persons and
practicing. He questioned the witness about his relations with
a number of men—Alfred Wood, Allen, Cliburn, blackmailers
to whom Wilde had given various small sums of money. Wilde
said he had taken Wood to the Florence Restaurant, but he had
not had immoral relations with him. Wood had gained possession of letters written to Alfred Douglas.

Did you consider that he had come to levy blackmail?—I did
and I determined to face it.

And the way you faced it was by giving him £15 to go to
America?—That is an inaccurate description. I saw that the
letters were of no value and I gave him the money after he had
told me a pitiful tale about himself, foolishly perhaps, but out
of pure kindness.

I suggest you gave him £50. Did you give him £5 more the
next day?—Yes. He told me that after paying his passage to
America he would be left almost penniless. I gave him £50.

Had you a farewell lunch at the Florence Restaurant?—Yes.

A farewell lunch with the man who had tried to blackmail
you?—He had convinced me that such was not his intention.

The lunch was in a private room?—Yes.

It was after lunch that you gave him £5?—Yes.

Did you not think it was a curious thing that this man with
whom you were on such intimate terms should try to blackmail you?—I thought it infamous but Wood convinced me that
such had not been his intention, though it was the intention of

other people. Wood assured me that he had recovered all the letters.

Out of the blackmailing class were the youths Edward Shelley and Alphonse Conway. Wilde denied improprieties with them. Shelley had been a clerk in the office of his publishers, whom he invited to dine at the Albemarle Hotel. With the youth Conway he had become acquainted at Worthing.

Counsel: He sold papers at the kiosk on the pier?—It is the first I have heard of his connection with literature.

Was his conversation literary?—On the contrary quite simple and easily understood. He had been to school where naturally he had not learned much.

The first day's proceedings closed with these questions. While his writings had been the subject of questioning Wilde had scored off Carson easily enough, though whether the jury were impressed by the brilliance of the impromptus is to be doubted. Simplicity, sincerity, and some sense of moral earnestness would have served him better. When Carson's probing passed on to the young men Wilde was seen at a disadvantage. The jury were invited to examine the gifts made to the Worthing newspaper boy, including a suit of clothes and a silver-handled, grape-vine walking-stick, presents made as a preliminary to a visit to Brighton. They had stayed the night at the Albion Hotel where Wilde had taken a sitting room and a couple of bedrooms.

On the second day the jury heard about the house with heavy curtains in Little College Street belonging to Taylor. Here Wilde had gone to afternoon tea parties in rooms that were "not luxurious but pretty." Various perfumes were burned in them—"a charming practice." The jury heard that the "artistic, clever and intellectual" Taylor had been arrested not many months before during a police raid on another London house, together with Charles Parker, whom Wilde had entertained at dinner. When they were taken into custody there had been men in women's clothing, music-hall artistes. The magistrate had dismissed the charges.

Through Taylor Wilde had made the acquaintance of several youths, grooms, valets or out-of-works. He had given them presents or money in return for the pleasure of their society. When they visited him at the Savoy Hotel it was possible they took whisky-and-soda and iced champagne.

Did you drink champagne yourself?—Yes; iced champagne is a favorite drink of mine—strongly against my doctor's orders.

Mr. Carson: Never mind your doctor's orders, sir.

Mr. Wilde: I never do.

Had he walked from his home in Tite Street to Taylor's place?—Never did he walk anywhere, always he took a cab.

The questioning concerned incidents at various London hotels and a visit to Paris. Towards the end Carson brought up the name of Walter Grainger, a youth of sixteen, servant at a house in Oxford where Alfred Douglas had stayed. There was then put the question which led Wilde to falter.

"Did you," asked Counsel, "ever kiss Grainger?"

"Oh dear no," Wilde answered. "He was a peculiarly plain boy. He was unfortunately extremely ugly. I pitied him for it."

Counsel: Was that [ugliness] the reason you did not kiss him?

Witness: Oh! Mr. Carson you are pertinently insolent.

Did you say in support of your statement that you never kissed him?—No. It is a childish question.

Did you ever put that forward as a reason why you never kissed the boy?—Not at all.

Why, sir, did you mention that this boy is extremely ugly? —For this reason! If I were asked why I did not kiss a door-mat

I should say because I do not like to kiss door-mats. I do not know why I mentioned that he was ugly except that I was stung by the insolent question you put to me and the way you have insulted me throughout this hearing.

Why did you mention his ugliness?—It is ridiculous to suggest such a story could have occurred under any circumstances.

Then why did you mention his ugliness?—Perhaps you insulted me by an insulting question.

Was that a reason why you should say the boy was ugly?

Wilde, according to the record, began several answers inarticulately and none of them did he finish. His efforts to collect his ideas were not aided by Counsel's staccato repetition—"Why? Why? Why? Why did you say that?"

At last Wilde succeeded in regaining self-control and he replied, "You sting me and insult me and try to unnerve me and at times one says things flippantly when one ought to speak more seriously."

From this incident the fable developed that his indiscretion was the cause of Wilde's undoing; that up to that time Carson had hammered away in vain; that he was about to sit down in despair; and that the single indiscretion caused the collapse of the Wilde case. The impression on the jury caused by Wilde's slip is not to be exaggerated, but without it his case would still have been lost, because of the evidence marshaled against him. Nor did it serve Carson to probe further and deeper. He had reached the close of his cross-examination. A couple of dozen questions more and he sat down. He could do so with the satisfaction of a task well done. The stolid, dogged, unimaginative had scored in the end over the man of brilliance.

Sir Edward Clarke, re-examining his client, endeavored to place a better light on some of the things that would not bear the light at all. Various of Lord Queensberry's letters were put in as evidence and read out in court. The object was to discredit the Marquis by showing him as a man who was treating his sons in a shameful manner. Strong as was the wording, the jury were more likely to have been impressed with the phrases, in which Queensberry protested that he would stop at nothing to save his son from the monstrous Oscar Wilde.

Thereafter, on the close of the case for the prosecution, Edward Carson took up this theme, calling upon the jury to say whether his client had not been justified in endeavoring, by every means in his power, to rescue his son from the baneful domination of the prosecutor. As to the man Taylor, who had kept a shameful den, he had been the right-hand man in all the orgies, as procurer for Wilde. More menacing to the prosecutor than Counsel's denunciations was the announcement that the man Wood, who had been shipped to America, was back in England and would be called as a witness to give evidence about the practices he engaged in with Wilde.

When the court rose that evening there was no longer any doubt about the result of the case. The question asked on every side was how Wilde could have had the temerity to bring it. Sir Edward Clarke had to consider the best course to pursue for the client who had so flagrantly deceived him. When the names of the associates had first come to his knowledge he had taken the view that Wilde had done no more than pose about these men. Carson's revelations had destroyed any lingering illusion. Sir Edward appointed a consultation for the following morning.

When the court resumed, Carson continued his speech, promising to call youths as witnesses. Wilde was not present to hear him. Those who noted his absence nodded significantly. Sir Edward Clarke and his junior were seen to leave the court. Carson pursued his speech. Outside, Sir Edward came quickly to the point with his client. There could be no hope of obtaining a verdict and it would be better to withdraw the prosecution forthwith. Were the case to continue to the end, the judge would inevitably order Wilde's arrest. Were it to be abandoned at that stage, there was just a possibility that no further action would follow. Wilde agreed without protest, almost with eagerness. Then Sir Edward gave a parting hint—there was no need for Wilde to remain in court while the announcement was being made. The warning was plain enough—he should leave the country for his own safety.

Carson was proceeding with his speech. The wonder, he said, was not that the gossip should have reached Lord Queensberry's ears but that "this man Wilde should have been tolerated in society for the time he had been."

Sir Edward was seen to pull Carson's gown. He asked for the indulgence of the court while he consulted his opponent. Some whispering followed and Sir Edward briefly addressed the court. He announced the withdrawal of the prosecution in a carefully phrased statement. "I think," he said, "it must have been present in your Lordship's mind that those who represent Mr. Wilde have before them a very terrible anxiety. They cannot conceal from themselves that the judgment that might be formed on the literature and upon the conduct that had been admitted might not improbably induce the jury to say that Lord Queensberry in using the word 'posing' was using a word for which there was sufficient justification to entitle the father to the utmost consideration and to be relieved of a criminal charge in respect of his statement." A verdict given by the jury at the end of the evidence might be regarded as a conclusive finding on all parts of the case. To go on would mean investigation of matters of a most appalling character. So he was willing to submit to a verdict having reference to the literary part of the case.

It was acceptance of the inevitable phrased to soften the

blow to his client. The judge brushed it aside. There could be
no terms and no limitations. The verdict must be guilty or not
guilty.

Mr. Carson: Of course the verdict will be that the plea of
justification is proved and the words on Lord Queensberry's
card were published to the public benefit.

Sir Edward Clarke: The verdict is not guilty.

The judge: The verdict is not guilty, but it is arrived at by
that process.

There was applause in court, a demonstration the officials
made little attempt to check. Over the side of the dock the
Marquis was seen to stretch out a hand towards his beaming
friends. Outside in the streets women were dancing in delight
—"a filthy business" said Sir Edward Clarke as he walked by.
"I shall not feel clean for weeks."

The morning by now was well advanced. Some time had
passed since Sir Edward Clarke, in the upper room at the Old
Bailey, had given the broad hint to his client. Wilde had then
left the precincts of the court in a brougham drawn by two
cobs. He was at liberty to go where he pleased. There was, as
yet, no authority to detain him. It was presumed that he would
leave the country without delay, in which view Queensberry
joined. "If the country allows you to leave," the victor wrote,
"all the better for the country. But if you take my son with you
I will follow wherever you go and shoot you." To this end the
Marquis instructed two private detectives to follow Wilde.

The brougham was driven only as far as the Holborn Via-
duct Hotel, where a large room had been reserved. Wilde was
joined by Alfred Douglas, Lord Douglas of Hawick and
Robert Ross. A leisurely lunch was taken at which Wilde, at
Douglas's direction, wrote a short letter to the "Evening
News," giving another version of the reason for dropping the
case:

It would have been impossible for me to have proved my case without putting Lord Alfred Douglas in the witness-box against his father. Lord Alfred Douglas was extremely anxious to go into the box but I would not let him do so. Rather than put him into so painful a position I determined to retire from the case and bear on my own shoulders whatever ignominy and shame might result from my prosecuting Lord Queensberry.

The concoction of this imaginative piece exhausted the last of Wilde's fading energy. It was nearly three in the afternoon when the party drove off. A call was made at the offices of Sir George Lewis and then at a bank in St. James's Square, where Alfred Douglas cashed a check. There was money for the journey to the Continent. All urged Wilde to catch the train for Dover while yet there was time. Wilde had sunk into a state of apathy from which he could not be roused. He had not the will-power left for action. All he could do was to send off little Ross to report to his wife. She broke down on hearing that her husband had lost his case. Sobbing helplessly she said, "I hope Oscar is going away abroad." It was a vain hope. He was too shattered. He collapsed in a chair in the Cadogan Hotel in Sloane Street waiting for what the fates had in store.

It has been asserted that the authorities held their hands to give Wilde time to make his exit. It is certainly a fact that not until after the last train had left for Dover was the warrant issued for his apprehension. Immediately on the close of the case Queensberry's solicitor had sent to the Public Prosecutor a copy of the witnesses' statements and a shorthand note of the trial. No indecent haste was shown by the Hon. Hamilton Cuffe in dealing with the matter. First the solicitor was asked to see him. Then Scotland Yard was asked for a detective, who was sent off to the Chief Metropolitan Magistrate at Bow Street. The Chief Magistrate adjourned the proceedings of his court and drove down Whitehall to the Treasury.

Meanwhile the Home Secretary, Herbert Asquith, who ten years later became Prime Minister, had been informed and had summoned the Law Officers of the Crown, the Attorney-General and the Solicitor-General to confer with him. It was late in the afternoon when the conference had been concluded and the Chief Magistrate returned to Bow Street to sign the warrant of arrest.

The press was ahead of the law in informing Wilde. Thomas Marlowe, later editor of the "Daily Mail" and then a reporter on the "Star," called at the hotel. He was seen by Ross who delivered the news. Wilde went gray in the face on hearing it. With the passing of the hours he and his friends—Reggie Turner as well as Ross was there—had begun to wonder whether the authorities would, after all, take action and Douglas had driven off to the House of Commons in the hope of learning from his cousin, the Hon. George Wyndham, what had been decided.

Wilde passed the hours of waiting drinking hock and seltzer. It was at six-thirty that there came a knock on the door and two detectives were admitted. The formalities were completed in the style befitting the occasion.

The detectives, on arrival at the hotel, asked for Mr. Wilde. The porter stated that he could not be seen. The detectives made themselves known and were conducted by a waiter to room 53. Inside Wilde was seated in an armchair smoking a cigarette. His friends were sitting on the table, on which were a number of glasses. "Mr. Wilde, I believe," said Inspector Richards, as if it had been Stanley meeting Livingstone. "Yes, yes," replied Wilde languidly.

"We are police officers and hold a warrant for your arrest."

"Oh, really," said Wilde.

"I must ask you to accompany me to the police station," said the Inspector. Asked where he would be taken thereafter the Inspector replied, "To Scotland Yard and Bow Street."

"Well," said Wilde, "if I must go I will give you the least possible trouble." Putting on his overcoat and taking hat and gloves, he followed the detectives from the room. They drove to Scotland Yard in a four-wheeled cab. He was allowed to take with him the novel he had been reading, which was mistaken by one of the waiting reporters for a copy of the Yellow Book. In fact it was a copy of "Aphrodite" written by his friend Pierre Louÿs to whom "Salomé" had been dedicated. On arrival at the Yard, Wilde offered to pay the cabman's fare. He was taken on to Bow Street where the warrant was read over to him. He made no reply to the charges. Removed to the cells he was searched and was found to have in his possession £200 in £5 notes.

Meanwhile Douglas had returned from the House of Commons to the hotel to find a brief note that Wilde had been taken to Bow Street and asking that bail should be arranged. He went into the West End to call at the theaters where Wilde's plays were running and asked the managers, Lewis Waller and George Alexander, if they would stand as sureties. Both declined. Ross had gone on another errand to Tite Street. He packed a change of clothes and some linen in a Gladstone bag and hurried to Bow Street where he was neither allowed to see Wilde nor to leave the bag. Ross found Mrs. Wilde had left her home to stay with relatives, and the only person remaining was Arthur the man-servant. Arthur had been devotedly attached to his master and he afterwards took his own life.

This was the last service Ross was able to render at that time. He feared that he, too, might be taken into custody in a general round up of Wilde's acqaintances. He withdrew to Calais where he was pressed to remain by Wilde's legal advisers. There was an exodus of apprehensive young men to the Continent during the next few days. Douglas had as good reason as any of them for apprehension but he remained to give his friend the comfort of his presence and support. Even had the risk been greater he would have stayed to face it. He was, as Wyndham told his father, quite insane on the subject. "If Wilde is released then Bosie will do anything he asks," Wyndham stated, "and no entreaty from you or his mother will weigh with him." Bosie regarded himself as being in many ways "the innocent cause of this horrible calamity."

14. THE ACCUSED

It is on account of the "love that dare not speak its name"
that I am placed where I am now.

THREE days at the Old Bailey had blasted the
fame of a lifetime. Oscar Wilde sat in the cell
of a man on remand with the sickening dread at his heart that
the present was the preliminary to an evil future. From the outside world he caught the sounds of execration and abuse. He
was dismayed by the intensity of the hatred he had roused. He
was disowned by his acquaintances. Scarcely a man dared to
raise his voice in his defense. To speak a word for him was
to invite the suspicion of being tainted, one of "that sort."

"The arrest," says Harris, "was the signal for an orgy of
Philistine rancor such as even London had never known before.
Everyone tried to outdo his neighbor in expression of loathing
and abhorrence." The press joined in with a license that would
not now be tolerated. The man had been charged. Comment, if
general abuse can so be called, that was then continued for some
days after the collapse of the prosecution of Lord Queensberry
would now be penalized for contempt of court. The "Echo"
was temperate in declaring Mr. Oscar Wilde to be "damned
and done for" with the addition, "He said he considered there
was no such thing as morality and he seems to have harmonized
his practices with his theory." Another paper took satisfaction
in painting for its readers a picture of Wilde confined in his
small cell like a caged beast. With ferocious glee, says Douglas,
it described how he paced up and down all night. "I do not
remember ever before or since reading such a revolting article,

so full of devilish malice and bestial cruelty." Pamphlets re-
producing meatier passages from the trial were hawked in the
West End streets.

For a month Wilde was the occupant of a cell in Holloway
Prison, a box of a place, twelve feet long, and ten across. High
up out of reach was the small, barred window. There were a
table, a jug and a Bible. The bed was of such limited dimensions
that not by any contrivance could he find room for all of his
considerable bulk. The rules for accused persons on remand
permitted him to provide himself with food from a public
restaurant and he was allowed to smoke. *Facilis descensus
Averno*—the descent to the prison abyss was made by graduated stages.

Over in Paris Robert Sherard was shown what the voice of
calumny could do against a loyal friend, even against prim,
puritanically-minded Sherard. Because of his friendship with
Wilde he was publicly insulted by a man of standing in the English colony. He took the slanderer into the French courts and
forced him to recant. The case was reported in the London
press and Sherard says: "It was necessary for me in self-protec-
tion to take action in London also. A serious effort was made by
the defendants to justify the abominable innuendo. My portrait
was hawked round all the London hell-holes and every effort
was made to associate me with any incident which might warrant the wicked assumption that had been made to my detri-
ment because I had not chosen to abandon an unhappy friend
abandoned by all." Till the day of Wilde's conviction Sherard
battled for his friend's good name.

Sherard's letters and Alfred Douglas's visits gave him some
sense of comfort. Sherard wrote daily, but Wilde did not feel
himself able to do more than send a message that his sympathy
and loyalty were deeply appreciated. Douglas lost no opportunity of being with his friend. "I saw him every day in the

ghastly way that 'visits' are arranged in prisons. The visitor goes into a box, rather like a box in a pawnshop. There is a whole row of these boxes, each occupied by a visitor and opposite, facing each visitor, is the prisoner he is visiting. The two sides of visitors and prisoners are separated by a corridor about a yard in width and a warder passes up and down the corridor. The 'visit' lasts about a quarter of an hour. The visitor and prisoner have to shout to make their voices heard above the voices of other visitors and prisoners. Poor Oscar was rather deaf. He could hardly hear what I said in the babel. He looked at me with tears running down his cheeks and I looked at him. Such as it was, as he told me in every letter he wrote (he wrote every day with clock-work regularity), this interview was the only bright spot in the day. He looked forward to it with pathetic eagerness. The world outside the prison, as represented by the newspapers, was howling for his blood like a pack of wolves."

On Saturday, April 6th, Wilde appeared in the police court. It was five weeks to the day since he had been driven to the court to play the prosecutor. Now he was conveyed there in another sort of carriage to be placed in the dock. The charge against him was under section eleven of the Criminal Law Amendment Act of 1885 involving offenses against male persons. He was dressed in a frock coat and according to an observer showed no great concern at any time during the proceedings. Evidence was no more than begun when Taylor was brought in to take his place in the dock. He was seen to be a dark-complexioned man of about thirty. Wilde received him with a bow. Taylor smiled and bowed in return.

There was one surprise during this hearing. Sidney Mavor, a well-dressed youth, appeared in the witness-box and described how he had been Wilde's guest for a night at the Albemarle Hotel. His bedroom led from Wilde's room. Counsel asked what took place to which the youth replied laconically, "Noth-ing." He declined to bear out in the witness-box the proof of evidence he had previously supplied for the prosecution. The explanation is given by Alfred Douglas.

"This youth was a gentleman by birth of an entirely different character and class to the other witnesses. I happened to see him in the corridor of Bow Street Police Court while he was waiting to give evidence. I went up to him and hook hands and said—'Surely you are not going to give evidence against Oscar?' He looked round in a frightened way and then whispered: 'Well, what can I do? I daren't refuse to give evidence now, they have got a statement out of me.' I said: 'For God's sake remember you are a gentleman and a public-school boy. Don't put yourself on a level with the others. Deny the whole thing and say you made the statement because you were frightened of the police.' He grabbed my hand and said, 'All right, I'll do what you say.'" And so he did.

The others of Wilde's associates gave their testimony under the compulsion that if they did not testify they would be prose-cuted. The same choice had been offered to Taylor who pre-ferred to take his chance in the dock rather than betray a friend. Douglas sent £50 to Arthur Newton, the solicitor, as a contri-bution towards the costs of Taylor's defense. Douglas, it needs to be said, was not one of those who had frequented the cur-tained, scented rooms in Little College Street.

At the closing of the hearing Travers Humphreys applied for bail, which was refused, the magistrate basing his refusal on the gravity of the case. "I think there is no worse crime than that with which the prisoners are charged." The same senti-ment—it was quite widely held—was more forcibly and pic-turesquely voiced by Frank Harris's Irishman, "Oi'd whip such sinners to death, so Oi would; hangin's too good for them."

At the second police court hearing, the accused, as they were driven up, were received by a hoarse shout from a crowd of roughs and toughs. As he took his place in the dock Wilde was seen to be paler and thinner. He seated himself with a languid air. The testimony of associates and chambermaids was continued. At the close, bail was again applied for, Arthur Newton remarking that his client came of a highly respectable family.

"In a case of this kind," commenced the magistrate, "a man's respectable connections are not in any way a reason to let him out on bail—rather the contrary."

Among the people in the crowded court was Jerome K. Jerome, who had been the first to draw attention in his periodical "Today" to some of the writings by Wilde which formed part of the Queensberry case. It was recalled that Wilde had said of this author that his famous "Three Men in a Boat" was "vulgar without being funny."

When he attended for the third time at Bow Street to be committed for trial, Wilde was seen to have been badly affected by his confinement. His face was haggard and gray, his cheeks fallen in, his hair, in which he had taken such pride, unkempt. He gave the appearance of great depression and sudden age. Even his clothes, the stylish gray coat with velvet collar and the silk hat and gloves, seemed to have deteriorated. In again refusing bail the magistrate reiterated, "I think there is no worse crime than that with which the prisoners are charged."

During these proceedings, and throughout those that followed, Sir Edward Clarke continued to act as Wilde's leading counsel. He did so without taking a fee for his service. His action exposed him to the taunts of the muck-throwers. In professional circles his conduct of the case was recognized as brilliant and his financial sacrifice was looked on as being in accordance with the best traditions of the Bar. As the leader gave his services gratuitously the two junior counsel, Charles Mathews and Travers Humphreys, were also unpaid. In fact

there was no money with which they could be paid. In a week
Wilde had become penniless.

His income, which had been rising to £3000 a year, had
dried up suddenly at its source. His books were withdrawn
from sale. His plays had soon ceased to run. At the Haymarket
"An Ideal Husband" was withdrawn on the day of the arrest.
At the St. James's the author's name was removed from the
playbills, but "The Importance of Being Earnest" survived only
for a few weeks. When the income was cut off, the creditors
came flocking for payment. Wilde's home was sold up.

Auctioneer's bills invited attendance at the sale "by order of
the Sheriff" to be conducted by Mr. Bullock, on the premises
of 16 Tite Street, on Wednesday, April 24, 1895, at one o'clock.
Auction sale? No rummage sale was a worse mêlée than the
disposal of Wilde's furniture and pictures and objects of art.
Auction sale?—Pillage of an unprotected house they called it
afterwards. The crowds got out of hand. There was no one
present to protect Wilde's interests. His wife had left Tite
Street, his brother Willie did not intervene, nor did Alfred
Douglas. The house was invaded by a mixed lot—a few genuine
purchasers, many of the curious, and a number of the acquisi-
tive and dishonest. The auctioneer was unable to control the
milling crowd and the police had to be summoned. By then
many articles of value had been carried off. The prices obtained
for the rest were scandalously low, the press of people being so
great that bidding was disorganized.

People walked through the house at will, through the rooms,
that is, where the auction was not taking place. An Irish publisher wandering upstairs found several persons in the study
treading over a floor strewn with documents in Wilde's handwriting—envelopes, letters and pages of what obviously enough
was a manuscript. It looked as if the various articles of furniture,
as they were taken out to be sold, had been emptied of their

contents which were strewn on the floor. In this way Oscar Wilde manuscripts vanished never to be traced. There were the scenarios of a couple of comedies, the text of a poetic drama "The Woman Covered with Jewels," the script of a completed prose work that had been sent back that very morning by John Lane. This was the extended version of the "History of Mr. W. H."

To the loss of these productions of his pen, Wilde had to add the dispersal of his library of presentation copies of their works made to him by almost every poet of his time from Hugo to Whitman, from Swinburne to Mallarmé, from Morris to Verlaine; the beautifully bound copies of his father's works; the array, so wonderful to him, of his school and college prizes. His china and works of art went for a song—his Burne-Jones drawings, his Whistler drawings. One fine Whistler picture of a girl was sold for £6, the script of a poem in Keats's handwriting, of which he was so proud, fetched only 38s. Rothenstein bought a Monticelli for £8 and sold it later for a much higher price to Wilde's benefit.

In his sudden poverty, which was handicapping him in presenting his defense, Wilde conned over his possible resources. His book rights were valueless. The rights to his plays he had disposed of except for "Salomé," which still awaited production, and he bethought him of Sarah Bernhardt. Sherard, in Paris, was asked to interview her and to invite her to purchase the rights for a lump sum. He had to report a series of evasions by the great actress. She had previously promised to produce it at her own theater and when she was first interviewed was most sympathetic, deploring the calamity that had befallen the poet, her friend. To produce "Salomé" at that time would be impossible, but perhaps she might be able to advance a loan as between friends. "What I can do," she added, "I will."

Sherard was asked to call again after the week-end. As soon

as he left the house, he sent off a telegram to Holloway Jail, promising funds for the following week and describing Sarah's display of sympathy and affection. When he called a second time, the actress's little black page informed him that Madame had gone out. A second time he called and the little black page stated that Madame was out again. A third call proving fruitless, Sarah was tracked down to some public function. She made an appointment for the Friday following. On the Friday following she was engaged with her daughter-in-law. On the Saturday she was working at her sculpture. There was to be no loan, not even a letter of refusal. Sherard was left to report his failure to Holloway.

When, in after time, Sherard came to write his account of his unhappy friendship, he noted with some satisfaction that Madame Sarah had thrown away the chance to strike an excellent bargain for herself. "Salomé," purchased in 1895 for two or three thousand pounds, could have yielded, he estimated, a thousand per cent. But who then could have foreseen the Wilde renaissance in which "Salomé" was to play the initial part? Sherard, lamenting the falsity of the Bernhardt's professions, continued to challenge the British colony in Paris by his championship of his friend.

From Alfred Douglas, Sherard received a long letter of how Wilde, ill and miserable, had scarcely the strength to prepare his defense against what Bosie termed "a diabolical conspiracy which seems to be almost unlimited in its size and strength." By what mental process Douglas transformed the truth about Wilde—of which he was fully informed—into a diabolical conspiracy it is difficult to understand. He added that despite the clamor of the daily newspapers that disgusted him, he thought the sympathy of "all decent men" was with Wilde, a conclusion to be reached only by some process of self-deception. He added: "I have determined to remain here and do what I possibly can though I am warned on all hands that my own risk is not inconsiderable and my family implore me to go away. . . . I should be a base coward if I did anything else, considering all I owe to him, and that I am in many ways the innocent cause of this horrible calamity." Here only the word 'innocent' can be objected to. It was to Bosie's credit that he remained in London at the call of his friend until Wilde's lawyers ordered him out of the country. He then crossed to Calais.

In his lonely hours of waiting Wilde drew much comfort from the letters that were sent to him by his old friend the "Sphinx"—Mrs. Ada Leverson. How good and kind she was to him in his loneliness, he reflected—"Not that I am really alone. A slim thing, gold-haired like an angel stands always at my side, whose presence over-shadows me moving in the gloom like a white flower." The "Sphinx" was more appreciative of the merits of Alfred Douglas than some of Wilde's friends. "Not only was he an admirable athlete, but he had a strong sense of humor and wit quite of his own, utterly different from Oscar's. His charm made him extremely popular and he wrote remarkable poetry."

Oscar was wretched when he did not receive a letter from his "Fleur de Lys," as Douglas now signed himself. The "Sphinx" sent books to Holloway to make the hours of confinement less tedious.

There was no arrival by carriage and pair when Oscar Wilde arrived at the Old Bailey on Friday, April 26, to stand his trial on charges under the Criminal Law Amendment Act of 1885. Accuser then he was, now the accused and he took his place in the "black dock's dreadful pen." He looked haggard and worn. His clothes were taking on an air of shabby gentility. Beside him in the dock was Alfred Taylor, neatly dressed by contrast.

There was a charge of conspiracy against the two men, which was the reason for their joint appearance.

There was the same press of people in court over which Mr. Justice Charles presided, and the same array of counsel, except that Edward Carson had dropped out. Carson was not prepared to appear against his old acquaintance in a criminal case, and so C. F. Gill moved up to lead for the Crown.

The trial, which lasted five days, had many points of legal interest. These may be read in the full record—How Sir Edward Clarke protested against the unfairness of the conspiracy charge; how the charge was dropped by the Crown; how the various charges were whittled away; how the blackmailing witnesses on whom the Crown relied were made to appear shoddy in the witnessbox; how the witness Atkins was exposed as a perjurer. The young man Mavor repeated his denial that Wilde had been guilty of any misconduct with him. The young man Shelley, who had worked for Wilde's publishers, emerged as a strange personality—troubled in a religious sense because of the sins he had committed with Wilde, and desirous of being in closer communion with his religion.

There was a touch of comedy when one witness gave an account of the trip on which he was taken to Paris. He said that he went to the Moulin Rouge, although Mr. Wilde had forbidden him to do so. "Mr. Wilde," he explained, "told me not to go to see those women as women were the ruin of young fellows. He spoke several times about the same subject and always to the same effect."

While the procession of witnesses passed through the box, Wilde lounged listlessly in the dock. He was said to have a dreamy air about him and a sickly pallor had seized upon his countenance. He was heard to sigh deeply as the more incriminating evidence was sworn against him. When he, in his turn, was called to give evidence he stood in the box in the same attitude of ease and assurance that he had shown a month previously when facing Carson. His cross-examination was made notable by his defense of "the love that dare not speak its name." It arose from the line of a poem by Alfred Douglas. Challenged on this he replied:

"The 'love that dare not speak its name' in this century is such a great affection on an elder for a younger man as there was between David and Jonathan, such as Plato made the very basis of his philosophy, and such as you find in the sonnets of Michelangelo and Shakespeare. It is that deep spiritual affection that is as pure as it is perfect. It dictates and pervades great works of art like those of Shakespeare and Michelangelo and those two letters of mine [to Alfred Douglas] such as they are. It is in this century misunderstood, so much misunderstood that it may be described as the 'love that dare not speak its name' and on account of it I am placed where I am now. It is beautiful, it is fine, it is the noblest form of affection. There is nothing unnatural about it. It is intellectual and it repeatedly exists between an elder and a younger man, when the elder man has the intellect and the younger man has all the joy and glamor of life before him. That it should be so the world does not understand. The world mocks at it and sometimes puts one in the pillory for it."

The words, finely delivered, animated by evident sincerity, made a great impression on the court. There was some applause mingled with hissing from the public gallery, which the judge immediately silenced. The avowal before a hostile world of the spirit of affection that inspired his relations with Alfred Douglas, was described as "the finest speech of an accused man since that of Paul before Agrippa." It had an evident effect on the jury.

Counsel invited Wilde to apply his principle of "misunderstood love" to the two letters he had written to Alfred Douglas. "There is," said Wilde, "nothing in that of which I am ashamed. The letters are full of deep affection. The first was more of a prose poem, the second more of a literary answer to a sonnet he had sent me."

Questioned about his visits to the curtained rooms in Little College Street, Wilde said that he had been introduced to Taylor by Mr. Schwabe, a nephew of Sir Frank Lockwood, the Solicitor-General. He had visited Taylor's rooms to meet actors and singers of many lands.

Counsel: A rather curious establishment, wasn't it, Taylor's?

Witness: I didn't think so. I thought it Bohemian.

Rather a rough neighborhood?—That I don't know. I know it was near the Houses of Parliament.

With regard to his friendship with the young men, valets, grooms, and others, was that to be described as the deep affection of an elder man for a younger? Certainly not. "One feels that," replied Wilde, "once in one's life and only once towards anybody."

Sir Edward Clarke had the material for an eloquent address to the jury and he made the most of it in a speech which, on its conclusion, drew applause from the crowded courtroom. He contrasted the position of Oscar Wilde, no ordinary man, but an author of poetry and prose, brilliant dramas and charming essays, with the perjurer and the blackmailers, flourishing in their frightful trade, who had given evidence against him. It deepened one's horror that his client was at the mercy of these persons. He appealed to the jury for a decision that would clear the reputation of one of the most renowned and accomplished men of letters and which would clear society of a stain.

Mr. Justice Charles charged the jury in a summing up which certainly omitted nothing that was favorable towards the accused. In considering the evidence he hoped that the jurors would free their minds from their reading of the newspapers which every day for weeks had contained references to the prisoner Wilde. Counsel had quoted Coleridge, "Judge no man by his books." His lordship thought it better to remark, "Confound no man with the character of the persons he creates." As to the letters to Alfred Douglas, his lordship dissented from the opinion Mr. Carson had expressed about them that they were of a horrible and indecent character. The accused was to be given the benefit of the fact that he was not ashamed of them. The evidence was reviewed with the caution that the witnesses were of a low class of morality, Shelley alone being untainted. One witness for the Crown had testified in Wilde's favor.

Having spoken for three hours, the judge directed the jury to retire, but he remained in his place on the bench for some time as if he did not expect that their consideration of the evidence would be long continued. Three hours, however, went by. Then the foreman announced that on the principal charges there was a disagreement, nor was agreement likely to be arrived at. Only on the charges relating to Mavor and Wood were they agreed—on a verdict of Not Guilty. An acquittal having been entered on these items in the indictment and on the charge of conspiracy between Wilde and Taylor, the case was left over to the following Old Bailey sessions.

To elope is cowardly—it is running away from danger
and danger has become so rare in modern life.

FOR three weeks Wilde was a free man again.
They were the last days of freedom he was to
live in London. He spent them in retreat. Like a hunted fox
he went to earth, and, like the fox, he lay in terror of the baying
hounds. There was no spirit left in him, not even the spirit to
fly to the refuge of the Continent.

He was in a state of extreme distress when he crept back to
his brother's home for shelter. Bail had at last been granted to
him on appeal to a judge in chambers. It was fixed at the total
sum of £5,000, for half of which Wilde was required to give
his personal surety. The other moiety was found by Lord
Douglas of Hawick, on the urgent request of Lord Alfred, and
by a Church of England clergyman.

The Rev. Stewart Headlam had no acquaintance with Wilde,
but admiring his bearing through the trial and deploring the
hostility of press and public, he came forward to help him. His
position in the Church was no protection for him against the
anti-Wilde partisans. A mob gathered outside his house in
Bloomsbury threatening to stone him for his intervention on
Wilde's behalf. "I became bail for him," he explained, "because
I felt that the action of a large section of the press, of the
managers of the theaters where his plays were running and of
his publishers was calculated to prejudice his case even before
his trial had begun." His fellow-members of the Fabian Society

received him at a meeting a few days later with a cheer that assured him at least of their support.

When the bail formalities were completed, Douglas of Hawick took Wilde to the Midland Hotel, St. Pancras, where a couple of private rooms had been reserved. They were about to sit down to dinner when the manager entered the sitting room to demand that Wilde should leave forthwith. He was driven to another hotel and was lying exhausted on the bed, when the scene was repeated. This manager was apologetic. "They will raise the street and sack the house," he said, "if you stay here." So again he had to leave pursued by Queensberry's gang of roughs who had been paid to follow.

It was long after midnight when Willie Wilde heard a tapping on the door of his mother's home in Oakley Street. He admitted Oscar, who reeled into the passage. "Give me shelter," he cried, "or I shall die in the streets." The astonished Willie saw his brother collapse across the threshold where he lay "like a wounded stag."

He had come back to his own people but it was to humiliation rather than to home. His mother could not forgive him for the shame he had brought upon the family name. His drunkard brother was insufferably patronizing—"he makes such a merit of giving me shelter." Wilde's physical condition was deplorable, and his nerves were in a worse state. It was thought that a stay in the country would help him to recover but he declined to travel alone. Someone thought of Robert Sherard, in Paris, and a telegram was sent appealing to him to come over to England. Sherard at once set off imagining that he was to act as companion on a journey to a country beyond the Channel.

Sherard found his friend in bed, in a poorly furnished room that was in great disorder. He was lying on a small camp bedstead in a corner between the fireplace and the wall. His face was flushed and swollen, his voice broken. He was a man altogether collapsed. "I sat down on the bed, took his hand in mine and tried to comfort him. He made no answer, only a gesture that he was too exhausted to do anything but lie inert. After a while he asked me, 'Oh why have you brought me no poison from Paris?' He frequently repeated this question, not only that evening but on many following days—not I am sure because he had really any wish to commit suicide, but because the alliteration of the phrase pleased his ear. It irritated mine under the circumstances, for I did not think the time opportune for insincerity and posturings."

With a grim touch of humor Sherard told him that prussic acid was easy to make. A friend in Paris, he recalled, had distilled a mash of bitter almonds and had sat smoking cigarettes while the dish was brewing. However, prussic acid was not always to be relied upon for rapidity of effect. "I looked up the subject on your behalf at the Club and found that death had been delayed forty minutes—forty minutes of indescribable agony." The realist has rarely silenced the romanticist more crushingly.

Flight was inevitably discussed. Sherard advocated it, offered to make all the arrangements and to carry the odium for it on his own chivalrous shoulders. Wilde's relations opposed it. Lady Wilde threatened that she would never speak to her son again if he were to go. Willie dramatically declared that a Wilde did not fly—an Irish gentleman would face the music. Willie became so indignant that he threatened to sell his small library of books to provide the funds to send Sherard and temptation packing. Sherard, realist ever, noted that Willie's few books included the essays of Montaigne with the passage—"If I were accused of stealing the towers of Notre Dame the very first thing I should do would be to cross the frontier."

It was in these days that Willie paid the celebrated tribute to his brother. "Oscar is not a man of bad character. You could have trusted him with a woman anywhere."

Alfred Douglas wrote from France—he had been ordered out of the country by Wilde's lawyers—imploring his friend to set out for the Continent forthwith. There was no need for him to be concerned about the estreatment of his bail. Douglas of Hawick would make himself liable for the entire amount, Mr. Headlam's as well as his own. Lord Douglas agreed. "It will practically ruin me if I lose the money at the moment," he said, "but if there is an even chance of his conviction then in God's name let him go."

Frank Harris called at the house in Oakley Street to add his voice more forcibly to the others. He found a man so low in spirit that he was reluctant to stir from the refuge of the house and brave possible insults by lunching in a public restaurant. Wilde was persuaded at last to enter a cab and drive off. Harris recounts how he argued at length and with all his force to induce Wilde to allow himself to be taken down to the Thames at Erith to be put on a steam yacht ready waiting, "a greyhound at the leash," to steam to France. The story is told in Harris's best style, the forceful dominating man haranguing the other in his weakness.

Harris had found the yacht; Harris had inspired the yacht-owner to offer the use of his vessel without thought of charge. Harris was prepared to pay the estreated bail. Harris expostulated and entreated for the journey to be started there and then. It was in vain—that, at least, is unquestionable fact. Wilde, Harris related, stood the picture of desolation and despair with tears pouring down his face, but he would not give way. In the book he is made to give an explanation that Harris may have invented for him, but which, it is likely enough, conveys something of his state of mind.

"You have no conception of how weary I am of the whole

thing, of the shame and the struggling and the hatred. To see
those people coming into the box one after another to witness
against me makes me sick. The self-satisfied grin of the barris-
ters, the pompous foolish judge, with his thin lips and cunning
eyes and hard jaw. Oh, it's terrible! I feel inclined to stretch
out my hands and cry to them—'Do what you will with me as
you will but in God's name do it quickly! Cannot you see I am
worn out? If hatred gives you satisfaction indulge it.' They
worry one, Frank, with ravening jaws as dogs worry a rabbit."

Harris reports the following conversation between himself
and Wilde:

"The chambermaid's evidence is wrong," Oscar declared.
"They are mistaken, Frank. It was not me they saw at the Savoy
Hotel. It was Bosie Douglas. I was never bold enough. I went
to see Bosie in the morning in his room."

"Thank God!" Harris said, "but why didn't Sir Edward
Clarke bring that out?"

"He wanted to but I would not let him. I told him he must
not. I must be true to my friend. I could not let him."

"But he must," said Harris. "At any rate if he does not I will.
I have three weeks and in that time I am going to find the chambermaid. I am going to get a plan of your room and your
friend's room and I'm going to make her understand that she
was mistaken. She probably remembered you because of your
size; she mistook you for the guilty person; everybody has
always mistaken you for the ringleader and not the follower."

After this disclosure—nothing of course came of it—Wilde
is represented as having told the truth about his practices to an
ignorant and astonished Harris.

"Oh, Frank," Wilde said, "you talk with passion and conviction as if I were innocent."

"But you are innocent!" Harris cried. "Aren't you?"

"No, Frank," he said. "I thought you knew that all along."

"No," Harris said. "I did not know."

Thereafter the big-hearted Harris reports that he gave an assurance to Wilde that his confession would not make any difference—it would have no effect on his friendship, or on his resolve to help. Anyone who has taken the trouble to read Frank Harris's book will scarcely credit the assertion that the confession (if made) could have caused him any surprise in view of what he states he had seen with his own eyes.

A confession of the same sort was made by Wilde later to Robert Sherard. This was undoubtedly the cause of surprise and dismay.

To Alfred Douglas across the water, Wilde wrote announcing his decision. He could not run away, or hide, and let down his bails. He could not live in exile with a dishonored name. Wilde had his illusions, and a man must live up to these or forfeit his self-respect.

Wilde went neither to France nor to the country, but was given a more congenial place of refuge with his friend the "Sphinx." This lady, a staunch admirer of the playwright, noted how unhappy he was as the unwilling and unwanted guest in Oakley Street. She thought he might be more at ease with friends than relatives and so she and her husband invited him to stay at their house in Courtfield Gardens. Before he moved in they called all the servants together—parlor-maid, house-maid, cook, kitchen-maid, even the old family nurse. They announced who the guest was to be and offered a week's wages to any of the employees who wished to leave, for the affair of Wilde had become such a scandal as had rarely been known. Each servant in turn agreed to remain.

"Then I went to fetch Oscar. He accepted with joy. He came back with me in the little pill-box brougham. When he arrived I showed him to his room. While all our friends as well as the whole of the public were discussing Oscar, no one had

any idea he was under our roof. He made certain rules to avoid
any embarrassment to us. He never left the nursery floor till
six o'clock. He had luncheon and tea up there and received all
his loyal friends there. He never would discuss his troubles
before me; such exaggerated delicacy seems today almost incredible. But every day at six he would come down dressed for
dinner and would talk to me for a couple of hours in the drawing room. As always he was most carefully dressed, there was a
flower in his buttonhole and he had received his usual daily
visit from his old hairdresser, who shaved him and waved his
hair as he had been accustomed to do in the past."

While he was staying at Courtfield Gardens Wilde was
visited by his wife who was in tears as the Sphinx received her.
She remained with her husband for two hours. She was the
bearer of an urgent message from her lawyer, urging him to go
away without waiting to face a second trial that would undoubtedly be his ruin. The lawyer's advice and the wife's entreaties produced no effect. That evening the Sphinx sent him
a note begging him to yield to his wife's supplications. "That
is not like you, Sphinx," was his reply.

It is difficult to understand the workings of his mind. Was
he, even at that stage, lured by the hope of acquittal? What
material difference would acquittal have made for him? Even
after acquittal he could not have remained in a London where
the clamor was being raised against him. Acquitted or convicted, his exposure and public disgrace was such that he would
have had to leave the country. By going then he could have
begun to serve his sentence of public ostracism in exile without
the preliminary hardships and humiliation of prison.

16. THE TWELFTH MAN

"For, do you know," said Oscar, "all my life I have been looking for twelve men who didn't believe in me and so far, I have found only eleven." When a friend brought me the news of Wilde's sentence I said, "Poor Oscar! he has found his twelfth man."—Richard Le Gallienne.

WITH the opening of the next sessions of the Central Criminal Court, Oscar Wilde attended for the third time, at the Old Bailey. During the interval Edward Carson had conferred with representatives of the Crown, urging them not to proceed further. Wilde, he submitted, had been sufficiently humiliated and his exposure was complete. These representations were rejected. Here the gossip about Lord Rosebery that had resulted from the indiscretion of the French journalist, was a contributary factor. Without the slurs on the Prime Minister it is possible that there would not have been the same determination to press the charges, but since there had been talk there must be no new occasion for giving scope to the voice of calumny.

It was decided that Sir Frank Lockwood, the Solicitor-General, should lead for the prosecution. He was a witty as well as an experienced advocate, whose robust nature was not to be affected by the fact that the Maurice Schwabe who had been mentioned in the case was his own nephew. While the Crown had reinforced their team, the indictment had been simplified.

The conspiracy allegation having been dropped, there was no single count on which both Wilde and Taylor could be

arraigned together. Sir Edward Clarke, therefore, applied for
the cases to be tried separately. The judge agreed. The Solicitor-General elected to take Taylor first. Sir Edward objected.
The judge ruled against him. It was a point gained for the
Crown. So Oscar Wilde had two more days on bail while the
first trial was held. This resulted in Taylor's conviction on two
of four counts. Sentence was postponed.

In the evening of that day, not long after the jury's verdict,
the Marquis of Queensberry and his eldest son Percy of
Hawick, came to blows. The incident occurred in Piccadilly,
not far from the Post Office where Queensberry had just sent
off a telegram to his daughter-in-law, Lady Douglas, expressing
his satisfaction over Taylor's conviction.

Must congratulate on verdict. Cannot on Percy's appearance.
Looked like a dug-up corpse. Fear too much madness of kissing.
Taylor guilty. Wilde's turn tomorrow, Queensberry.

Seeing his father in the street, Lord Douglas went up to
him to ask him to stop writing offensive letters to his wife and
other members of the family. The fight then began. Twice they
were separated by a policeman. When they engaged for a third
time they were taken off to the police station. They appeared
at the police court the next morning charged with disorderly
conduct. Who struck the first blow? There was a conflict of
evidence. Said one witness, "It was a near thing but I think the
Marquis was quicker." On this his son's solicitor commented,
"He naturally would be seeing that he is a boxer." At the
police station, the Marquis had offered to fight his son for
£10,000. Father and son were bound over to keep the peace.

On May 22, 1895, Wilde stood in the Old Bailey dock for
the second time to plead not guilty to the charges against him.
These were now reduced to acts of gross indecency with the
three men Parker, Wood and Shelley and with two persons

unknown. The evidence given previously was gone over again. On the evidence, the judge struck out the counts dealing with Shelley. At the first trial Mr. Justice Charles had described Shelley's as the only untainted evidence. Now, Mr. Justice Wills dismissed it as lacking corroboration.

The Solicitor-General's conduct of the prosecution was more forceful than that of Treasury Counsel at the previous hearing. Sir Edward Clarke, who had himself been Solicitor-General from 1886 to 1892, made Sir Frank Lockwood's advocacy a matter for complaint. "I had the honor to hold his office for a longer period than any man during the past hundred years. It is not likely that I at any time or place will speak lightly of the responsibilities of that office. But I always look upon the responsibility of a Crown Counsel, and especially the responsibility of a law officer of the Crown, as a public rather than a private interest. He is a minister of justice, with a responsibility more like the responsibility of a judge than that of a counsel. . . . I say these things without the least unfriendliness or feeling, but in the hope that I may do something to induce my learned friend to remember—what I fear for a moment he forgot yesterday—that he is not here to try to get a verdict of guilty by any means that he may have, but that he is here to lay before the jury for their judgment the facts on which they will be asked to come to a very serious consideration."

There was no ground for complaint against Lockwood's cross-examination of the accused. It was sharp and to the point. It had not the force of Carson's, but no opportunity was presented for Wilde to repeat the success of his harangue at the previous trial on "the love that dare not speak its name."

In his closing speech Sir Edward Clarke denounced the blackmailing witnesses. "This trial," he said, "seems to be operating as an act of indemnity for all the blackmailers in London. Wood and Parker in giving evidence have established for themselves a sort of statute of limitations. They have secured from the Crown an immunity from past rogueries and indecencies. The position should be changed and these men made accused not accusers."

There were heated exchanges between counsel when the Solicitor-General, in his closing speech, referred to the convicted Taylor as Wilde's intimate friend.

Sir Edward Clarke protested against a rhetorical description that had never been proved in evidence.

Solicitor-General: It is not a rhetorical statement, it is a question of fact. They call each other by their Christian names. No doubt my learned friend wishes to disconnect them. He wishes as a result of this trial that one should be condemned and the other left free to continue his grand literary career.

Sir Edward: I protest.

Solicitor-General: My friend hopes to preserve Wilde by means of a false glamor of art.

Sir Edward: My lord, I must strongly protest against this line of argument.

Solicitor-General: Oh! You may protest.

His Lordship: So far no allusion has been made to the verdict in the other case.

Solicitor-General: I am alluding, my lord, and I maintain that I am right in alluding to my learned friend's last appeal to the jury as to the literary position of his client. I am dealing in connection with that with his connection with the man Taylor and I say that these men must be judged equally.

Sir Edward: They ought to have been tried fairly in proper order.

Solicitor-General: Oh, my lord, these interruptions should avail my friend nothing.

His Lordship: Mr. Solicitor is quite within his rights.

Mr. Solicitor-General dealing with Wilde's "madness of

kisses" letter to Alfred Douglas went on: "I contend that such a letter found in the possession of a woman would be open to but one interpretation. How much worse is the inference to be drawn when it is written from one man to another. It has been attempted to show that this was a prose poem, a sonnet, a lovely thing which I suppose we are too low to appreciate. Gentlemen, let us thank God if it is so. We do not appreciate things of this sort save at their proper value and that is somewhat lower than the beasts. If that letter had been seen by any right-minded man it would have been evidence of a guilty passion."

Sir Edward Clarke had complained about blackmailing witnesses and the giving of a verdict that would enable this detestable trade to rear its unblushing head. "Gentlemen," declared Sir Frank, "I should have as much right to ask you to take care lest by your verdict you should enable another vice as detestable as abominable to raise its head with unblushing effrontery in this city. The genesis of the blackmailer is the man who has committed these acts of indecency with him. And the genesis of the man who commits these foul acts is the man who is willing to pay for their commission. Were it not that there are men willing to purchase vice in its most hideous and detestable form there would be no market for such crime and no opening for the blackmailers to ply their calling."

You might imagine that the man in the dock might have been crushed, his head bowed at these fierce denunciations. It was not so. With something of the detachment of other persons in court, Wilde was appreciating Lockwood's eloquence—like a thing out of Tacitus, he thought, like a passage in Dante, like one of Savonarola's indictments of the Popes of Rome. Being sickened with horror at what he heard, it suddenly occurred to him that it would have been magnificent had he been making the denunciations of himself.

Mr. Justice Wills began his charge to the jury with the observation that he had not had a university education. The precise bearing this had on the matters before the jury he did not indicate. It was not possible for him to proceed with consideration of the charges without reference to the position of Lord Alfred Douglas, a young man on the threshold of life, against whom he was anxious to say nothing that might have the effect of blasting his career. Even though his family was a house divided against itself, and there was no filial love or parental affection, even though there was nothing but hatred, what father would not have attempted to save his son from an association suggested by the two letters the prisoner had written to Lord Alfred? Lord Queensberry had drawn from the letters the conclusion most fathers would have drawn, though he seemed to have taken a method of interfering "which no gentleman would have taken in leaving at the defendant's club a card containing a most offensive expression."

"Which no gentleman would have taken"—Lord Queensberry was in court occupying a seat near the bench to hear the judge's stricture.

His Lordship was dealing with the evidence of the witness Wood, when the foreman of the jury intervened with questions about the position of Lord Alfred Douglas. In view of the intimacy between the young man and the accused had any warrant, he asked, been issued for the apprehension of Lord Alfred?

The judge: I should think not. We have not heard of it.

The foreman: Was it ever contemplated?

The judge: Not to my knowledge. I cannot tell you nor need we discuss that, because Lord Alfred Douglas may yet have to answer a charge. You should deal with the matter on the evidence before you.

The foreman: But it seems to us that if we are to consider these letters as evidence of guilt, and if we adduce any guilt from these letters, it applies as much to Lord Alfred Douglas as to the defendant.

The judge: Quite so. But how does that relieve the defendant? Our present enquiry is whether guilt is brought home to the man in the dock. I believe that to be the recipient of such letters and to continue the intimacy is as fatal to the recipient as to the sender, but you have really nothing to do with that.

At this stage his Lordship adjourned the court for lunch. Having meditated on the logic of the foreman's proposition he resumed his summing up with the observation: "There is a natural disposition to ask, 'Why should this man stand in the dock and not Lord Alfred Douglas?' The supposition that he will be spared because he is Lord Alfred is one of the wildest injustice—the thing is utterly and hopelessly impossible."

Since Lord Alfred never was charged, the ultimate logic would appear to have been that guilt could not be adduced from the letters and that Wilde was entitled to the advantage of that conclusion.

Thereafter his Lordship reviewed the testimony of the witnesses in detail, with clarity and impartiality, as befitted an authority on circumstantial evidence. It was for the jury to decide whether it was evidence of guilt or of suspicion only.

It was 3.30 when the jury retired. Time passed and they were still out. When five o'clock came the view began to be formed that there would be another disagreement.

"You'll dine your man in Paris tomorrow," Sir Frank Lockwood remarked, but Sir Edward Clarke dissented. "No, no," he said.

At 5.30 there was a request for writing material to be supplied to the jury. Shortly afterwards they filed back into court. It was not to return their verdict but to ask for the judge to read his note of the evidence of a waiter. Again the jurors retired but this time for a few minutes only. When they had taken their seats the Clerk of Arraigns invited them to give their decision. It was one of guilty on seven of the counts in the indictment.

Sir Edward Clarke raised a point of law, submitting that sentence should be deferred until the opinion had been taken of the Court of Crown Cases Reserved, the forerunner of the Court of Criminal Appeal. His application was rejected. Taylor was brought up from the cells to be placed in the dock beside his fellow defendant. The judge then addressed them.

"Oscar Wilde and Alfred Taylor," he said, "the crime of which you have been convicted is so bad that one has to put stern restraint upon one's self from describing in language I would rather not use the sentiments that must rise to the breast in every man of honor who has heard the details of the two terrible trials. It is of no use for me to address you. People who can do these things must be dead to all sense of shame and one cannot hope to produce any effect upon them. It is the worst case I have ever tried. That you, Taylor, kept a kind of male brothel it is impossible to doubt. And that you, Wilde, have been the center of a circle of extensive corruption of the most hideous kind among young men it is equally impossible to doubt. I shall, under such circumstances, be expected to pass the severest sentence the law allows. In my judgment it is totally inadequate for such a case."

Each prisoner was to serve two years' hard labor. There were cries of "oh" and mutterings of "shame." Taylor heard the sentence unmoved. Wilde made a gesture as if he wished to address the judge. He was directed to leave the dock and stumbled down the stairs, out of sight.

The proceedings which brought Wilde to jail and ruin have been the subject of searching scrutiny and much criticism. It has been argued that the defense was handicapped by the conspiracy charge which originally put the two men in the dock together. It has been asserted that had Wilde been tried alone at the first trial before Mr. Justice Charles he would have been acquitted. It has been the cause for complaint that at the second trial the Crown elected to go first for Taylor, against whom the evidence was much stronger. There was never a major trial yet where ingenious minds have not discovered some target for complaint.

That Oscar Wilde had any legitimate cause for complaint only those swayed by sympathy will assert. He knew the law. He had invoked the law. He had sought to have Queensberry condemned to prison. The man who accepts a challenge to a duel has no ground for complaining about the wounding effect of the chosen weapons. Nor, in fact, did Wilde complain. His own account of these matters contains a reference to wrong and unjust laws, a wrong and unjust system. But, he says, "Of course there are many things of which I was convicted that I had not done, but then there are many things of which I was convicted that I had done, and a still greater number of things in my life for which I was never indicted at all."

It is in the irony of things that whereas the judge before whom he was convicted at his second trial imposed a sentence of two years, the judge before whom he had been tried when the first jury disagreed would have imposed a sentence only of six months.

17. THE CONVICT

Circumstances are the lashes laid on to us by life. Some of us have to receive them with bared ivory backs.

OSCAR WILDE was sentenced to prison on May 25, 1895, served his term at Wandsworth and Reading, and was released on May 19, 1897. For the greater part of the time he experienced the rigors of the silent system then in force. Permitted the use of pen and paper, Wilde wrote the letter of Reading jail, extracts from which were published as "De Profundis," but which was not made public in full in England until 1949. His prison experiences also provided the inspiration and the material for "The Ballad of Reading Gaol," his last completed work.

With the closing of the prison doors the curtain came down on the public life of Oscar Wilde. His name was wiped out from the consciousness of men. Where he had been there was a void. Neither his name nor his works could thereafter be mentioned in polite society. The dining-tables had lost their most brilliant ornament and Mr. Punch his favorite target. The unimaginable amongst bad punsters could not pursue the unmentionable.

The gates that closed behind him confined the prisoner in a universe of silence. The imprisonment of the convict today is of a different order of confinement than it was under the silent system in force half a century ago. Deprivation of liberty, subjection to orders—that is prison, but no longer is the convict utterly cut off from the society of his fellow men, denied the privilege of speech, the faculty that marks man off from brute creation. The silence of solitary hours was the feature of the system designed to break the spirit of the hardened criminal. Habitual offenders preferred five years in penal servitude rather than two years of hard labor under the silent system.

No specimen of the human race could have been selected on whom the penalty of such punishment could have fallen with more oppressive force. The man of fashion had to put on the prison garb, the coiffure ceased to be Neronian. From hours of pampered ease he passed abruptly to days of privation. The man who had never walked a street along which a cab could convey him, had to toil at unaccustomed physical tasks. What had been the fashionable exquisite was transformed into the convict with untrimmed beard, nails broken, fingers bleeding from picking oakum. Instead of the honeyed praise of sycophantic companions there was the harsh, sharp voice of the menacing warder. And, worse to support for the man who had passed his days in talk, were the hours of unbroken silence.

Pages of a narrative cannot convey the emptiness of existence of the man in the silent prison cell. A narrative is a record of change. For the solitary prisoner in the world of silence there is no change. Day after day it is monotonously the same. Day follows day with only the warder's orders to break the silence. Words precariously whispered in the exercise yard are the only communications that pass to link a man with his fellows. The exchange of speech, the flow of ideas, the exchange of feelings that make up the companionship of living, this is ruled out. The days are relieved by toil. The nights, the long interminable hours are void, monotonously void of speech or action. Only the brain goes on, thinking, brooding, with thoughts racing on, in a chain never to be broken. The flesh is exhausted by the stress of interminable thought, but the brain denied relief of expression, continues in the interminable labor of thinking. Hardship, toil, fatigue, these take their toll of the

Robert Baldwin Ross, devoted friend and literary executor of Oscar Wilde.
(Photograph by Hoppé)

Autographed photographs exchanged between Oscar Wilde and his friend Bosie, Lord Alfred Douglas. (From Montgomery Hyde's book of the Wilde trial, William Hodge & Company)

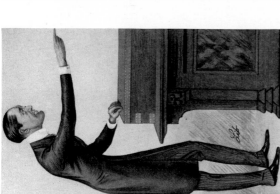

Cartoons of three of the leading figures in the trials: Sir Edward Clarke, Q.C., Wilde's counsel; Edward Carson, Q.C., who cross-examined him; and Lord Queensberry, who was the cause of his exposure. (National Magazine Company)

The original manuscript of Wilde's poem, "The Sphinx," preserved in the British Museum. It will be noted that Wilde did not follow the accepted spelling of "sphinx." Also preserved at the British Museum is the complete manuscript of the long letter Wilde wrote in Reading prison that was published under the title of "De Profundis."

The portrait shows Wilde at the height of his career, not long before the catastrophe of his fall. He is also seen shortly after his release from prison, when he had begun the last phase of his life as an exile on the Continent. (Picture Post Library)

The tall figure of Robert Sherard was often to be seen at Wilde's side during the period of their close friendship in Paris. Sherard was Wilde's first biographer. Frank Harris, adventurer and man of letters, also wrote a book about Wilde. (Photography by Elliott & Fry)

The statuary from the tomb of Oscar Wilde in the cemetery of Père Lachaise, Paris, the work of Sir Jacob Epstein, by whose courtesy the picture is reproduced. Wilde's remains had previously lain in an obscure grave and it was not until ten years after his death, when his debts had been paid off, that they were transferred to their final resting place among men and women of genius in a tomb provided by Robbie Ross, who himself was later buried by the side of his friend.

Lord and Lady Alfred Douglas, poets both like Elizabeth Barrett and Robert Browning. The couple completed the Browning parallel by eloping, to the indignation of Olive's father, Col. Custance, who disapproved of his daughter's association with a former friend of Oscar Wilde. (By courtesy of Secker & Warburg, Ltd.)

body, but the wearied flesh has still to support the fever of the brain. Most fortunate is the man of dull mind, most miserable the lot of the sensitive, the imaginative, the intellectual and the artist. Any chronicle of the incidents in Wilde's two years of prison, must give a false picture of his existence behind the bars of Wandsworth and Reading jails.

During the first months of his confinement it seemed that Wilde would succumb to the rigors of the prison routine. He was undernourished. His stomach was revolted at the food doled out to him. He became too weak to perform his allotted tasks. He was continually breaking the rules and exposing himself to penalties. He could not sleep on the plank bed and suffered the consequences of insomnia. He began to fear that his reason would desert him. The doctor suspected him of malingering. The chaplain looked on him as a hardened sinner.

"Mr. Wilde," he asked, "did you have morning prayers in your home?"

"I am afraid not," was the reply.

"You see," said the chaplain, "where you are now."

Within two months he was a physical wreck whom not even a prison doctor could suspect of malingering. Thereafter he found some relief in the infirmary.

To complete the humiliation of the opponent he had broken, Lord Queensberry took immediate steps to have Wilde made bankrupt. The bankruptcy petition was lodged in June, a receiving order was issued in July, and in August the first meeting of creditors was held. A deficiency was reported of £3,591. Queensberry's claim in respect of his costs amounted to no more than £677. Wilde's income had ceased with the withdrawal of his plays and he was in no position to make any offer to his creditors.

The public examination of the debtor, fixed for September, was deferred in the expectation that friends, by whom nearly

£1,500 had already been subscribed, would by their assistance enable his creditors to be paid in full. This expectation was not realized and on November 12 Wilde was brought up for public examination. The courtroom was crowded with spectators. Wilde, who mentally and physically was in a deplorable condition, was acutely conscious of the humiliation to which he was exposed.

He had had to submit to the questioning of the Official Receiver into the details of his earnings and spendings. He had, of course, kept no accounts. His income from royalties had run to about £2,000 a year. For the previous three years his expenditure had been at the rate of £2,900. Item by item he had had to go through the list of his debts. They were reminders of the days of luxury he had shared with Alfred Douglas, stabbing reminders of the days of sensual ease.

The public examination was soon concluded. Wilde gave a brief account of his finances and was taken back to prison to brood over the indignities to which he had been subjected. There had been one solace in his distress. As he was marched between two policemen down the long corridor of the Bankruptcy Court, he saw Robbie Ross standing there, waiting so that he might raise his hat, a silent token of his sympathy, as his handcuffed friend passed by. Wilde was deeply touched.

In the alarm that had followed Wilde's arrest Ross had withdrawn to the safety of the Continent. He had now returned to London and began to occupy himself with Wilde's affairs. Throughout the remainder of his prison days Wilde received a quarterly letter in which Ross gave him news of the literary world, chatty, charming and witty letters.

The first visitor Wilde received in jail was Robert Sherard who was admitted on the first quarterly ticket. A second visitor would have been permitted but none of the friends who had remained was available. Sherard had been bowled over by the shock of his friend's conviction—"one of those crushing blows of fate under the first impact of which one hopes not to recover." He had no heart left for his work in Paris, where he had established himself as a journalist of rising reputation. Throwing everything aside, he returned to London to live for a time not far from Wandsworth prison. He made his visit to the jail one afternoon in August and was so moved that he was able afterwards to recall little of what took place at the melancholy interview.

"We were separated by a double row of stout iron bars. In the passage between stood a warder who kept his eyes on the clock. We both clung to the bars and both for support. I noticed that his hands were disfigured, his nails broken and bleeding." Wilde was in fair spirits, but his punishment was obviously weighing terribly upon him. He complained that he was allowed only one book a week to read.

Sherard was most painfully affected. He considered that the best service he could render to his friend was to promote a reconciliation with his wife, who was then being pressed by her family to take action for divorce. Were she to abandon him, Sherard thought, his ruin would indeed be complete, so loyal Robert wrote asking her to forgive her husband.

In the natural kindness of her nature, Constance would have responded immediately to the appeal, but the family advisers were urging her to free herself from the man who had brought shame upon their name. Sherard had to write several times but in the end she gave way. Her brother wrote to tell Wilde that if he would write to his wife, she would take no action for divorce. Apparently he wrote. She crossed over to England from her refuge on the Continent and obtained a permit to meet her husband.

It was the saddest meeting of her life—indeed awful, more so than she had any conception it could be. "I could not see him and I could not touch him and I scarcely spoke." Wilde talked to her of the past. He had, he said, been mad during the three previous years, the years of his friendship with Douglas. He told her that if he saw Bosie he would kill him—"So he had better keep away," she commented, "and be satisfied with having marred a fine life—few people can boast of so much."

Sherard was much encouraged to find that his intervention promised so well. Once his punishment was over Wilde would find a home once again with his wife and children.

"I was much affected," Sherard wrote after meeting Constance. "She showed like an angel—an angel of beauty and goodness in the horrid night that hemmed me in." He again visited Wandsworth under a special permit and found Wilde to have been greatly cheered by his wife's visit. This time the interview took place in a room without bars between, and the attendant warder was shocked when, at parting, Sherard threw his arms round his friend and embraced him.

News of the reconciliation between husband and wife reached Alfred Douglas on the Continent. It was a development he had not foreseen. He feared the consequences it might have on his relations with Wilde. He wrote off to Sherard in angry terms threatening that if Wilde's friendship were to be lost to him in the future through any words used by Sherard he would shoot him "like a dog."

One who interested himself on Wilde's behalf was R. B. Haldane, Q.C., the eminent lawyer, later Secretary for War and Lord Chancellor. Then serving on a Home Office Committee on prison organization, he had a warrant that authorized him to require the governor of a prison to produce any of his prisoners. He had known Wilde in the days of his social success and was haunted by the idea of what this highly sensitive man might be suffering under ordinary prison treatment. The chaplain, whom he saw first, reported that the prisoner had wholly failed to make headway. In the cell Wilde at first held himself off, refusing even to speak.

"I put my hand," Haldane relates, "on his prison-dress clad shoulder and said that I used to know him and had come to say something about himself. He had not fully used his great literary gift and the reason was that he had lived a life of pleasure and had not made any subject his own. Now misfortune might prove a blessing to his career for he had got a great subject. I would try to get for him books and pen and ink and in eighteen months he would be free to produce. He burst into tears and promised to make the attempt."

They discussed the books he might wish to be supplied with. Until then he had only been given the "Pilgrim's Progress," which did not satisfy his needs. He asked for Flaubert's works, but Haldane thought that these were scarcely likely to be sanctioned seeing that they carried a dedication to the advocate who had successfully defended that author on a charge of indecent publication. At this Wilde laughed and he became more cheerful. Finally they agreed on St. Augustine's works and Mommsen's history of Rome. These Haldane procured and they followed Wilde from cell to cell. After the sentence had been served, Haldane received, anonymously, a copy of "The Ballad of Reading Gaol"—"it was the redemption of his promise to me."

On Haldane's recommendation Wilde was transferred from Wandsworth to Reading where it was thought conditions might be easier. During his journey to Berkshire he was again exposed to the public gaze. Even in the disguise of prison attire there was no mistaking the tall, familiar figure. He was extremely distressed by the experience, exposed to the taunts of a jeering mob.

Fears were at that time entertained that death would cut his prison term prematurely short. Ross, visiting him soon after his transfer from Wandsworth, was seriously impressed by his friend's condition. He was thinner, emaciated, his face dull brick in color, his eyes horribly vacant. "If I asked about Oscar before a Commission I should say that 'confinement apart from all labor or treatment had made him temporarily silly.' If asked whether he was going to die: 'it seems quite possible within the next few months even if his constitution remained unimpaired.'" But there were other reports on the prisoner.

At the Home Office they had been sufficiently impressed by the representations they received to send down two officials to report. Wilde at the time was a sick man in the infirmary where the rigor of the silence was relaxed. There were other convicts in the ward, companions, an audience. Wilde began to talk. The charm began to work. The audience registered enjoyment. The entertainer was for a space brought back to life.

The two officials, watching through the peep-holes, found no sign of a prisoner in repine, but an animated man who appeared to be in the best of spirits as he sat discoursing to fellow-patients, who were in high delight. The report to the Home Office testified that the prisoner C.33 was in good condition physically and mentally.

There was small benefit to Wilde in the transfer Haldane had promoted. The governor of Reading, a Colonel Isaacson, was a martinet among disciplinarians. The silent system was nowhere enforced more rigorously than in his imperium. The story is told by Gide of how Wilde and another convict were brought before the governor for having broken the rules by talking. The other man confessed to having been the originator of the conversation, thus exposing himself to the heavier penalty. Wilde thereupon asserted that it was he who was responsible for the offense. "The governor then got very red, because he no longer understood. 'But C.48 says he's the one who started, I cannot understand. I gave him two weeks; all right, if that's how things stand I'm going to give you both two weeks.' "—two weeks of solitary confinement.

Having promoted the reconciliation between Oscar and Constance Sherard was alarmed to learn that Alfred Douglas had written for a French review an article that was an apology for and a glorification of the "Greek movement." It would have been disastrous to Wilde's interests and could have turned his wife against him, so he busied himself to stop publication. He received a remonstrance from Douglas that he should have written to the editor of the review asking for the article to be suppressed—"Such conduct on your part was exceedingly impertinent."

Sherard was sunk in melancholy at this time, grieving over the fate that had overtaken his friend. Having thrown up his newspaper work he was given up to gloomy thoughts. At one prison interview Wilde had the painful task of revealing the truth about himself, to which Sherard had obstinately closed his eyes, even after the Old Bailey disclosures. To Wilde he insisted on proclaiming his belief—he did not believe a single word that had been said by the witnesses for the Crown; Wilde, he considered, had been the entirely innocent victim of a hideous plot.

This faith made the prisoner burst into tears. He explained, then and there, that though some of the charges had been untrue, his life had in fact been "full of perverse pleasures"; unless that were accepted they could not continue to be friends in the future. The truth came upon Sherard as a terrible shock, but it did not disturb his loyalty.

On a later visit to the jail, Robbie Ross found him an embarrassing traveling companion for so delicate an occasion. Robbie's picture—in a letter to his friend Adey is revealing as to character—"I went yesterday to Reading and met Sherard at

Paddington. We got on like two turtle doves. He told me of all the murderers he had known, mentioning that the last Parisian murderer was an intimate with whom he had stayed. He mentioned that he had heard from Bosie and seemed anxious that the third person in the railway carriage should know on what mission we were bent." Discretion was not one of Sherard's qualities.

It was on the occasion of this visit that Wilde asked him to absent himself for a space while he talked with Ross. Sherard withdrew. "In the gray gloom of the prison corridor when I waited till this conference, from which I was excluded, was over, it dawned upon me that my long friendship, fruitful as it had been in sorrow, might reserve for the future another sorrow, and the disappointment of a wasted effort."

Wilde had served nearly half his term when his mother died. The news of his loss was brought to him by his wife. Rather than that he should be informed in cold, official tones, Constance, though herself in ill-health, traveled across the Continent to be the bearer of the news of his bereavement. Wilde had loved his mother with the strongest affection. When he had been in London a day had rarely passed that he had not visited her. His sorrow, with none to share it in his prison cell, was heightened by the sense that he had saddened her last days by the shame he had brought upon her.

Though neither knew it at the time the prison meeting between husband and wife was the last that was to take place. Constance was already suffering from the onset of the disease to which she succumbed a few months after her husband's release from jail.

In the depths of his misery, a letter from the outer world gave him a slight diversion for his thoughts. "Salomé" had been staged in Paris by Lugne-Poë. It was something to Wilde to know that at a time of disgrace and shame he was still regarded as an artist. He wrote to Robbie Ross asking that his thanks should be conveyed to Paris. The writing of the letter was a scrawl, he was aware of it, but he had not been allowed writing material for so long that he was beginning to forget how to write.

One hope that sustained him in the days of his deepest despair was that his sentence might be shortened. Attempts had been made by various of his friends to organize petitions on his behalf. One set out that even were the prisoner to survive and complete his sentence, it was feared that he would be incapacitated from following his profession. It was not submitted to the authorities. The leading writers of the day were not prepared to support it with their signatures. It is improbable that any petition would have had effect. Sir Edward Clarke interested himself on behalf of his client and had an interview with the Home Secretary, but to no avail. Informing Robbie Ross of what had passed, Sir Edward wrote: "I am glad that Mr. Wilde should have faithful friends like yourself to stand by him, but it is impossible for me to forget that before I undertook the most painful case I have ever been engaged in, he gave me his word of honor as a gentleman that there was no foundation whatever for the charges which were afterwards so completely proved."

Consideration was given to the case at the Home Office and it was announced that the Minister had found no grounds, medical or otherwise, to justify a reduction in the prison term. Wilde was reduced to new depths of dejection by the Minister's decision.

In July 1896, the first half of the two years' sentence having been served, Isaacson was posted to Lewes and Major Nelson ruled at Reading in his stead. There was an easing of the rigors of the silent system. C.33 benefited from the change. From the Home Office directions had been received that he was to be permitted to receive books from friends. Now came a greater concession—the use of pen and paper that had previously been denied him. Later changes in staff placed Warder Martin in charge of convict C.33. Warder and prisoner were soon on excellent terms.

Warder Martin was of a literary turn of mind and he wrote an account of Wilde's latter days at Reading. By that time he was a model prisoner, taking a pride in keeping the tin utensils of his cell scrupulously clean. He was distressed that he could not polish his shoes, brush his hair, or shave himself—"these awful bristles are horrid." There is a picture of him in the prison chapel, a figure of boredom, another of him standing with his face to the wall while "star class" first offenders passed along the corridor, and a description of him in his cell at night.

"It was when he was alone in his cell, when the doors were double locked, when the gas was flickering, when the shadows of night were falling, when all was quiet, when all was dead. He underwent a transformation or it might be more appropriate to call it a transfiguration. He is pacing his cell,—one, two, three. Three steps when he has to turn. Three steps and turn again. His hand behind his back, a wrist encircled by a hand, and thus backwards and forwards he goes, his head thrown back, smiling—but heavens! what a smile! His eyes —those wonderful eyes!—are fairly dancing. Now they are looking towards the ceiling—but far beyond the ceiling, looking into the infinite. Now he laughs, what a laugh! Piercing, poignant, bitter—all and more are condensed in that awful laugh. His powerful imagination is at work. Though his body is in fetters his soul is free—for who can chain the soul of a poet. . . . What that poet was before he went to prison I care not. What he may have been after he left prison I know not. One thing I know, however, that while in prison he lived the life of a saint, or as near that holy state as poor mortal can ever hope to attain."

18. LETTER OF READING JAIL

It often happens that the real tragedies of life occur in such an inartistic manner that they hurt us by their violence.

IT was in the evenings of the latter months in prison that Wilde wrote his last prose work, the long letter from Reading jail. Never has a piece of writing been so distorted by partial publication. The extracts were the passages of generalities in which he described some of the emotions he experienced in confinement—his sense of humiliation, repining over the life that had been ruined, his hopes for the future. At times he seemed to verge perilously towards the seat of penitence.

These extracts, skilfully linked together, gave a completely false notion of the letter that had actually been composed. It was addressed to Alfred Douglas. It was a letter of reprobation, an indictment of the friend whom he charged with having contributed to his downfall and his ruin. Incident by incident he followed the course of the fateful friendship. Incident by incident was made to serve as cause for censure of his friend. Seated in his cell, at the desk improvised from the planks of his bed placed across a couple of trestles, he discharged at Bosie all the heartburning regrets and supercharged resentment that had been stored up during the long silence of the solitary prison life.

"He says that if he saw Bosie he would kill him." The phrase in Sherard's letter had been the first indication of the transformation that had taken place in Wilde's feelings. That was a twelvemonth before he sat down to write. Already old affection had been changed into aversion. Since then twelve months of brooding had augmented the burden of his resentment.

The letter of Reading jail was the product of the interminable hours that Wilde had passed without the support of human companionship, solitary hours, hours in the tomblike silence of the cell in a long gallery of cells. Animals are spared by nature from the burden of supporting unoccupied hours of time. Watch a dog that is not occupied. It is relieved by the oblivion of sleep. There is no such relief for man, whose brain must continue to think on in a circuit of repeated thought. Wilde's mind during the empty days and longer nights was given over to thoughts that revolved in their interminable circuit around Alfred Douglas and the friendship that had brought him to the place of shame, his career, his brilliant career, shattered, his reputation blasted in infamy—"In the lowest mire of Malebolge I sit between Gilles de Retz and the Marquis de Sade."

He found a phrase for it, always there was the phrase, throughout the length of the long letter there was no page without its phrase. But these were the literary decorations for the adornment of his thought. Savoring the beauty of the phrases, the reader may miss some of the bitterness in the thought. The style natural to the man was ill suited for the thoughts that were then to be expressed, the pent-up resentments that had festered in the solitary hours, when time stood still but thought raced on. The adornments of the phrases impart an insincerity to the more elevated passages of the extracts in "De Profundis." They soften the asperity of the passages of bitterness. Strike out the phrases and the sharp, stark residue of reproof emerges a record of the bitterness of thought rethought and thought again during the months of solitary brooding.

Night after night he spent in writing down the expression of his loathing, bitterness and contempt for the young man who once had been his companion spirit. Reproaches inspired by such inflamed resentment could not be objective truth. What is disclosed is the accumulation of bitterness that had silted up the man's mind, blotting out the memory of his former affection.

Throughout his prison days Wilde had been haunted by the shadow of his friend. It was a shadow that never seemed to leave him. He came to think of himself as one who had been betrayed by the weakness of his own nature, ruined by a friendship that had been intellectually degrading. Why had he been confined to prison? It was not because of his relations, real or supposed, with the witnesses who had given evidence against him, the youths from the streets. His relations with persons of that kind were not a matter of interest, so he thought, either to the Government or to society. He was there because he had tried to put Queensberry into prison and Queensberry had turned the tables on him. But it was not Queensberry who was ultimately responsible, it was Queensberry's son.

The mind of a man exposed to the effects of solitary confinement is in a state to be worked upon by trifles light as air. There had been matters to release brooding fancies in Wilde's brain. First there had been the sale under the hammer of the charming things he prized—his drawings, his china, his library. The best of the books, his pride, irreplaceable, had sold for less than £150, about as much as he had been accustomed to spend in an ordinary week on Bosie's entertainment. Yet Bosie had never thought of troubling himself to buy up the books and so preserve them for his friend. It was Queensberry who had been the petitioning creditor in making Wilde bankrupt. It had been an extra refinement of pleasure for the Marquis, completing his victory by Wilde's crowning point of humiliation. Wilde's thoughts went back to the time when he had launched his prosecution, when Bosie had assured him that all the costs would be borne by his family, that if he were to come forward as the champion of the family to have Queensberry shut up, then they would look on it as a privilege to pay all the expenses that would be incurred. While these things were rankling in Wilde's mind, there had come the news, through Robert Sherard, that Douglas was writing an article for one of the French literary papers on their friendship, in which some of Wilde's letters were to be included. It was wounding to him to think that he was to be further exposed to the world and he forbade it. Thereafter came an application on Douglas's behalf for permission to publish in the "Mercure de France" an article, with extracts from the letters he had written when he was awaiting trial in Holloway, letters of too intimate a nature to be made public. It was the source of deepest pain to him, circumstanced as he was, that Bosie should have been so lacking in sensitiveness as to disclose such writings to a curious, hostile world. These things festered in his mind, were magnified into crimes against friendship. Imagination touched up what resentment suggested and the result, when the opportunity for self-expression came, was the discharge of that long sustained reproach of the "De Profundis" letter.

Few characters in fact or fiction have been analyzed with such minute exposure of their faults. Bosie was vain, Bosie was shallow. He had no motives in life, but merely appetites. The gutter and the things of the gutter were his interest. He had been idle at school, worse than idle at the university. He was lacking in the Oxford temper, could not play gracefully with ideas but had arrived merely at violence of opinion. He was wrong about money, insisted on a life of reckless profusion; he outstripped taste and temperance; he demanded without grace and received without thanks. He was grasping, ungracious, unscrupulous. In anger, his mind and body grew distorted and he became a thing as terrible to look at as to listen to. He was given to sudden fits of almost epileptic rage. His talk was invariably centered on one thing, which, in the end, became monotonous and boring. He was possessed by the terrible alchemy of egotism. He was a person consumed by hatred, blinded by hatred.

Wilde pictured himself as a weak, easy-going, good-natured man dominated by the weaker character. He had tried unavailingly to end a friendship and rid himself of a friend who had proved the absolute ruin of his art. Wilde tore up the vesture of his old affection and trampled the fragments in the mire.

The writing of the letter of upbraiding was a task that occupied many nights of loneliness. It gave expression at last to the piled up, rankling indignations, fomented by the long months of suppression.

The monotony of the prison cell was broken. The hours were no longer empty. The circle of his thought was broken. Thinking was no longer brooding, reiterated thought festering in the mind. Thinking was now the prelude to writing that gave a vent to the pent-up store of his resentment. In the daytime he gave himself over to preparation. At night time, when the planks of his bed had been placed over the trestles, he yielded himself to the pleasure of composition. Never before had he welcomed the drudgery of writing. Always it had been drudgery to which he had forced himself—or he had succeeded in forcing himself when the force of his self-discipline had been slight. Now he surrendered himself to the joy of self-expression, that was followed by the balm of peace. The plank table in the bare cell was the best desk he had ever had for writing. Never before had he been able to pursue his writing without the risk of interruption to break in upon the sequence of his thoughts. The bare walls, the barred window —there was nothing to disturb the flow of his words.

When he first sat down it was to write a letter of accusation and reprobation to his friend. It began as letters do begin with the greeting—"Dear Bosie" and the opening passages were such as an infuriated man might write when venting his anger. But before the final subscription came to be added many weeks of writing afterwards, the purpose of the writer had changed. He was still addressing, still abusing his friend, but the scope of his letter had been enlarged and he was writing not merely to accuse the friend but to defend himself. The words were still addressed to Bosie, but he was writing to the world at large. It was no longer a personal letter of accusation to a friend but a self-justification for the world to read. He was writing for publication. He did not defend himself, he explained. Like Cardinal Newman he was writing his apologia. As things stood his conduct must appear to the outside world as a combination of absolute idiocy with vulgar bravado. Some day the truth would have to be known—he would tell the truth. He was not prepared to sit for all time in the pillory in which he had been placed. He would write so that his friends might have the psychological key to the secret of his conduct. He wrote, at times, of resignation to the will of fate in his newly assumed humility, but he was not prepared to accept without challenge the verdict that society had entered against him—that Queensberry should live as the hero of a Sunday School tract, that Bosie should rank with the infant Samuel and that he should take his place between Bluebeard Gilles de Retz and the Marquis de Sade.

It is the double purpose of reprobation and self-justification that gives to this letter its strange quality—a record of complaint, much of it concerned with the trivialities of the tea-cup storms of friendship, interspaced with passages relating to art and philosophy. A quarrel in a sick-room and a young man's extravagances ranked almost with the eternal verities as they were set down in the purple phrases of his orchidaceous prose.

Having settled accounts with his friend, and released the black discharge of his hours of brooding, he passed on to loftier things, to discuss matters of art and philosophy, his beliefs and his lack of belief, the approach of the artist to the faith of Christ. He surveyed his own past. There was no expression of regret. There had been perversity but that was no more than one other aspect of the varied experience of life. His life had been wrong on two counts. His experience had been limited to the satisfactions of the hedonist, to pleasure without suffering. Prison had completed the range of life's experience. The other count against himself was that by his material and sensual indulgences he had been unworthy of himself as an artist.

Nothing, I think, is more revealing as to the nature of the man who was Oscar Wilde than the entire absence of any notion of regret, or repentance for the conduct that had been the occasion of his imprisonment. All the long months of loneliness in prison during which there had been so little to interrupt the flow of his meditations had not brought to him the consciousness of sin some men might have felt. Throughout, then and thereafter, he looked on himself not as one who had been in the wrong, but as one who had followed the course his own character, or his nature had imposed upon him. He was not in charge of his own destiny. His character was stronger than his consciousness and his reason. He had capitulated in his weakness to his character in its strength.

Looking towards the future, he found cause for the highest hopes. Not even the privations of prison could take away from him the sense of his own capabilities as a creative artist. What had been done could be done again. Achievements of the past could be repeated in the future. In a mood of exaltation he declared his high resolve. He would show the world that the artistic life did not end in the infamy of convict clothes. With his capacity for self-dramatization he pictured himself passing on to new triumphs, eclipsing his former successes, that would wipe out the memory of his follies and his fall. The world of liberty, when he emerged into it, was to prove a harder place for achievement than the prison cell.

When the extracts of "De Profundis" were first published they were acclaimed by some as the record of the emotions of a soul in anguish, the most moving expression of the feelings of a sensitive soul exposed to the privations and indignities of captivity. The book was hailed as the most poignant document in the literature of prison. But, even in those carefully selected extracts, the note of anguish was difficult to catch.

Suffering speaks simply, without design or affectation, as the words are forced from the mind that has suffered. Repentance, as Dr. Johnson pronounced, has no leisure for cadences and epithets. There is nothing simple about Wilde's colored prose with its phrases, its adornments and its flowing rhythms. There is a phrase too many in every sentence that robs the writing of spontaneous sincerity. Of art he writes with art, of religion as a man toying with ideas, not with the conviction of the converted. He did not profess himself to be one of the converted but proclaimed that he belonged to the confraternity of the faithless.

When the letter is read not in extracts but as the whole piece in which it was composed, the false impression of the "De Profundis" version is immediately apparent. You can see it as an expression not of anguished feelings but as the outpourings of a brain that for too long had been denied the expression of the ideas fermenting in it. Having rid himself of these accumulations, Wilde sat down with relish to indulge in the long

denied luxury of writing about the subjects of his intellectual
occupation after the companionship of books had been restored
to him.

It was to be said later that prison destroyed his creative faculty. It is a suggestion that cannot survive a reading of the letter. The writing is as good as anything he wrote, the wit and
the phrases as felicitous as ever. It is rhetorical and rhetoric has
gone out of fashion, but as rhetoric the passages roll superbly
on.

He was too consciously the artist not to be aware of the
quality of his writing. He anticipated criticism. The reason
he had polished up his writing, erased some words and substi-
tuted others, was that he was seeking for exactitude, seeking
to render his real impression and to find for his mood its exact
equivalent. All the same, the soul in anguish does not pause to
tune the language "like a violin." Conscious art is not the spontaneous voice of suffering.

His resentments discharged in the long opening section of
denunciation, had already spent some of their force. There
were further censures but the letter closed on the hint of
a kindlier note. Perhaps after he had been released he would
arrange through Robbie to meet Bosie in some quiet foreign
town. The mighty denunciations had ended on an anti-climax
and an invitation. Despite all the reprobations he was by then
ready to begin all over again.

As the time for his release drew nearer his friends began to
make preparations for his future. There was no home for him
to go to. His wife and family had found refuge on the Continent, their identity concealed under another name. Where
was he to find refuge? He thought it necessary for the fulfilment of his literary intentions that he should live in London.
It was essential for him as a dramatist, but there was danger in
this, as he realized. He might again expose himself to the pen-

alties of the law. It would be infamous, he considered, if he were to be punished in the future for conduct that he regarded as pathological rather than criminal—it would be infamous, but he realized that it might happen.

Isolated, as he was, in prison, it was understandable that in his more optimistic moods he should be buoyed up by hopes of a literary come-back, of new successes in the theater that would cancel the catastrophe of his fall. These were delusions. Never in England while he lived could he have wiped out the shame opinion had branded on him. The doors of the theater were shut against him as firmly as those of society. In despondent moments he realized something of this, and saw himself as a pariah with whom none would associate. There were times when he was almost unnerved by the thought of returning to a world that reviled him. It was well for him that outside there were faithful friends to take charge of him.

Robbie Ross now came forward to take charge of his affairs. Henceforward Robbie was to be administrator-in-chief. Business matters, domestic matters, literary affairs and finances, everything was to be done through him. At first Oscar was critical. In his neurotic condition he was easily upset. A careless phrase harrowed his feelings. He was prompt to make complaint.

Through Ross arrangements were made for an allowance to be paid from his wife— £150 a year was the sum agreed upon. Wilde made protest about this, considering that a larger sum should have been secured for him. Ross was accused of bungling. Wilde was vigorous in his reproaches. With exemplary forbearance that was to be continued through the years Robbie accepted the upbraidings.

After much debate it was decided it would be better that Wilde should make his home in France, within easy traveling distance of his friends in London. Dieppe was suggested to him.

He demurred at this. He was too well known in Dieppe and there would be unwelcome visitors—he remembered Queensberry's gang of roughs. Better a quiet retreat in the country not far from Dieppe. So it was agreed.

The chief subject of his thoughts during his final weeks at Reading was the handling of his prison letter. It had been begun as a letter to Bosie Douglas, but his purpose had changed as he wrote and as the nights of writing continued he found himself addressing not merely Bosie but the world at large. He came to think of his letter as an Epistola, ranking with the encyclicals in which Popes make their pronouncements *urbi et orbi*.

Ross was entrusted with the responsibility for making the necessary arrangements. He was given detailed instructions to follow. Copies must be taken by typists whose discretion could be relied upon. Since his was to be the responsibility, he must be armed with the necessary authority and so Ross was formally named as Wilde's literary executor.

Wilde announced that he was sending the text of the prison letter to Ross under a separate cover. In fact it was not released by the Governor. The writings of C.33 were collected sheet by sheet as he wrote them to be taken to Major Nelson's office, where they were preserved, to be handed to the prisoner on his release.

The letter, extending to more than 60,000 words, was written on blue foolscap paper, with the prison stamp at the head. According to the strict interpretation of prison rules, the MS. should have been retained by authority and preserved among the archives of the prison. By wise dispensation, however, the author was not deprived of the results of his long hours of writing.

One of the last visitors C.33 received in Reading jail was Frank Harris who arrived in an ostentatiously generous mood over the disposal of £20,000 he reported he had made in South Africa. He promised to give Oscar a present of £500, an offer that reduced Wilde to tears. Before he left prison, however, Wilde had received a note from the intending benefactor regretting that the promised check could not be sent. Wilde was disgusted.

At last the appointed day drew near. In anticipation of Wilde's release two American journalists attended at the office of the Governor seeking to buy an account of his prison experiences. Wilde indignantly refused their offer. "I cannot understand, sir," he said to the Governor, "that such proposals should be made to a gentleman."

On May 18, 1897, Wilde was taken to London, in compliance with the regulation that a prisoner should be released from the prison to which he had been first committed. There was the further point that Queensberry's gang of toughs would be in wait at Reading. Early on the morning of May 19, the doors of Wandsworth jail were opened for him. He walked out into the world a free man once again. He handed over his Epistola to Robbie Ross.

He was seen to be dressed in the clothes he had worn when he first passed from the Old Bailey dock. They had been fumigated and preserved against the day of his release and in his pocket was half a sovereign, the earnings of two years' hard labor.

A reception had been organized to greet the released prisoner. The Sphinx, one of those who were present, recalled the scene: "Very early one May morning, my husband and I and several other friends drove to meet Oscar at the house, in Bloomsbury, of Mr. Stewart Headlam. We all felt horribly nervous and embarrassed. He came in and at once put us at our ease. He came in with the dignity of a being returning from exile, smoking a cigarette, with waved hair and a flower at his button-hole. His first words were, 'Sphinx, how marvelous of you to know exactly what hat to wear at seven o'clock in the morning.' It was then that he wrote a letter and sent it by cab to a Roman Catholic Seminary, asking if he might be allowed to retire there for six months. The cabman returned. They could not accept him on the impulse of the moment. Then he broke down and sobbed bitterly."

It was the end of his life in England. On the morrow his days of exile had begun.

19. REFUGE AT BERNEVAL

*What consoles one nowadays is not repentance but
pleasure. Repentance is quite out of date.*

OSCAR WILDE emerged from prison to find that
the two years he had served inside formed
the preliminary period of his punishment. A life sentence of
ostracism remained before him. The lesser man is less heavily
penalized. When his term in jail is over he is reckoned to have
purged his offense and can start afresh with the slate wiped
clean. For the celebrity it is otherwise. It is not enough for
him to say: I have done my time. The reply is made: Your
crime was not merely an offense against the law, it was an
outrage against society: The law has dealt with you, but society
has not; now you will serve the sentence of society, which is
that you be an outcast for life.

Wilde might hope for forgiveness in the next world. In this
there could be none in England. Herein it seems the righteous
man anticipated the devil's work, for to him, according to
competent theologians, is entrusted the torture of the damned,
whereas God's mercy is infinite.

Of compassion the man Wilde now stood in the utmost
need. His world had come tumbling down about him. His
family were estranged. His home had been disposed of, his pos-
sessions sold. He was a bankrupt. His disgrace had ruined his
future as a playwright. All this by his folly he had caused, but
the consequences were none the lighter because he had brought
them on himself. By their wilfulness and folly men bring many

misfortunes upon their heads, but they are not thereby to be debarred from human sympathy.

Any prisoner returning to the world after an absence of two years needs a prop to sustain him while he accustoms himself once more to operating the machinery of living. Wilde needed some sustaining presence more than most. Not for years, hardly ever in his forty years, had he had to undertake the fashioning of life for himself. He had been reared by a fond mother, cloistered in school and college. There were a few years when he was on his own, then he resumed family life with a wife at his side. There had been a circle of admiring friends in London and in Paris. Always he had led a cushioned existence. Even life in prison, with all its hardships, had been a life of complete dependence, where all arrangements had been made by others. Self-reliance is the last quality required of a convict.

It was fortunate that Wilde had been able to count upon a few faithful friends to arrange for his reception in a hostile world. They had planned his existence for him and provided him with the means to live. Robbie Ross was henceforth to be the administrator of his affairs and through him the annuity from his wife's estate was paid. But Ross had his work in London. Wilde in France was alone, solitary, in exile. There was no prop to sustain him.

He reached Berneval with high hopes he would be able to pick up the threads that had been broken and fashion life anew. Robbie Ross and Reggie Turner went with him to France to see him through the first days of acclimatization. At Robbie's suggestion he adopted the name of Melmoth, from the Archdeacon's novel, and joined Sebastian with it, the saint of the arrows, whose picture had so impressed him at Genoa twenty years before. Sebastian Melmoth—there was a fine sound about it that he relished. It would serve to spare the susceptibilities of strangers, but there was no disguising the figure of Oscar Wilde from those he had known.

The days of companionship passed quickly. The two friends had to leave him. He was alone. He was more conscious of his solitude in his room at the hotel, or walking beside the emptiness of the sea than he had been in his Reading cell. Life was not merely lonely, it was empty—there was nothing, no family, no admiring friends, not even warders with their threatening voices.

For the first time he realized the isolation of the exile. Gusts of self-pity swept over him. He had thought that in his newly found humility he would be able to accept obscurity in exile. It was worse than anything he had been able to picture to himself. By day as he walked on the cliffs he raged, rebellious and bitter in heart. At night visions of his mother, stern and reproachful, disturbed his sleep. Behind, in his thoughts, were his days of gilded infamy, his Neronian hours, rich and profligate. With him in the present, the present that was to be his future, was the loneliness of disgrace. He bowed before the verdict of society, but when rebuffs came they were hard to endure. His first harsh experiences came at Dieppe where, at the prompting of English visitors, he would be refused admittance to the best restaurants. When he sat down with friends the restaurateur would apologize—"dinner enough for three but not enough for four."

Although released from prison he was not entirely free from police attentions. Soon after his arrival in France he received official warning from the Sub-Prefect at Dieppe that any irregularity of conduct would bring upon him the penalty of immediate expulsion from the country by *ordre administratif*. His movements were watched and reported on by detectives hired by Queensberry. The penalties of his follies were not to be avoided merely by crossing the English Channel.

To Robbie he poured out the sadness of his thoughts. It was
Robbie on whom he could rely, Robbie who had braved
everything, even association with disgrace to help him in his
need.

He received a letter from his wife. She was prepared sometimes to meet him—twice a year she suggested. With her letter
she sent him photographs of their sons, such lovely little fellows
in their Eton collars—but she did not suggest that he should
see them as well. He was deeply grieved.

The peace of the Normandy coast gradually restored his
calm. The oppression of his loneliness began to lift. He attended
at the Catholic Church. His spirits mounted. He was glad he
was alone, it made him free to devote himself to work. He
rhapsodized on Berneval. He must make it his permanent home.
He was afraid of life in the cities of men.

June was not far advanced before he had seen about a permanent home. A chalet was available and he took it for the rest
of the season on payment of £52. He felt himself lucky to be
free to enjoy the sun and the sea of this beautiful world. In
brain and body he was conscious of power and health. He made
Will Rothenstein a sharer in his delight. In the old days Wilde
had given encouragement to the young artist in Paris, and
though most of his friends and acquaintances had abandoned
him, Rothenstein did not forget the kindness he had been
shown. He wrote to Berneval offering to visit if as an old
friend he would be welcome. Wilde was greatly pleased and
looked forward to a meeting with delight.

It was necessary for him to make money—he did not know
how he was to live after the summer was out unless he made
money. A new play was the thing. It would achieve what he
most wanted—his rehabilitation as an artist. He began to toy
with dramatic ideas. There were two subjects which had been
stirring him during his imprisonment, subjects from the Bible,

a piece about Pharaoh or about Ahab. The ideas were toyed with, but the play was not begun.

Wilde rejoiced that there were a number of old friends who remained to him, who would travel to Berneval to relieve his lonely days. There was Rothenstein's friend Conder, creator of exquisite fans, who divided his time between the Rabelaisian diversions of Montmartre and the apple orchards of Normandy. Wilde appreciated the vein of melancholy of the man who found life so beautiful that he thought it must end soon. "Conder," he said one day, "is so wonderful, my dear Will—he persuades you with that irresistible acumen which is the peculiarity of poets, to buy a fan for £5 for which you are perfectly prepared to pay £50."

Little Ernest Dowson, of the frail figure and sensitive face, was another visitor, Dowson, the poet of Cynara—"I have been faithful to thee, Cynara! in my fashion." Dowson was normal in his reactions and it is related that he attempted to induce Wilde to revert to normality. Together they visited an establishment but Wilde reported afterwards that the experience had chilled him—"the first time these ten years and the last: it was like cold mutton."

Dalhousie Young, the composer, had the right of entrée at Berneval as the champion of the fallen. He had braved the displeasure of the censorious by publishing a defense of Wilde when he was in prison at a time when only the most steadfast or imprudent of friends would in public have ventured to challenge the law's dealings with Oscar Wilde. The Stannards, husband and wife, offered Wilde their hospitality which touched him deeply. She was the novelist who wrote as John Strange Winter.

The twins of art—Charles Ricketts and Charles H. Shannon —did not forget the author whose "House of Pomegranates" they had so exquisitely decorated. Wilde had been a frequent visitor at their Chelsea house in the Vale—and it was he who had first suggested to Ricketts the idea of designing books that resulted in the starting of the Vale Press. Did Wilde in his present loneliness think with envy of the association of these two inseparables? Never was there any hint of discord in their partnership; so close was their identity that Ricketts in giving his opinions always said not "I" but "we." How different would life have been for Wilde had he been able to establish such harmony with Alfred Douglas.

Frank Harris would have joined the company at Berneval, but Wilde repulsed him. He declined the offer to go on a riding-tour with the maker of false promises.

There were woods in which he found an idyllic touch about life at Berneval. You might almost picture him as the sinner reformed, the penitent seeking grace. It seemed that the reconciliation between husband and wife was to be completed. Constance bore no hatred against him, did not share the detestation of her family advisers. From her refuge in Geneva, she began to write to him regularly, two letters a week. Reconciliation there was to be, but first there must be a period on probation, a year in which to prove himself. Furthermore, there must be no more Bosie. Wilde was affronted by this condition. It was too humiliating, this offer to take him back on terms. Weeks afterwards he was still trembling with anger as he spoke of it. Not by these priggish, old-maidish devices was reconciliation to be brought about. It is to be imagined they were the suggestions not of the wife but of the family advisers. Whoever was responsible, the bar was conclusive. Constance remained in Switzerland.

At Berneval amidst high resolves there were gnawing pains for something closer and deeper in emotion than friends on their occasional visits could yield. No high hopes and literary intentions could fill that void in his life. The idyll of Berneval was a vision of the early days of regained freedom. It was a vision that was doomed to fade. There are men self-contained and self-sufficient, who feel no need for the solace of companionship. Wilde, emphatically, was not one of these. The idyll of Berneval made provision for everything but this essential necessity of companionship. It was on a mind becoming conscious of starvation of the affections that Bosie began to exercise his arts, by daily letters and by frequent telegrams.

At first sight it must appear incredible that Alfred Douglas should have wanted to resume relations with the man who had denounced him in the letter from prison. The only explanation conceivable is that he had not read those blistering reproaches. Did Douglas receive at that time a copy of the letter that had been addressed to him? It is an unsolved mystery with the probabilities neatly balanced. From the time Wilde handed over the rolls of writing on his release from prison, the letter disappeared from sight. There is no reference to it in any of the correspondence. What happened? Did Ross hand a copy to Douglas? Ross swore later that he did so. Douglas denied it. On the face of it, Ross would be credited. It was in his interest to have handed over a copy of the letter. He was jealous of Bosie. Anything he could do to stop a renewal of the old association he would have done. What more effective barrier could there be between Oscar and Bosie than the denunciations of the letter? Bosie could not have swallowed such insults and still wish to resume his former place with Wilde. It is an argument that applies with equal force in either direction. Bosie could not have swallowed the insults, therefore he could not have read them. This conclusion is almost irresistible. Everything known of the nature of the man and his vanity makes it impossible to credit that he could for a moment have tolerated contact with the friend who had so scathingly reprobated him. And that is all that can be said. It may be that a copy of the

letter was handed over and that Douglas, affronted by the reproaches of the first few pages, flung the thing on the fire. This
was his brand of treatment of another and lesser letter of reproach.

Wilde had not been many days at Berneval before Bosie
had started writing to him. They were bitter letters. You can
imagine their nature, the reproaches of the old favorite who
had been cast aside. They did nothing to melt Oscar's resentment. His first reply was made in distant terms, a letter that
almost ostentatiously kept away from any personal note and
discussed, merely, his own and Bosie's literary work. Bosie
remained excluded from the fold.

The Douglas spirit was proof against rebuffs. Bosie continued to plead his case. Oscar, he was assured of it, hated him, but
he had not changed towards Oscar. He had given his promise
to stick to him, and stuck he had despite all appearances to
the contrary. He was longing to see him again. The pleadings
and the professions of loyalty produced their effect. There was
a thawing at Berneval. Bosie could note with satisfaction a
distinct rise in the emotional barometer.

More letters were exchanged and then on the fifteenth day
of June came the capitulation to his own dear boy. They must
meet—of course they must meet. It had taken a mere twenty-
five days from the release from jail for Oscar to wipe out
resentments of the past and to take back the friend he had
denounced as the author of his ruin. It is the only valid commentary on the letter of Reading jail. In fewer days than it
had taken to draw up the catalogue of iniquity, Wilde's anger
had melted away. Like a child passing a duster over his slate,
he erased from his mind his letter of accusation.

Wilde wrote the letter of acceptance to Bosie on the fifteenth
of June. On the seventeenth he telegraphed in alarm to cancel
the arrangement. Somehow news of the proposed reunion had

gotten abroad. Bosie had been indiscreet and friends had taken prompt action to stop the renewal of the association they deplored. They communicated post haste with Wilde's solicitor and he in turn with Berneval. It took Wilde by surprise, left him distressed in nerve and full of apprehension. Bosie made light of the solicitor's warning, ridiculed the idea of "Q's" intervention. Wilde was not so easily persuaded. There was the visible evidence of the detective hanging about Berneval, day after day. The marquis might arrive at Berneval and that was more than he could face.

Midsummer came and the great Queen's Jubilee. There was no more devoted subject of her Majesty than the exile of Berneval and he gave a fête for the village children in honor of the occasion. It was an unqualified success, delighting the giver of the feast equally with the fifteen gamins he entertained on strawberries and cream, apricots, cakes and sirop de grenadine.

It was without doubt a unique Jubilee celebration. It would have been diverting to have heard the Queen's comment on the proceedings. Douglas was not apparently much entertained, complained indeed, in his next letter, that he found life boring.

There was a celebration of another sort when a party of young poets from Paris traveled to Berneval as a deputation to make a formal greeting to Oscar Wilde on his release from jail. The main item in the proceedings was a banquet at the Café des Tribunaux. It was a highly acceptable tribute, a boost for Wilde's wavering morale. The sentence he had received for conduct that was no offense in French law seemed so harsh that they made almost a martyr out of him. What more could he ask?

Wilde was at work again, discharging himself of his reactions to imprisonment. He wrote the two letters on prison life that were published in the "Daily Chronicle," and he began the composition of his last major contribution to literature, "The Ballad of Reading Gaol," on which his fame as poet has come to rest. He was swift in composition, but slow beyond measure in revision, so that he was occupied on the nicer points of the Ballad long after leaving Normandy. Other work was available for him in Paris where, had he wished, he could have contributed to two literary papers and been handsomely paid for it. The editor of "Le Journal," for instance, offered 300 francs a week for a weekly chronique, or causerie from the pen of Oscar Wilde. He rejected this and similar offers, being unprepared to agree to the exploitation of the notoriety of his name. It was a strange reluctance on the part of the man who twenty years before had been prepared to exploit any notoriety to get his name before the public.

Sherard visited him in July, finding him in excellent health and high spirits. He found a new manliness in the Wilde who took a daily swim in the sea, and was ready to walk for miles through the Normandy countryside. Sherard, with Robbie Ross, took part in the game of alphabetical authors in which Wilde, with his wide reading and retentive memory, held the advantage over his two competitors. They had not completed the alphabet before they retired for the night. Towards midnight Wilde, in his dressing-gown, poked his head around Sherard's door to shout Xerxes, and then retreated. Sherard ran on to the landing to counter with Xenophon. A distant voice muttered Xavier. For this there was no riposte.

It was during this visit, presumably, that Sherard was the witness of an incident that enlightened him as to his friend's tendencies. It was an incident, he relates, "which at the time impressed me not at all, but which under the blinding light which has since been shed on the character and morale of the

other actor in this episode leaves me no room for doubt. It was
at Berneval that a deliberate attempt was made to drag Wilde
back into Malebolge."

As the summer wore on the simple delights of Berneval
began to pall and money difficulties to mount. Wilde had been
started off with about £800, which with careful management
would have sufficed him for many months, but thrift was a
quality unknown to him. The released prisoner, after his enforced abstinences, does not favor a life of sustained self-denial.
The chalet, the entertainment of friends, the feting of gamins
had to be paid for. M. Melmoth was known for his generosity.
The local tradesmen asked no more than for a couple more
Melmoths to be assured of a comfortable season. It was extravagant and it was understandable, but it could not continue,
unless he could supplement the allowance of £3 a week he
received from his wife.

The first enthusiasm for work was beginning to fade. Money
alone could not move him to undertake the long drudgery of
composition. He needed, always he had needed the splendid
spur of fame. How could there be fame in his days of infamy?
The repulse from his wife and the emptiness of his days weighed
more heavily upon him. At last he could endure no more. He
capitulated to Bosie.

The two friends met at Rouen rejoicing at their reunion.
Douglas twenty years afterwards gave a brief account of it:
"The meeting was a great success. I have often thought since
that if he or I had died after that, our friendship would have
ended in a beautiful romantic way. We walked about all day
long arm-in-arm or hand-in-hand and were perfectly happy.
Next day he went back to Berneval and I returned to Paris, but
we had settled that when I went to Naples about six weeks
later he was to join me there."

M. Melmoth returned to Berneval for the last time. The days

of waiting were almost beyond bearing. Berneval was no longer to be tolerated. He worked himself into such a state that he fancied he must commit suicide. He wished he had never consented to part from Bosie at Rouen, there were such abysses of time and space between them. All his hopes now centered on Naples and Bosie. The only chance left for him of doing creative work was to be with his friend.

The final departure from Berneval was a hurried one. Wilde had been told that information about the life he was leading had been lodged with the authorities and that an expulsion order was to be made against him. Warned in time, he went to a friendly farmer who drove him away to Dieppe. There he caught the train to take him towards Naples and to Bosie.

There are moments when one has to choose between living one's own life fully, entirely, completely, or dragging out some false, shallow, degrading existence that the world in all its hypocrisy demands.

OSCAR WILDE and Alfred Douglas met again at Aix and traveled together to Naples. After a short stay at the Hotel Royal, they took a villa at Posilippo, the Villa Giudice, where they remained for three months. They made no attempt to conceal that they had come together again. The news of their reunion was quickly spread abroad.

Opinion in England was outraged by the renewal of the old scandal. Oscar's friends were offended, his wife and her advisers indignant. By his friends Wilde's action was regarded as the worst step he could have taken. This companionship was looked upon as the least desirable the world of men offered to his choice. Douglas was regarded as no less than a gilded pillar of infamy.

There were immediate protests. First to make complaint was Robbie Ross who, having labored with such zeal and affection to refashion Wilde's life, was chagrined by the renewal of the old association. To what purpose had he and other loyal friends exerted themselves if it was but to pave the way for the rekindling of the scandal? What hope was there for rehabilitation and an artistic come-back? Against Robbie's reproaches Oscar found little to submit in answer. It was futile to urge that it was necessary for the sake of his literary work. There was the letter of Reading jail to attest the contrary—that with Bosie artistic work was impossible. The plain fact was that Wilde and Douglas, like any other couple infatuated with each other, thought the world well lost to gain the solace of each other's society. For Wilde the world he had known was lost in any case. What he had gained by the new affront to society was quickly to be shown. The rebukes of the indignant Robbie left him the more angry because there was so little he could reply. He had the sense to let his resentment cool and pleaded that in a world that had rejected him he had been in need of the companionship that Douglas could give him. He and Bosie were together again and they asked to be left alone.

Left alone they could not be, there was too much outraged concern. From London Wilde heard of tittle-tattle in the clubs in which Sherard had become involved. In the smoking room where he was seated, two of Wilde's traducers came upon Sherard to taunt him over the new development in the scandal. The faithful Sherard was baited into saying that it was an unfortunate mistake, that it would give a new theme for calumny to seize upon and that it would alienate what sympathy for Wilde still remained. His words were twisted in the course of being transmitted to Naples and a reproof was quickly on its way. Sherard was pained that he had drawn such unmerited censure upon himself. He drew the conclusion that things were not well at the Villa Giudice. Reports that reached him confirmed his fears, sad stories of how Wilde had been slighted and insulted whenever he showed himself to members of the English colony.

Attempts were made to put an end to the association. The British Ambassador sent his Attaché to the villa to see Douglas and reason with him. It was a fruitless mission. Bosie was not to be detached. But it was all very depressing. Wilde was conscious of the ostracism of his countrymen. It pained him that none of the English colony called at the villa to leave cards.

While the voices of scandal and censure were freely engaged, the two friends had settled down in troubled and uncomfortable companionship to devote themselves to their literary work. Douglas turned to poetry and wrote some of his best sonnets, Wilde to his prison Ballad. While funds lasted, life was entertaining enough, except for the rats that drove Douglas in alarm from the villa. A ratcatcher was called in and his services were supplemented by the ministrations of a witch, a bearded woman rich in incantations. The rats vanished. Bosie was able to return.

Many hours at Posilippo were devoted to the completion and revision of Wilde's last work, the piece of rhetoric in ballad form called "The Ballad of Reading Gaol." It is his best-known poem, dedicated "To the memory of C.T.W., sometime trooper of the Royal Horse Guards, obiit H.M. Prison, Reading, Berkshire, July 7, 1896." Trooper Woodbridge was confined in Reading jail while awaiting execution for the murder of the young wife who had been unfaithful to him—

> *The poor dead woman whom he loved*
> *And murdered in her bed.*

Wilde had seen him walking in the yard at exercise and a voice behind him had whispered the news, "That fellow's got to swing." The poem conveys the feelings of the condemned man, and the dreadful scene of the morning of the day of dark disgrace. It is written in simple language, quite unlike Wilde's earlier verse, with short telling sentences and starkly presented images, an impressionist piece of vivid realism, with a verse or two of satire, and an imaginative section in which the horror of the other convicts in their cells is portrayed in lines that echo phrases of Coleridge's "Ancient Mariner." The power of the verses triumphs over a mixture of ill-consorting styles.

There are stanzas in which the ex-convict gives an account of some of the ill-deeds he had known to be done behind the bricks and bars of prison.

> For they starve the little frightened child
>   Till it weeps both night and day:
> And they scourge the weak, and flog the fool,
>   And gibe the old and grey,
> And some grow mad, and all grow bad
>   And none a word may say.

The flogging of the fool he had previously described in the letter of Reading jail. The case of the frightened children, sent to prison because they could not afford to pay a fine for poaching, he had aired in the first of his two letters to the "Daily Chronicle." His sympathetic guardian, Warden Martin, had been dismissed from the prison service for having broken regulations by giving the poor children biscuits to eat. There are phrases in the poem that had done duty in his letter, to Alfred Douglas, for example—"With midnight always in one's heart and twilight in one's cell." The concluding stanza has been abundantly quoted:

> And all men kill the thing they love
>   By all let this be heard,
> Some do it with a bitter look
>   Some with a flattering word,
> The coward does it with a kiss,
>   The brave man with a sword.

Wilde, for once, was sufficiently detached to see the short-comings of his poem. His criticism is shrewder than most poets have been able to apply to their own verses—"The poem suffers under the difficulty of a divided aim in style. Some stanzas are realistic, some romantic, some poetry, some propaganda. I feel it keenly, but as a whole I think the production is interesting—that is interesting from more than one point of view, and that is artistically to be regretted."

No poem Wilde wrote gave him more concern as he polished the lines to perfection. This, doubtless, was due to the fact that he was writing in an unfamiliar style. Never before had he been so uncertain about the merits of what he had done, but never before had he written anything of this kind—nor would he ever again attempt to out-Kipling Henley. He went over it verse by verse, line by line, word by word.

He discussed the phrasing by letter with Robbie Ross. Alfred Douglas heard the lines of the Ballad repeated meal-time after meal-time until he became bored, for Bosie had not Sherard's enthusiasm in acting as poet's mate.

When the piece at last was finished a publisher had to be found and this was not easy. Publishers no longer sought the writings of Mr. Oscar Wilde. At last, no reputable firm being willing to undertake publication, it was entrusted to Smithers. It was the type of thing to appeal to this publisher of the fantastic and the bizarre. "I'll publish anything that the others are afraid of," was the declaration he made to describe his policy. Leonard Smithers, Yorkshire by birth, solicitor by profession, had on his publishers' list the names of Beardsley, Dowson, and, strangely enough, Max Beerbohm. On the side as a bookseller he trafficked surreptitiously in pornography of the crudest sort. He went about the production of the Ballad as if it had been one of his riskier adventures in eroticism, so that Wilde said of him he was "so accustomed to suppressing books that he suppresses his own."

Everything about the publication of the Ballad was in a minor key. It could not come out in the glory of his own name —C.33 must hide his identity from readers who did not know his secret. To have publication undertaken by a man like Smithers would reduce any author's self-esteem.

Smithers nerved himself to print a first edition of 800 copies. They sold in a few days. There was a reprinting. That too was soon sold out. The reviewers had ignored the poem on first publication. When it was a popular success they praised it. It was not long before several thousand copies had been sold. A bolder publisher would have achieved success with it.

Despite the semi-clandestine fashion of publication, well over five thousand copies were sold during the lifetime of the author. This was some consolation but the poet was depressed by lack of recognition of this work. He had sent out a number of presentation copies. One alone was acknowledged. It was chilling.

When the MS. of the Ballad had been sent off to London, Wilde toyed in his mind with other projects. There was the "Florentine Tragedy" which he had in process, but he made no progress. He corresponded with Dalhousie Young about writing the libretto for an opera "Daphnis and Chloe." It had first been discussed at Berneval. On his way south to Naples Wilde had written to the composer about the financial terms, suggesting the payment of an advance of £100, with a further £50 on production. Dal Young complied, and that was the end of the matter. "Daphnis and Chloe" did not proceed beyond the specimen lyric. Years afterwards Ross repaid Dal Young the £100.

It was not long before financial pressure made life difficult in the Villa Giudice. With the funds at their disposal the two friends should have been able to support themselves for some months, but they soon ran through their resources. The Lady Queensberry wrote threatening to stop her son's allowance if he continued in association with Wilde. The friends were to be starved into parting.

There was an ultimatum from Mrs. Wilde's solicitors—the allowance from his wife would be forfeited if Wilde lived with any disreputable person; any member of the Queensberry family was regarded as coming within that category. This was the final blow. The Naples experiment had been entered upon with great hopes, and against the warnings of previous experience. To share the solicitude of the villa with Bosie was wonderful while things went well between them, but the continuous, unbroken contact was a test that only the most harmoniously based association could survive. In the rejoicings over their reunion the strains and tensions of the past had been forgotten, but it was not long before the soreness of old wounds had been revived by fresh hurts. There had been quarrels, and quarrels with Bosie were devastating. It was just as it had been before—long resentful fits of sullen silence, sudden fits of almost epileptic rage. By November there was small need for family intervention to drive the friends apart. Alone, in their isolation, they were becoming a torment to each other.

So, in the end, Bosie capitulated to his mother's ultimatum. There was no reason which even the punctilio of honor could suggest for standing out. He would leave Oscar for the sufficient compelling reason that Oscar no longer wanted him. Nor did he feel the former irresistible compulsion to be with Wilde.

Each of them wrote a record of the parting, an epilogue to their association. Alfred Douglas, in a letter to Lady Queensberry, set out his feelings for once in simple and quite moving sincerity. He addressed his letter to his "Darling Mamma" from Rome a few days after what he termed his "escape" from Oscar.

I am glad, O so glad! to have got away. I am so afraid that you will not believe me, and I am so afraid of appearing to pose as anything but what I am, but I am not a hypocrite and you must believe me. I wanted to go back to him, I longed for it and for him, because I love him and admire him and think him great and almost good, but when I had done it and when I got back, I hated it. I was miserable, I wanted to go away. But I couldn't. I was tied by honor.

If he had wanted me to stay I would never have left him, but when I found out that he really didn't want me to stay and that I might leave him without causing him pain and without a breach of loyalty, then I was glad to go. Even then I hid it from myself, I struggled not to let my inward thought get the better of me, and it is only since I have been here two days that I have completely realized and admitted how glad I am to be away. Even when I got here I persuaded myself that I was miserable and that I wanted to go back and I wrote to you in that sense. But now I know what a relief it is to have escaped *honorably* from a sort of prison.

I still think it was right to go to him when he asked [1] and at that time I longed to go to him. I felt I must clear up the matter. And as long as I was there, I was bound to fight in his interests and I did it even to the last bitter point. The knowledge that I didn't really want to stay with him only made me more determined not to show the least disloyalty. I was prepared to carry it to the very end. If he had proposed joint suicide I would have accepted it.

He pressed his mother to let him have £200 to send to his friend immediately, with £300 more, in instalments, afterwards. These payments represented to him an honorable discharge of his debt and he added:

Don't think that I have changed about him or that I think him bad or that I have changed my views about morals. I still love and admire him and I think he has been infamously treated by ignorant and cruel brutes. I look on him as a martyr to progress. I associate myself with him in everything. I long to hear of his success and artistic rehabilitation in the post which is his by right at the very summit of English literature, nor do I intend to cease corresponding with him or not to see him from time to time in Paris and elsewhere. I give up nothing and admit no point against him or myself separately or jointly. Do not think either that he has been unkind to me or shown himself to me in an unfavourable light. On the contrary

[1] This is an adaptation of the facts for Mamma's eyes. That he had pressed Wilde to join him, that he was the author of the reunion, the Wilde letters leave no doubt.

he has been sweet and gentle and will always remain to me as the type of what a gentleman and friend should be. Only this, I am tired of the struggle and tired of being ill-treated by the World, and I had lost that supreme desire for his society which I had before, and which made a sort of aching void when he was not with me. That has gone and I think and hope for ever.

Up to this, however, I had no excuse to leave him. I simply couldn't do it. If he had been disagreeable to me of if he had turned out different from what I thought, if he had ever behaved in any way differently from how a man of honour and humanity should behave I would have seized the chance. But he didn't. He has always behaved *perfectly* to me. The only thing that happened was that I felt and saw that he really didn't wish me to stay and that it would really be a relief to him if I went away. So at last I was able to get away with a clear conscience.

And it is no use wishing I hadn't ever gone with him to Naples. It was the most lucky thing that ever happened. If I hadn't rejoined him and lived with him for two months, I should *never* have got over the longing for him. It was spoiling my life and spoiling my art and spoiling everything. Now I am free.

That reads as a manly letter from a young man rich in enthusiasm. In contrast with this was the letter Wilde wrote to Robbie Ross in which he tried to excuse himself for having rejoined Alfred Douglas. Years afterwards the terms of the letter were read out in a London court of law to establish that Douglas had abandoned Wilde, deserted him and ruined him. Wilde's accusations were fatal to Douglas in his lawsuit. By the letter the whole blame for the Naples reunion was placed on Bosie—he was the tempter who had lured Wilde astray, for the second time, with the siren promises of a home and financial support. The promises, Wilde asserted, were false; Bosie was expecting to be financed as he had been in the earlier days and when no funds were forthcoming it was Bosie who had walked out and abandoned his friend.

Admirers of Wilde must wish that he had never written

that letter. There are allowances that can be urged for him—
that Bosie had been selfish and infuriating; that Wilde was
writing to his staunchest friend, guardian of his affairs, whom
he had offended, writing with an eye on the future and his
finances, writing for the ultimate information of his wife and
her advisers. But having made these allowances, it is distressing
to find that Wilde could write in these terms of the friend
who had written in such boyish admiration of him. Even had it
been the truth it was not generous and it was far from the truth,
certainly not the financial truth. Bosie on leaving provided
Wilde with £200 given him by Lady Queensberry, and he
had paid the rent of the villa for the entire quarter.

It was the end of the friendship. The two men were to meet
afterwards in Paris, to meet frequently with financial advantage for Wilde, and with no manifestation by him of the feeling of outrage against Alfred Douglas of which he had written
in his letter to Ross. But never again was the old fire of their
friendship rekindled.

Of the attraction that drew them to each other what is there
to be said? There was an urgently compelling force behind it
of great strength. Of the nature of it only those can write
who have experienced it.

When Wilde left Berneval for Naples it was in pursuit of a
phantom. It had at that time the embodiment of Alfred Douglas.
It is the nature of phantoms to be caught only where the rainbow ends. All the world knows this save only those who are
lured by phantoms of their imaginings into vain pursuit. From
them the truth about phantoms is concealed.

The phantom Wilde was pursuing is one that lures all the
sons and daughters of men who are born with the craving for
perfection in companionship. It was Wilde's misfortune to feel
the longing and to be unable to realize the fulfilment in a person of the other sex. He had tried to fulfil himself in marriage

and he had failed. Many marry and fail and marry again. He failed once and was never tempted into a second attempt. Thereafter he pursued his phantom among members of his own sex. There were a succession of attachments, some casual and ephemeral, some of deep and continuing affection, some based on physical satisfaction of the moment, others rooted in loftier emotions. None of them was enduring. In a public confession of his faith he championed the love that has no name. It was his fate to find in his hour of need that the love that dare not speak its name was one that could not yield him the consolation that he craved.

21. WANDERINGS IN EXILE

Society often forgives the criminal, it never forgives the dreamer.

WHILE he was staying in Paris in the spring (1898) Wilde was informed that Constance had died at Genoa, on April 7, following an operation. While she was convalescing Mrs. Wilde had been staying as the guest of the Ranee of Sarawak, who had a villa near Genoa. She had driven into the town when she had a sudden seizure. She was taken into a hotel, where she collapsed and died. According to the record of Alfred Douglas, Wilde was tormented by sad dreams about her on the night of her death and woke up in tears. "I dreamed she came here to see me and I kept saying— Go away, go away, leave me in peace."

Wilde was distressed by the news and sent off a telegram of summons to Robbie Ross: "Constance is dead. Please come tomorrow and stay at my hotel. Am in great grief." In spite of all that had happened, Wilde had preserved an affection for his wife, the feelings of an elder brother towards a favorite younger sister. He had been deeply moved by the visits she had made to him in prison. When there had been talk of divorce, he had acquiesced—to tie his wife to him against her will would be wrong. When she had been prepared for a reconciliation, he had welcomed it and only the Sunday school device of the year's probation had prevented their reunion. One can but wonder what the consequence would have been had husband and wife gone together again on his release from prison. It may be that he would not thus have reverted to his former life of

257

self-indulgence. When he left prison he was in good health physically, far fitter than he had been at the time of his fall. He had a firm resolve to work to restore his finances and his fame. A few weeks with Alfred Douglas and he had fallen back into the old ways of sensual ease. His new resolves had faded, never to be rekindled. Restored to his family the relapse might never have occurred.

Alfred Douglas was to censure Constance for not having stood by her husband. "There have been wives," he wrote, "as I have good reason to know, who have stood by their husbands through thick and thin and borne it out 'even to the crack of doom.' Mrs. Wilde, alas, was not one of them. . . . I hate appearing to attack Mrs. Wilde whom I liked and admired and respected, but I am obliged to say that I think in the long run she let him down, rather badly. If she had treated him properly and stuck to him after he had been in prison, as a really good wife would have done, he would have gone on loving her to the end of his life." There is more of this stuff and the further assertion—"Towards the end of the time before the catastrophe, the relations between them were distinctly strained. To try to make out that this had anything whatever to do with me, is simply dishonest and not truthful."

How Douglas contrived to square this assertion with his conscience is beyond human comprehending. Apart from the difference of sex, Douglas stood in relation to Mrs. Wilde as "the other woman" to the wife in a divorce case. One of the complaints Douglas voiced frequently against his own father was that Queensberry had tried to introduce his mistress into Lady Queensberry's home. That, in the person of Alfred Douglas, was precisely what had been introduced into the home of Mrs. Wilde. Is there in the whole realm of English letters anything so nauseating as this insufferable Douglas reproaching the gentle Constance, this man who, to a greater degree than

Wilde, made the best (or worst) of both sexes, and who as a husband added straightforward adultery to his diversions?

Now that his wife had passed beyond the possibility of reconciliation, what was to become of Wilde? While she still lived it was always possible to contemplate that a home with his family might be his. Now where was his home to be, or was he never again to have a home of his own? What was he going to do with his life? In his growing mood of fatalism he found himself wondering what life was going to make of him.

Robbie Ross, pondering on the problem, made the inquiry whether Wilde thought of marrying again. With his knowledge of his friend it was curious that Ross should have had such a thought in his mind. To Ross's knowledge Oscar had been continuing the casual associations that had been the occasion of his downfall—he was to continue this conduct, without qualm or compunction, to the time of his death. How then could he embark again on marriage except on marriage in the terms of securing the domestic convenience of a housekeeper?

Wilde knew better than to consider this solution of the problem of his future. Hearth and home were not for him. Hotels, a succession of hotels, were to be his home as he wandered aimlessly about France, and Italy, a restless itinerant, an exile without roots.

Robbie Ross did all that a friend could do to ease the burden of his difficulties, but Robbie was not free to devote himself to Wilde as Watts Dunton labored for Swinburne. There was something pathological about Swinburne's submissiveness to his custodian. The wastage of Wilde's years of exile was deplorable, but better to have lived vagabond days as a Bohemian of the Boulevards than to have been shepherded into respectability with Swinburne at the Pines. At least Wilde escaped the insufferable tedium of suburban decline.

From the time of the collapse of the Naples experiment until the end, Ross was guide and guardian of his friend. Ross was the confidant from whom little was concealed. Ross was applied to in time of trouble. It was Ross who sent a new suit over to Paris. It was Ross who retailed all the news from literary London. When things went wrong it was Ross who crossed over the Channel to put them right. When Wilde was undermining his health, it was Ross who hurried South to Italy. Oscar was comforted and reformed. There was urgent need for reformation. Oscar had been indulging himself with absinthe which, owing to his strong constitution, he was able to drink deeply without obvious effect on his sobriety. There was some plain speaking by Robbie and Oscar was frightened into more sober ways. The lecturing in no wise marred the pleasure of the visit. Indeed Wilde "liked being ordered about by people he knew were fond of him."

On the anniversary of the release from prison, there was a lecture from Robbie on lost literary opportunities and time that had been misspent. Oscar, for the moment, was spurred towards new endeavors. He defended himself against the charge of idleness; he had some achievements to his credit and he could point to his prison Ballad. But though he made promises for greater industry he knew that he was promising more than he could fulfil. He placed the blame for his failure to write on the privations of prison life that had destroyed him as a creative artist. This was no more than an excuse, for his letters were as fresh, his talk, by the unanimous verdict of his acquaintances, as witty as ever.

The fact was that to undertake the drudgery of composition he needed the encouragement of admiring friends and the spur of fame. Those incentives were denied him and their absence was fatal to him as an author. His creative faculties remained with him to the end, but he lacked the driving force that would enable him to translate the inventions he squandered in talk at the dining-table into the disciplined achievement of essay or play. Other men gained the profit from his freely flowing fancies.

He was induced to undertake the task of preparing his plays for publication. He revised the texts with care, calling upon Ross to aid him with his grammar. Ross was rewarded with the dedication of the finest of the comedies, "The Importance of Being Earnest." It was no more than Robbie deserved. This task of revision, begun in the summer of 1898, was the last sustained literary task Wilde was to undertake.

Creative work would have been his salvation in his years of exile. Without disciplined employment the days passed tediously by. He could not sustain the hours of loneliness. When literary folk met him they were charming to him, but there were so many weeks in which the tedium was unrelieved by their company and he was forced to seek companionship where he could find it, necessarily among his intellectual inferiors. He was excluded from society in Paris. Even in literary circles he was not welcome. "Je ne fréquente pas les forcats" was the verdict of one French man of letters. It served as the excuse for most of them. So he was reduced to passing his time with chance acquaintances of the Boulevards and to finding escape once again in the comforts of absinthe.

Most of the chroniclers draw a woeful picture of the final phase of Wilde's career. The story is pitched on a note of tragedy, darkened by penury, squalor and misery. Here the chroniclers have erred, though not by intention and design. It was difficult for them to give an objective account after years of eclipse. They had known the man in the splendor of his success. They were conscious that it might have been a continuing splendor of achievement. They saw the actual through the haze of what might have been. It tinged and darkened their pictures.

Oscar's existence was by no means the life of squalor and penury they depicted. Slights and rebuffs he had, of course, to suffer. There was no glittering triumph to sustain him and he never completed, scarcely attempted another literary work. He was ostracized, but loyal friends remained, and there were young men to give him some of the balm of admiration. Sometimes he was short of money, living in what he termed penury, but, as was said of D. H. Lawrence, he insisted on a high standard of destitution. He would have known no financial difficulty at all had he managed his money with the slightest regard for economy, but the association with Bosie had robbed him of any notion of good husbandry.

There is no certain reckoning of his receipts but it is evident that from the time Wilde was released from prison in May 1897 until his departure from Naples later in the year he had received well over a thousand pounds thanks to the benefactions of his friends. Thereafter he must have had over £500 a year —probably double that sum—and the pound sterling was still a golden sovereign in those easy days. Money trickled through his fingers. He was lavish in his kindness, lordly in his almsgiving. It was by his extravagances that he brought himself into difficulties and the difficulties were not long persisting, for there was always someone whom he could touch— "toucher," he liked the word. Douglas or Frank Harris could usually be approached; Leverson or Claude Lowther could be tapped; or, if all else failed there was always the dependable Robbie, dear little provoking Robbie. Oscar soon learned the beggar's arts and begged unscrupulously, without blushing.

The records of his journeyings about the Continent from Naples to Paris, from Paris to Napoule (financed by Frank Harris), from Napoule to Gland (as the guest of Harold Mellor) on to Geneva, Genoa, back to Paris, to Italy (on £50 from Mellor) and to Rome attest that for a man in reduced circumstances he traveled surprisingly well.

It was in the winter of 1898 that he went South to the French Riviera as the guest of Frank Harris to stay near Cannes at the little village of la Napoule. In those days it was a charming enough place, a few cottages and villas and one hotel, where he spent Christmas Day alone, for Harris, rather mysteriously, had failed to appear. Oscar celebrated the occasion a day late in the company of a nice young fellow named Harold Mellor, who had come over for golf. Son of a North of England manufacturer, Mellor was well off, with a place of his own at Gland. He had soon succumbed to Wilde's charm. Napoule was agreeable (nice and dull) and Oscar passed the time walking in the pinewoods. Once the past leaped out at him as George Alexander appeared suddenly, riding on a bicycle. Alexander rode on without stopping. Oscar was deeply hurt. There was another and happier reminder of former times a few days later when he was taken to Nice and saw the Bernhardt in "La Tosca." There was an emotional meeting between them.

Several visits were made divertingly to Nice, which was pretty and gay, with music everywhere. Then he went to Cannes to see the Bataille des Fleurs.

In February (1899) Oscar left for Switzerland to stay at Gland as the guest of Harold Mellor. The visit did not turn out well. Mellor as a host was not the Mellor of Napoule, but proved to be unsocial, taciturn, wretched company, who took no pains to please or gratify his guest. Oscar longed to get away, he had never disliked anyone so thoroughly. By April he had gone from Gland. At parting Mellor had apologized and implored him to stay. The truth was that Mellor was neurasthenic. For a quarter of a century he was to pass miserable days until, despairing of "the affair called life," he opened a vein in his arm and died, like a Roman, in his bath.

During his trip to the South Wilde made a pilgrimage to his wife's grave at Genoa. He was very moved as he stood by the marble cross. It bore her Christian names, "Constance Mary, daughter of Harold Lloyd, Q.C.," and an inscription from the Book of the Revelation. His own name was not recorded. He abandoned himself to a passion of grief. As he covered the grave with a carpet of crimson roses he broke down and sobbed bitterly in the anguish of his sorrow and regret.

In March 1899 a telegram announced the death of his brother, with whom, for years past, he had not been on friendly terms.

Willie's life had ended in the ignominy of alcoholic excesses. He had never recovered from the ill fortune of his first marriage to an American woman, Mrs. Frank Leslie, who later became a Baronne. When she had made up her mind to dismiss Willie as her mate she called the reporters together to announce —"I have decided to divorce Mr. Wilde, as he is of no use to me by day or by night." Returned to England Willie made a second and happier marriage, but according to his friends, he had been unmanned. "He went to America a fine, brilliantly clever man. The Baronne sent him back to England a nervous wreck, with an exhausted brain and a debilitated frame. His power for sustained effort was gone. His fate in some ways was as pathetic as his brother's. He suffered bitterly from the loss of his powers. He had been robbed of his golden years and seemed to me like some unhappy Samson."

On Willie's death the property in Ireland, that had belonged to Sir William Wilde, came to Oscar by entail. It was his to sell and he thought hopefully that it would fetch £3,000, but there were his creditors to consider, for he was still an undischarged bankrupt.

There is a sympathetic picture of the Wilde of these days from the pen of Laurence Housman. The account of the meeting is the more valuable as Housman, an impartial witness, completely disposes of the idea that Wilde, broken by prison, had suffered any sort of mental decline. "The impression left on me is that Oscar Wilde was incomparably the most accomplished talker I had ever met. The smooth-flowing utterance, sedate and self-possessed, oracular in tone, whimsical in substance, carried on without halt or hesitation or change of word, with the quiet zest of a man perfect at the game and conscious that for the moment, at least, he was back in his old form again . . . what I admired most was the quiet, uncomplaining courage with which he accepted an ostracism against which in his lifetime there could be no appeal. To a man of his habits and temperament, conscious that the incentive to produce was gone with the popular applause that had been its recurrent stimulus, the outlook was utterly dark; life had already become a tomb."

In Paris that summer (1899) Wilde found the awful heat very trying and he longed to be away. Where was he to go? He could change the scene but there was no abiding contentment. Paris had its consolations. He was dining at the Café de la Paix when he saw Augustin Daly and Ada Rehan, who were most charming to him. Her hair had turned quite white and he accused her of having dyed it so, which delighted her. When he visited a Montmartre café frequented by young poets, he was received with great honor and everyone was presented to him.

Christmas of 1899 was his last. He passed it in Paris, pleasantly, though the weather was wet and cold. His health was beginning to trouble him and he suspected poisoning by mussels. The specialist he consulted diagnosed not mussels but neurasthenia. The symptoms would make a physician murmur allergy today, but allergic mysteries were beyond the range of the medico of the Nineties.

Robert Sherard was in Paris and they met. They went about

in each other's company as they had done sixteen years before, but there was no renewing the old spell. Robert was sentimental over the past. Oscar was not and found the meetings tedious. The glamor had gone, Sherard had lost the good looks of his youth. It is curious to note how Wilde's interest, and with that his friendships and affections, was conditioned by the attraction of physical appearance. Alfred Douglas complained that it was the loss of his youthful beauty that contributed to the fall in Wilde's affection for him. Sherard's friendship—and for that matter Bosie's—was not influenced by such a physical appeal. Poor Sherard! For the joy of a few months of Wilde's close companionship he had to pay the price of disillusionment. His loyalty stood the test. In his friendship he never wavered.

There were frequent meetings now with Alfred Douglas, who was living in Paris. Queensberry was dead and Bosie was coming into his patrimony, some £15,000, which he regarded as a smallish sum, "a modest amount of money." Oscar looked for benefactions. Frank Harris, also, was responsive to appeals. Frank had been forgiven for his former errors and was Oscar's frequent host. There was something exhausting in the turbulence of his conversation but when he was "full of wine and libel" he was stimulating company. There were delightful evenings at Paillards, the Café de la Paix, Maire's or the Grand Café, sometimes with Harris, at others with Douglas. To each host he spoke in confidence of the parsimony of his other benefactors. Harris heard how tight Bosie was; Douglas was informed, so frequently informed of the "meanness and want of imagination" of Harris; to both there were lamentations over the niggardly ways of Ross.

In the spring of 1900 Wilde traveled South again. Harold Mellor, perhaps to make amends for his lapse as host, offered to finance a trip to Italy to the extent of £50—it is a tribute

to Wilde's charm of manner that his friends were so generous
in supporting him. So his thoughts turned to Rome and to Ross
who was wintering there with his mother. In April he went
on his way to Rome, traveling by way of Palermo, a place
that delighted him. His visit did not pass unnoticed and the
record in the local paper gave him a stab of satisfaction. He
might pass himself off as Sebastian Melmoth, but was glad
enough when he was remembered as Oscar Wilde. "My in-
cognito," he tells Ross, "vanished in three hours. The students
used to come to the café to talk—or rather to listen. To their
delight I always denied my identity. On being asked my name
I said every man has only one name. They asked me what my
name was. 'Io' was my answer. This was regarded as wonderful
reply, containing in it all philosophy . . ."

It was Thursday of Holy Week when he reached Rome and
he remained there for a month absorbed, lost in the ecstasies
of admiration of artistic beauty and of devotion in this the
"only city of the soul." He was assiduous in his attendance
before the Pope, whose blessing he contrived to receive on
seven occasions. He had gone to the Eternal City with the old
expectation that he would be received into the faith. Once
again conversion eluded him. He did, however, find relief from
his malady and this he attributed to the papal grace.

His experiences gave zest to his writing. Never were his
letters so inspired. The grandest portraits in the world, the
beautiful voluptuous marbles and the saintly figure of the Pope
—sacred and profane are curiously mingled. You cannot wonder that conversion eluded him as you read the record of his
impressions—the note of religious fervor mounting and then,
just as it should unfold, in rapture it dissolves, lost in his genial wit.

Ross, who met him in Rome, noticed that though he was
in good spirits, a great change had come over his health. Oscar

pressed him to introduce him to a priest so that he might be received into the Church. Nothing was done for Robbie did not consider him to be really serious and so the opportunity was lost. Later Ross reproached himself over this, but, being a Catholic himself, he had feared there might be a relapse to Paganism. Furthermore, he was not friendly enough with any priest in Rome possessed of enough high scholarship to prepare for the rather grave intellectual conflict of Oscar Wilde's conversion. "It would have been no use getting an amiable and foolish man who would have treated him like an ordinary person, and would have entirely ignored the strange, paradoxical genius whom he had to overcome or convince. Wilde was equipped, moreover, for controversy, being deeply read in Catholic controversy, especially in later years."

When the heat of Rome became insufferable Wilde turned for the North. Mellor was available with his automobile—he was one of the motoring pioneers—to assist him over the final stage to Paris. He returned with vivid memories to sustain him and photographs he had taken, for he had become an enthusiast of the camera.

Photographs and memories, they were a solace in the difficult days of his last summer. By now he had surrendered himself to the life that was, in another man's phrase, "the leavings of a life." With a mounting sense of fatalism he abandoned himself passively to living the existence that was imposed on him. Sitting back he watched, almost with the detachment of an onlooker, the process of his living. No longer was there any effort to intervene to direct the course that his life was taking. He surrendered himself to the forces of his own character. No longer was he in charge. It was his character that imposed life on him. He had abdicated the captaincy of his own soul.

22. THE PASSING OF A JESTER

*Nowadays most people die of a sort of creeping com-
monsense and discover when it is too late that the only
things one never regrets are one's mistakes.*

LIFE was closing in upon him now. The circle of
his acquaintance grew smaller. Respectability
was offended by his tippling and his other habits. "I must make
my society of thieves and assassins now," he explained to a
friend who made protest over his acquaintances.

Generosity was dried up by the persistency of his demands.
Will Rothenstein was about to cross to Paris hoping to see
Oscar, but was afraid of his wanting to borrow money: what
was Ross's advice about that? There were others who would
have liked to share in the advice on this problem, not that
Oscar should have been in any sort of financial need.

Considering the hospitality he had received from his friends,
Wilde's improvidence was nothing short of recklessness. In
this his last year (1900), he was known by Ross to have received £150 from his wife's trustees, £300 from the Queensberry family and £100 from one theatrical manager, while his
trip to Italy had been financed by Mellor's £50. George Alexander was making him an allowance and Beerbohm Tree was
sending him gifts in the guise of "fees," with a message of
goodwill—"I am indeed glad, and we shall all be, to know that
you are determined to resume your dramatic work, for no
one did such distinguished work as you." Alfred Douglas
claims that he gave Wilde, in the last year of his life, at least
£1,000. Between February and September 1900 checks on his

269

account to the amount of £332 were made out to M. Melmoth. There were many other donations in cash.

Wilde by this time had developed a technique in cadging. He would complain to Harris that Douglas was treating him meanly and make the same complaint about Harris to Douglas. Each man was induced to help him. The scenario of a play was another source of income. It was promised in turn to several benefactors, some of them paying in advance for work they knew would never be written as a means of relieving Wilde in his apparent poverty.

While the credits were enough to keep him in easy circumstances, Wilde did not pay for his lodgings at his hotel, the Alsace, where the kindly Dupoirier, contrary to the fundamental instincts of a French hotelkeeper, allowed his account to run up to over £150. It was these later days of his decline that gave rise to the stories that were told about him, of his pitiable plight as he sank lower, the convict poet of the boulevards. The pity of his case was not his imaginary poverty, but the life to which he reduced himself. Even the pretense of work and rehabilitation had gone. The visits of his friends dropped off, his loneliness grew. Absinthe was the never-failing solace for depression.

Sherard, reflecting mournfully on the condition of his friend in his pitiable plight, thought of him as one of the children of sorrow who followed the paths of letters to an evil goal— Chatterton, Poe, Baudelaire, from whom Wilde adopted absinthe, de Nerval, who was found hanging from the railing of an evil house. During the days of his own exile, Beardsley, wandering around these cheap hotels, had found an earlier exit from life. Ernest Dowson, three-quarters gone, had been rescued from drink and the Latin Quarter to die in an English cottage in Sherard's arms. Of the people whom he still met, some, like Conder, were "counselors neither of discretion nor prudence." The wretched Smithers, profuse and prodigal, was a tempter at his side. So he promenaded the boulevards to be remembered as a bloated phantom by Vaunce Thompson.

"He came into Henry's bar one evening. The barman drove him away. We saw him go to the Chatham Bar, to be chased off with ignominy, tears running out of his eyes, his thick mouth quivering as he drifted into the night. Then in a little café he found a refuge. He squeezed his fat, soft body into a corner behind a marble-topped table and sat there hour after hour, drinking. Paris had nothing for him save the few dingy places where, unknown, he could find warmth and alcohol. One evening he told us he had been poisoned by eating bad mussels. His thick loose body was full of pain, and he poured into it glass after glass—and he talked. It was as if he were trying to tell everything at once as he hiccoughed out fantasies and dreams, plays, stories, shining paradoxes and memories. He was going to write them all—some day, and then he damned the mussels, said they were killing him, and at the thought of death he got frightfully pale and heaved himself upon his feet and went away bulbous and shaking."

Sometimes Robert Sherard would pass him in the streets and they would wave faintly to each other. Robert had not been forgiven for his indiscretion at the time of the reunion with Douglas. One evening, braving the resentment of his ancient friend, Robert mounted to the small gloomy bedroom in the Alsace. A bottle of absinthe stood on the washstand. Pointing to the writing at which the other was engaged Sherard remarked that Oscar was working again. "One has to do something," was the reply. "I have no taste for writing now, but as was said of torture, it helps pass an hour or two."

The conversation lapsed. Oscar threw himself on the bed exhausted. "Come and see me again," he remarked, "though I hardly like to ask people to see me in this room." When Sherard

answered what mattered the *mise-en-scène* Wilde threw back
at him, "Qu'importe la verre pourvu qu'on ait l'ivresse." Sherard felt sad as he went down the malodorous staircase—it was
the last word he heard his friend say, the dismissal to close a
friendship of eighteen years.

There was one last friendship with a young man Louis Wilkinson, a pen friend, for the two never met, but by their letters
they began to establish friendly, even affectionate relations.
Son of a Suffolk Parson, Wilkinson was a schoolboy in his
final year at Radley before going up to the University, being
then about eighteen years of age, when first he wrote to Wilde.
This youthful and enthusiastic literary admirer, a rare intruder
in the last years, charmed Wilde by his homage. "I read your
'Ballad of Reading Gaol' and have never been so deeply affected
or fascinated by any other work of prose or verse before. . . .
I cannot help but think very deeply of your cruel and unjust
fate as I pass Reading on my way back to school here at Radley,
and I trust you will not be insulted by my earnest sympathy as
well as deepest gratitude."

This gave Wilde the greatest pleasure he had known for
months. After years of ostracism it was a new gift of manna,
and he invited Wilkinson to send to Paris a photograph of himself with another letter. He followed it up with a presentation
copy of "The Importance of Being Earnest."

When Wilkinson's photographs reached him he was very
much moved, for the pictures evoked memories of the past and
as he looked at them he saw a reminder of the youth Oscar
Wilde had once been. Wilkinson, who later wrote novels under
the pseudonym of Louis Marlow, was then trying his hand at
verse. Oscar received a poem and acknowledged it with a note
of encouragement.

In the summer, Wilkinson wrote to announce that he was
shortly to visit the Continent and he suggested that he might

stay at the Alsace. Wilde was not prepared to receive him in those dreary apartments, feared perhaps the chilling effect they might have on the young enthusiast. He put the young man off with tender words that almost bade him come, and with the tale, his own tale of Narcissus. "I loved Narcissus," whispered the pool, "because as he lay on my banks and looked down at me, in the mirror of his eyes I saw ever my own beauty mirrored." Wilde saw himself playing Narcissus in Louis's eyes.

When later, young Wilkinson had crossed the Channel and was as near at hand as Dieppe, Oscar could no longer resist the attraction of a meeting. What was there left that life had to offer as sweet as the company of a young, admiring friend? Young men had been the milestones of affection on the road of life, Robert Sherard, Robbie Ross, Alfred Douglas. But milestones do not keep pace with the traveler as he passes on. Here offered to him was an opportunity for rekindling the affections of the past. Louis was bidden to come and then, as all was concluded, Oscar fell ill. A telegram canceled the invitation. The next communication Wilkinson received, after some months of silence, was from Robert Ross, announcing Oscar's death and returning the young man's photographs.

In the summer of 1900 Wilde was permanently installed in the Hôtel de l'Alsace. It was not the sort of place he had been accustomed to, but it was comfortable in its shabby fashion. The drainage—that was the trouble; but the hotel was not the tenth-rate lodgings some termed it, indeed as Dupoirier protested it was officially classified as being of the fifth class. Dupoirier had won Wilde's patronage a season before when he had been evicted from another establishment, his baggage retained as security for payment of a trifling bill of £5. Dupoirier immediately bade him in God's name to return to his old room at the Alsace, and the kindly man set off himself to redeem his lodger's belongings. At the Alsace, which bore the number thirteen in the Rue des Beaux Arts, Wilde passed his remaining days, not troubled by an irate landlord over the mounting score. For numéro treize, the entrance was painted green, light shell-green, his favorite color, and the sign showing its name was yellow.

In the late summer of that year that was seeing out the century the foreboding of death came upon him. He did not think that life was to be his much longer.

One of his last acts of kindness was to go to the assistance of the widow of Augustin Daly and Ada Rehan. Daly's sudden passing in Paris had left them unable to cope with strange affairs in a foreign land. Mrs. Daly capitulated before them. Ada, having all to face, was confused and frightened. "Then Oscar Wilde came to me and was more good and helpful than I can tell, just like a very kind brother. I shall always think of him as he was to me through those few dreadful days."

There was one more reminder of the past—a visit from his brother's widow. Lily had not been long in mourning for Willie before she had found consolation in one of Smithers' team—Taxeira de Mattos, the brilliant translator, among other authors, of Maeterlinck. "An excellent idea," was Oscar's comment on learning of her intention to marry. Now, here they were, husband and wife, on a visit to Paris to see the Exhibition. They passed a happy day together, the happiest he had known since the shadow fell on him. They talked about the London from which he was exiled, the London of his triumphs, the London that was never long out of his thoughts.

In exile he remained always the Englishman, for neither against the country that sent him to prison, nor against the society that had passed sentence of ostracism upon him, was he known to have said anything of bitterness or of reproach. When war broke out in South Africa he followed events in the Transvaal with all the interest of a patriot at home, though opinion around him in Paris was by no means pro-British.

As the summer of 1900 turned to autumn he complained of pains in the head. They grew worse as the days passed, intolerable, incessant. The absinthe he consumed aggravated his sufferings. The doctors pronounced that an operation alone would yield relief, but the operation was a delicate one calling for the highest surgical skill. The probable fee was indicated. "Ah well then," said the patient, "I suppose I shall die as I have lived beyond my means."

The kindly Dupoirier was the sympathetic witness of his sufferings—"He kept raising his hands to his head to try to ease the torture. He cried out again and again. We used to put ice on his head and I was forever giving him injections of morphine." Some relief was afforded by a minor operation for an abscess in his ear. This took place on October 10. On the eleventh Ross, in London, received a telegram—"Operated on yesterday try to come over soon." Robbie, who had planned to pass through Paris a few weeks later, put forward his arrangements. He reached Paris on October 15 and found Wilde looking well. He was seeing various of his friends during the day and was at times in the highest spirits.

His friend, he found, had had no lack of attention. He had the services of a special nurse; food was sent in from a restaurant nearby. Dupoirier, out of his own pocket, paid for the necessities and for the luxuries ordered by the doctors. As long as it was allowed him, the patient had champagne throughout his illness. The doctor from the Embassy (Tucker by name) attended him. A specialist well known in Paris performed the operation, and a second specialist was called in when meningitis was diagnosed.

In the last weeks of his life Wilde was distressed in mind over Frank Harris and the publisher Smithers. The rights and wrongs of the affair are now past ascertaining. It arose over the scenario of a play that Harris had bought from him—"Mr. and Mrs. Daventry." In addition to the scenario, Wilde wrote much of the first act and the piece was completed by Harris, who paid £50 to Wilde. It was put on in London at the Royalty Theater, with Mrs. Patrick Campbell in the lead, ran for over a hundred nights and paid Harris very handsomely. Wilde complained that Harris did not honor his agreement over royalties. It was a further point of complaint that Harris, with his heavy touch, had spoiled the delicate fabric of Wilde's play. According to Douglas, Wilde's rage and indignation against Harris hastened his death.

The publisher Smithers had a hand in the transaction and Wilde worked himself up into such a state of distraction that the doctor feared his recovery would be retarded. Wilde wrote a long letter of complaint to Harris, of which only some pages remain. It was probably the last communication Harris received from him. Smithers was charged with having trapped Harris, or blackmailed Harris into parting with money (£100 is named) that Wilde considered to be his due.

Harris brought peace of mind to the invalid by sending some money due for the play. It is estimated that Harris made £4,000 out of the piece from which he paid Wilde, at the most a mere £200. In addition to the scenes and first act, Wilde contributed considerably to the rest of it. In his usual fashion he talked dialogue for the play over the dinner-table with his friends. Harris had the advantage of listening in. In happier circumstances Wilde would have produced the play for what it was—his own work.

Wilde was now sufficiently encouraged to make plans to travel South when convalescent, to be with Robbie at Nice. The doctors, however, were not as sanguine as the patient. Tucker took Ross aside to tell him that though he was recovering Oscar's general condition was "serious"; unless he pulled himself together he would not live five weeks. Robbie had had no idea that such was the state of the case. He delivered another of his frightening talks to Oscar, who laughed and said he could never outlive the century as the English would not stand for it. Already he was responsible for the failure of the Paris Exhibition, as English visitors seeing him there had turned away.

Wilde was thought to have recovered sufficiently to be allowed out of doors. He was taken for drives in the Bois. On one of these he caught a slight cold in the ear and this rapidly developed into an abscess, causing great pain. No importance was attached to this by the English doctor, but the French confrère regarded it as a grave symptom. It was this abscess, according to Ross, which eventually produced inflammation of the brain.

There was a temporary improvement and in mid-November Ross arranged to resume his journey South to his mother at Nice. He came to take his leave. Wilde was excited and distressed. Sending the others out of the room he burst into hysterical tears because Robbie was leaving him. He would never see him again. Ross's perceptions were not of the keenest. Afterwards he was to reproach himself for not having realized how gravely ill his friend was, and in what distress of mind. "I knew he had been taking morphia a good deal and I became rather stern, as you are always told to be with people in hysteria. I simply attributed the whole scene to general weakness after his illness."

They none of them knew the end was near. How could they know? The doctors themselves were unaware of it. The patient, when free from pain was the light-hearted jester. Lying in bed he would jest at the thought of death. "When the last trumpet sounds and we are couched in our porphyry tombs [porphyry was one of those words in which he had always found sensual satisfaction] I will turn and say 'Robbie, Robbie, let us pretend we do not hear.' " Reggie Turner joined in the jesting. Said Oscar one morning, "I have had a dreadful dream —I dreamed I was dining with the dead." To which Reggie immediately rejoined, "I am sure, my dear Oscar, you were the life and soul of the party."

When Ross left for the South, it was Reggie Turner who was left in charge of the invalid. Every day he came around to keep him company and to take him out for a drive. Oscar laughed and talked in his usual good spirits, but tired easily and slept long. He was still planning to go South with Ross. Then, on November 25, which was a Sunday, he was not so well, complained of giddiness and stayed in his bed. Towards night he became light-headed. The doctors now gave it as their opinion that the abscess in the ear had produced inflammation of the brain. His condition was so evidently worse that Ross was summoned by telegram.

On one of his last nights of consciousness the dying man's thoughts turned to his boys and he wept over his memories. He related how his son Vyvyan, when a child of eleven, was lying on a sofa. "I asked him what he was doing. He waved me aside and said, 'Leave me, I am thinking.' " Again and again he repeated the little anecdote, imitating the childish voice and gesture.

Ross reached the Alsace to find that Wilde was in extremis, no longer able to articulate. He then, at this last stage, fulfilled his friend's wish to be received into the Roman Catholic Church. There was to be some uncertainty, controversy and doubt over the validity of his reception. Ross's account of what took place is clear: "When I went for the priest to come to his death-bed he was quite conscious and raised his hand in response to questions and satisfied the priest, Father Cuthbert Dunn, of the Passionists. It was the morning before he died and for about three hours he understood what was going on (and knew I had come from the South in response to a telegram) that he was given the last sacrament."

On the afternoon of November 30 the dying man finally lost consciousness, and sank into a coma. His breathing altered, his pulse began to flutter. He heaved a deep sigh, the limbs seemed to stretch, the breathing became fainter. He passed beyond at ten minutes before two o'clock. Ross and Turner were not in the room at the time. The faithful Dupoirier was holding him in his arms as he breathed his last. Death was certified as having been due to cerebral meningitis.

What were Ross's thoughts as he stood surveying the still figure on the bed, the silvery voice now silent for ever? What was uppermost in his mind—regret at the passing of his friend or relief that the exile of the outcast had at last been ended? Some relief mingled with his grief—"Though his death is a great shock to those who knew him as well as I did, it was in many ways for the best. He was very unhappy and would have become more unhappy as time went on. In most cases this is said merely as a matter of form and a convention of comfort. In this particular instance it really can be said with perfect truth."

The body was left to the care of the bearded English priest, himself a recent convert, who in so short a space had performed the initial and final rites of baptism and extreme unction. He kept a solitary vigil till dawn, when the croque-morts came with the coffin. Anna de Brémont, climbing the stairs to the back bedroom to take her farewell, looked down on a figure that seemed wrapped in slumber. The coarseness that of late years had marred his features had been, to her eyes, refined by the land of death. She saw the beauty of his youth again, while the striking likeness to his mother smote her heart with a pang of remembrance.

Upon Ross had fallen the duty of coping with the worldly affairs of his friend. It was the beginning of a task that was to occupy him for several years to come. There were the creditors who came bustling to the hotel to claim their dues. There were the authorities to satisfy before the funeral could be arranged, for, in dying, a foreigner living under an assumed name, Sebastian Melmoth had transgressed the law. It was with difficulty that Ross averted the humiliation of the removal of the remains to lie dishonored in the dismal morgue. Friends had to be informed, among them Alfred Douglas, then far away in Scotland. Bosie arrived in time to be the chief mourner at the funeral. The service was held at the Church of St. Germain des Près, where James Duke of Douglas had been buried in 1645, and where the ashes of the poet Boileau and of Casimir, King of Poland, rest under their monuments.

It was on the third day of December that Oscar Wilde was borne for the last time down the narrow stairs of the Alsace. Anna de Brémont noted that there were thirteen mourners gathered at 13 Rue des Beaux Arts to follow the hearse that bore the number 13. Among the wreaths, to some of which the senders had discreetly omitted to attach their names, was one from the faithful Dupoirier ("A mon locataire") and another from "Le service de l'Hôtel." There was no funeral pomp that day. The cortège was admitted to the church by an obscure side door. No bell was tolled. Low mass was said without music, the bearded priest mispronouncing his Latin so that La Jeunesse heard not the Latin liturgy but a nonconformist jumble. From the church the remains were taken for interment to the cemetery of Bagneux, on the outskirts of Paris, in the presence of Alfred Douglas, Robert Ross, Reggie Turner and a few Parisian men of letters.

An unhonored end? Did it matter that there was no pomp, no ceremonial tribute? Was it not enough that he had died

with two friends to attend him at his passing? Will Rothenstein could not help contrasting the description of Oscar's
funeral with that of Sir Arthur Sullivan—"At St. Paul's, Had-
don Chambers, Comyns Carr, Mrs. Beerbohm Tree and others
of the same stock in a national cathedral, all duly announced
as helping the impressiveness of the scene. In Paris, you and
Reggie—friends. If I cared what could happen to me after my
death, I could wish for no nobler end."

For nine years the grave at Bagneux was marked by a simple
inscription giving the name and dates. Then in the year 1909,
when all the debts of Oscar Wilde had been discharged, the
remains were transferred to a place of honor in Père Lachaise,
which is the last resting-place of men and women of genius—
Balzac, Chopin, Sarah Bernhardt, Adelina Patti, among them.
A monument by Epstein was set up to mark the place to which
admirers of Wilde's genius make their pilgrimage. Carved in
stone are the lines of his own epitaph:

> *And alien tears will fill for him*
> *Pity's long-broken urn,*
> *For his mourners will be outcast men,*
> *And outcasts always mourn.*

23. BATTLES OF THE FRIENDS

Every great man nowadays has his disciples. It is in-
variably Judas who writes the biography.

IT is again in the irony of events that the artistic
rehabilitation Oscar Wilde had hoped for, but
had not been able to bring about in his own lifetime, was not
long deferred after his death. In the years that followed his
passing in the Hôtel d'Alsace the world heard much about his
life's story and his works. The friends he left fell out amongst
themselves. There were acrimonious disputes in print and
bitterly contested lawsuits in the courts. The battle of the
books was continued until the disputants passed from the
scene. Ross died in 1918. Sherard lived until 1943 and Lord
Alfred Douglas until 1945. With Lord Alfred's death no im-
pediment remained to the publication in full of the letter of
Reading jail and this, the last completed prose work of Oscar
Wilde, was made available for the English reader in 1949.

In 1895, five years before his death, the name of Oscar Wilde
had been wiped out in polite society. Five years after his
death his re-establishment as a man of letters had begun. It
had proceeded on the Continent before it got under way in
England. "Salomé" made his name famous in Germany. The
play was first put on by Reinhardt in Berlin in 1902 and it ran
for two hundred nights, establishing an Oscar Wilde vogue.
His books were translated into German and sold better than
ever they had done in England. When "De Profundis" was
issued in a German translation, the bookshops were plastered
with the name of Wilde. "Salomé" was played on both sides

of the Rhine, and "An Ideal Husband" was produced. Wilde's fame quickly spread across Europe. In Vienna a complete edition of his works was brought out. Translations were soon popular in Italy and in Spain.

In England the first literary memorial was discreetly offered by Robert Sherard. Wilde had not long been dead when Sherard began to write his "Story of an Unhappy Friendship." It was privately published in 1902, the author explaining in a prefatory note that he had adopted this discreet method for the avoidance of scandal. He made an appeal for the fairer consideration of the case of his friend, "one of the brightest geniuses of the last century." The book had so encouraging a reception that Sherard set to work on a full-length biography. It took him some time to complete and it was issued in the normal manner of publication in the year 1906.

Sherard declared his object to be the removal of some of the mis-statements of fact, false impressions and lying rumors that in five years had gathered around the name of Oscar Wilde. Again he wrote with what was described as "admirable tact and discretion." From neither of these books could an uninformed reader have gained more than an inkling of an idea about the true story behind the Wilde catastrophe. The name of the Marquis of Queensberry appears only twice. Lord Alfred Douglas is not referred to at all by name. There are references to Douglas as the friend—"the most fatal for him to remember," a man who offered Wilde "the least desirable of companionships" and "whose friendship had brought disaster and ruin to him." At this stage Sherard was violently anti-Douglas. For Robbie Ross his admiration was unbounded. It was to Ross that he dedicated his first book "In remembrance of his noble conduct towards the unhappy gentleman who is the subject of this memoir, whom in affliction he comforted, in prison he visited, and in poverty he succored, thus showing an elevation of heart and a loyalty of character." The biography contains a long testimonial to Robbie whose conduct towards Wilde had been "the most beautiful thing the history of noble friendships records." In after years Sherard was to transfer his support to Douglas.

Ross, as literary executor, was busily occupied. The Wilde vogue, that had begun in Germany, produced financial benefits for the estate. By 1904 only a small amount was outstanding to Wilde's creditors. Next Ross set about the business of arranging for the publication of a standard edition of the works in English. Wilde had disposed of rights in his works to the various publishers who had produced them. Six firms had to be approached and, as he had died bankrupt, it was necessary to obtain the assent of the trustee in bankruptcy, not that difficulties were met with there. At the time of Wilde's death the public interest in his writings was rather less than nil. A bankruptcy official, when the business was raised with him in 1901, asserted that not merely were Wilde's works of no value, but that they would never command any interest whatsoever.

Ross was not deterred. With patience and determination he set about the undertaking, becoming in the course of it, an expert in problems of copyright. He was not to be discouraged by the chilling discovery that "the copyrights of an author in bankruptcy belong to everyone except his creditors, his family, or his literary executor." As a first step towards promoting interest in Wilde's works he proposed to make a book out of the prison apologia. Obviously the Epistola he had received from Wilde at the prison gates could not be made public in its entirety, in view of the gross libels it contained on Lord Douglas. But there were the other passages, enough of them to make a book. They were skilfully extracted, the actual work being undertaken by E. V. Lucas, that graceful essayist who wrote with the touch of Charles Lamb. Lucas declined to accept payment for his help. "I really like to think it possible," he wrote, "to do something for your friend. I hope, if I had known him personally, I should have been able to muster some of your fidelity. I have always felt a little guilty in making no effort— for strangers can do these things if they like—to let him know that he had a few friends after he left prison even among those whose names he had never known."

Early in 1905 "De Profundis" was issued by the house of Methuen. The reception it met with surprised and delighted compilers and publishers. Doubts were naturally expressed about the authenticity of the work. The sceptics had even had their doubts about the announcement of Wilde's death—Ross received over 300 letters of inquiry on this point—and when the book appeared there were challenges. How was it possible that a convict in jail could have written a book in his cell? These doubts were easy to remove and three gentlemen gave their guarantee of authenticity for the MS.—Hamilton Fyfe (later editor of the "Daily Herald"), Dr. Max Meyerfeld of Berlin (who was responsible for the publication of Wilde in German) and the English publisher, Mr. Methuen.

The book was widely reviewed—which would not have been possible five years previously—and the notices on the whole were sympathetic. From friends to whom presentation copies were sent, Ross received letters of appreciation, some of them with shrewd comments. Major Nelson, during whose prison governorship the writing was done, considered it to be "one of the grandest and saddest efforts of a truly penitent man." This opinion was also expressed by various clergymen who received copies. The more penetrating minds pronounced otherwise. Thus Cunninghame-Graham: "I am glad he never repented—how one hates penitents. . . . Christians, one might think, should say that Christ died for Oscar, too, and should not be hard on him." Bernard Shaw found that Wilde had

come out of prison the same man that he went in. Prince
Kropotkin found some passages to be sublime, but the note of
humility "repulsive—it never is sincere." Sir George Douglas,
with whom Wilde once stayed at Kelso, considered that there
was always something unreal about Wilde when he was trying
to be serious.

Rothenstein in a letter showing how thoroughly he understood the man, wrote of the "false emotionalism" of Wilde's
nature. "Had he lied the book would have been worthless. As
it is it shows all his life not to have been a mistake, but one
led according to his understanding and pleasure, not an affected
life but his real one. It was an undesirable life to lead, but at
any rate it was part of his real nature to choose it and it is clear
to me that it would have been false to him to have pretended
to care for anything less real to him than false emotions were."
Of all who were friends with Oscar Wilde, Sir William Rothenstein seems to have known him best.

Praise for Ross was general, for the work he had done and
for his courage in undertaking it. It was suggested to him that
he should write the life of his friend, or at least a book of
table talk. It is to be regretted he did not play Boswell to
Wilde's Johnson. At one time he seems to have toyed with
that idea, but he had lost his notes. He had written down some
of Wilde's conversation but "I gave him my notes and he
used a great deal of them for one of his later plays, which was
written in a great hurry and against time, as he wanted money."
Even had he retained his records it is doubtful whether he
would have adventured for he remembered the Master's saying
—"It is always Judas who writes the biography."

The success of "De Profundis" was an encouragement to
proceed. Thereafter a limited edition of the works was produced and was old out. A uniform edition followed. Later

came the popular shilling volumes which, in their blue-gray covers, became familiar on the bookstalls.

Robbie Ross had successfully promoted the artistic rehabilitation of Oscar Wilde. In recognition of his success and to mark the publication of the first collected edition of the works, Ross was entertained at a dinner at which nearly 200 guests were present at the Ritz on December 1, 1908. His health was proposed by H. G. Wells and Willie Rothenstein. In a speech of becoming modesty Ross said: "A disciple of Mr. Wells, I have always anticipated posterity and never doubted for a single moment that time would readjust those small and greater injustices which ethics, pursuing conduct, invariably impose upon art. I did not, however, anticipate that I should be so generously complimented for the fulfilment of a promise I made myself at the deathbed of Oscar Wilde. . . . May I take your hospitality this evening as a symbol that in after years it will be my privilege to boast that I was the occasion, though never the cause, of giving back to Oscar Wilde's children the laurels of their distinguished father untarnished save by tears."

Before that occasion for compliments, the creditors had received final payment. As sharer in Lord Queensberry's estate, Lord Alfred Douglas received, with four per cent interest, a quarter of the amount of his father's debt in respect of the legal costs of the Old Bailey prosecution.

With the debts paid off, Ross was free to transfer Wilde's remains from the obscure grave to a new resting-place among those honored in France in the cemetery of Père Lachaise. When the grave at Bagneux was opened it was Ross who "went down into the yawning pit of death and corruption and with his own hands dug out and transferred to the new coffin the still decaying remains of his friend's body." Later, on his death in 1918, Ross himself was to lie in the same tomb beneath the monument by Epstein, erected through the generosity of a faithful friend, the beautiful Mrs. Carew, mother of Sir Coleridge Kennard, who made a gift of £2,000 for the purpose. Epstein's piece has been much criticized. It is as alien to Wilde's conception of beauty as Beardsley's pictures had been to the spirit of Dorian Gray. Wilde, at the last, was again unfortunate in his illustrator.

It was not long after the dinner at the Ritz before Lord Alfred Douglas was known to be on the war-path. Almost alone amongst the faithful friends he had taken no part in the celebration of Wilde's literary come-back. The limelight had been focused on Robbie Ross. Some of the new luster had fallen on Sherard with his books. Bosie had had no share. The effect of this neglect may be imagined on the jealous mind of the man who conceived that Oscar had cared for his little finger more than for all the other friends together. In his literary paper, the "Academy," Douglas had held himself out to be the repository of the ark of the covenant. The "Academy," in O'Sullivan's phrase, set up to be the only protector or promulgator of Wilde, but the shrill hysterical voice of this periodical had a limited range. Compared with the trumpetings that heralded Ross's achievements it was the sound of a penny whistle. In the year 1913 Douglas found occasion to attract the blare of notoriety to himself. As challenger in a lawsuit he came forward, as his father had done before him, to capture the headlines of the newspapers. The Oscar Wilde scandal, fifteen years buried, was displayed anew.

Alfred Douglas was repeating with a filial fidelity little to be expected of him the experiences of the father he had detested. Not long after Wilde's death he had run through the £15,000 he had inherited from Queensberry. To repair his fortunes he had crossed the Atlantic to finance himself with an American bride. He came posting back to England on hearing that the girl he had left behind him had become engaged to marry one of his friends. He eloped with her and made her his wife. She was Olive Custance, handsome and gifted, poet in her own right. This love affair was a little drama of its own, with Douglas's sonnet to the traitorous friend ("I shall know his soul lies on the bosom of Iscariot"); the love letters that passed between him and his bride, he the "prince" and Olive his "page"; and the fury of the father, Colonel of the Grenadier Guards, who appealed to Scotland Yard for aid against the eloping couple.

The union of the two poets (alas, for romance!) ended in unhappiness. Bosie, by Wilde's emphatic testimony, was difficult to live with. Olive with the years lost the good looks Bosie had so prized. They parted. Douglas, following his father, found consolation elsewhere. Again, like his father, he was estranged from his son, and yet again, in the parental pattern, sent letters of vilification to his father-in-law. The Colonel took him to the Old Bailey on a charge of criminal libel on which he was ignominiously bound over. Almost coincidently Douglas himself was plaintiff in the libel action that brought the Oscar Wilde scandal sensationally before the world with a mass of detail not previously disclosed.

Douglas brought his action against Arthur Ransome, a young journalist who had published with Methuen a critical study of Oscar Wilde. Ransome was named defendant in the case, but Douglas was aiming his attack at Robert Ross, to whom Ransome dedicated his book. It was Ross who had provided the biographical material. Douglas's complaint was that the book made it appear that he had been responsible for Wilde's disgrace and that, after the reunion at Naples, he had deserted Wilde, leaving him penniless. Only those with full knowledge of Wilde's life story could have identified Douglas, who was not mentioned by name in Ransome's book. By his lawsuit

Douglas made the public at large acquainted with facts against himself that would otherwise have remained unknown.

The climax of the case came when, under cross-examination, Douglas had to submit, as he stood in the witnessbox, to hearing read out before the court the passages from Wilde's prison letter that had been suppressed from "De Profundis." It would have been an ordeal for any person not encased in an impenetrable armor of self-conceit. Douglas in his vanity was pitifully exposed. It was excruciating pain for him to listen to the opening passages of the letter to "Dear Bosie" and the words of castigation that came upon him from the tomb.

"You must read this letter right through," Wilde had written, "though each word may become to you as the fire or knife of the surgeon that makes the delicate flesh burn or bleed." When he wrote in his prison cell, he had had no conception that the reading would be more wounding to his friend than any searing of the flesh a surgeon could contrive.

It was beyond the Douglas capacity for endurance. Reading the prison letter had not proceeded very far before it was noticed that Douglas was no longer in his place in the witnessbox. He was not in court. The judge directed that he should be found. At length he was brought back. He explained that he had not wished to be present to hear the reading of the letter. He was told that he must remain; if he again absented himself judgment would be entered against him. So, he had to stand for all the court to see while the blistering passages of castigation were read out—"You had no motives in life, appetites merely; the gutter had begun to fascinate you; absolute ruin of my art; unscrupulous, grasping, ungracious always." The book "De Profundis" had suppressed all passages about Douglas. The reading in court suppressed all passages but the catalogue of reprobation.

This mortification Douglas had brought upon himself. In

the preliminaries to the trial his lawyers had been supplied with
copies of these writings and other condemnatory letters upon
which the defense based their case. Douglas courted exposure
when he went into the court. As had Wilde before him, and
with even less cause, he had resolved to brave it out in public,
and like Wilde he lost his case. It was a superfluous self-
humiliation.

Having failed in the courts, Douglas resorted to book publication to get even with his dead friend. In 1914, a year that
was also distinguished by the outbreak of the first World War,
there was published by John Long a book of 300 pages entitled
"Oscar Wilde and Myself" bearing as author the name of Lord
Alfred Douglas. It is one of the most lamentable publications
in the range of English letters. It was an attack on Oscar
Wilde inspired by rancor and disgraced by distortion, deception and prevarication from title page to colophon.

There is no taunt imagination could suggest that was not
flung at Wilde. He was a poor poet, an indifferent playwright,
ridiculously overrated. By his pernicious habits he had caused
harm to the whole body of English literature. He was a snob,
always referring to his "rank" in society and prating of his
Oxford days: "he tells us that in prison he became a great
individualist; apparently it was in prison he became a great
aristocrat." He was too much of a "tuft hunter" to be liked
by the persons whose acquaintance he sought. He was twitted
over his personal appearance—that his mouth was too large, his
face spoiled by a great expanse of jowl, he had the disfigurement of a broken tooth. He was reproached for his habits—
he took great care of his complexion, he brushed his hair more
times a day than any other man, he was a tailor's man. He was
a doughty and assiduous trencherman—"I would have backed
him to eat the head off a brewer's drayman three times a day;
his capacity for whiskey-and-soda knew no bounds." He was

twitted over his ancestry—"His father was once a Dublin apothecary keeping a chemist's shop in some obscure part of Dublin; who his grandfather was heaven knows."

These were pitiful reproaches. On the subject of Wilde's abnormality the passages were deliberately conceived falsehoods.

I considered he was a man of decent life and I never heard from him a word or sign which made me think otherwise. . . . When I heard on one or two occasions hints of tendencies of his I repudiated them with indignation believing that as I was his friend I knew him through and through and feeling that there could not be any truth in what was suggested.

My father had accused Wilde of certain abominations. Those accusations it seems were true. Wilde denied the truth of them to me and proceeded to take up what in view of the facts known to himself and not to me was a ridiculous prosecution.

The real fact is that he had something inside him that I knew nothing about—namely and to wit a guilty conscience. He was too much of a coward to tell me the truth that he was guilty of the charges the Marquis of Queensberry was leveling against him.

Anyone who knows me must be well aware that when it came to the question of his ultimate vices such influence as I had over him was on the side of goodness. . . . It was plain on every showing that our friendship was a harmless proper friendship.

There were medical and scientific grounds for supposing that he was not responsible for his actions— It is unthinkable that a sane person could flounder into the loathsome depths in which Wilde was taken red-handed.

Even the name on the title page of this book was a misnomer. Douglas supplied the information on which the book was based. The actual writing was done by his paid assistant, W. H. Crosland. The unspeakable Crosland, a journalist with certain talents for invective, once described himself as a "jobbing poet." Douglas, who employed him as his assistant and chief executive on the "Academy," wrote of him as a genius who "looked like an inspired bus-conductor." It was at Crosland's own suggestion, according to Douglas, that he was entrusted with the writing of the book. "You will never write it as it ought to be written . . . you are still too soft about the unspeakable swine Wilde to put it across." Douglas supplied the facts and Crosland did the job, receiving for it "at least £250." Douglas, in his Autobiography, pictured himself as proposing a fairly scathing piece of criticism of Wilde, with Crosland reproving him for being much too soft, and strengthening the passage, so that "in the end the book was more his than mine."

This explanation cannot relieve Douglas of responsibility. *Qui facit per alium facit per se.* On Douglas must fall the odium for a lamentable performance. Wilde had written his bitter reproaches when his mind was distorted by his broodings in solitary confinement. He upbraided in suffering and indignation. He believed in every one of his assertions. Douglas was moved by injured pride to taunt with malice, spite and perjury. The Douglas-Crosland production was a piece of tepid, styleless writing that cannot stand comparison with the prison letter, where the sweep of Wilde's periods gives distinction to his pettiest accusations.

Douglas lived to regret his offenses and to recant. In his Autobiography (published in 1929) and his Apology (1938) he formally withdrew the perjuries of his first book. He had offered, he wrote, a blacker and more biting portrait of Wilde than the truth warranted. Crosland's chapter—by then Douglas sought to disavow responsibility as far as he could contrive to do so—on Wilde's prose and plays was unfair. His excuse was that he had been half out of his mind with grief and indignation. It is to be conceded to him that he had been most grievously wounded in his vulnerable pride, but it was he who had brought about the occasion for his own public humiliation. Even so, need he have stooped to vilify his friend? There have been friends, with greater understanding, who, to use the words he employed against Constance Wilde, "have stuck through thick and thin and borne it out even to the crack of doom."

The most contemptible passages in the Douglas book were not those of accusation against Wilde, but the professions of innocence and ignorance in which he disclaimed complicity in the practices to which Wilde was addicted. Douglas had known and had shared in all that Wilde had done, an equal participant. He wrote later in disgust of Wilde's paramours as Wilde had written in contempt of Bosie's associates. There was not the semblance of a pretext for differentiation between their way of life. Of their own relations, Douglas gave an account in his Autobiography:

> Familiarities were rare but they did occur spasmodically. They began about nine months after I first met Oscar Wilde as the result of a long, patient and strenuous siege on his part. They were completely discontinued about six months before the final catastrophe. Wilde always claimed that his love for me was ideal and spiritual. I once, after he came out of prison, in the course of a somewhat acrimonious discussion, brought up against him that this was not strictly the case and that there had been another side to it. He said, "Oh, it was so little that, and then only by accident; essentially it was always a reaching up towards the ideal and in the end it became utterly ideal."

There is no need to pursue this further, but it is to be noted that even in the franker state of confession Douglas referred to Wilde's "vices," where the reference should properly have been to "our" vices. Having found grace as a convert to the Roman faith, he reckoned himself entitled, it seems, to reprobate another the sins of his own youth. His writings are disfigured by the lasting note of sustained, sanctimonious self-righteousness.

It took Douglas a dozen years or more to recover from the shock his vanity had received. He could then realize that

Wilde's attacks, though certainly unfair, were harmless enough, the simple results of his prison sufferings. In kindlier mood he recalled the days when Wilde had weaved his enchantments, days when they were equal in their devotion each to the other, days which offered no greater pleasure than to be with Oscar Wilde. Perhaps his memory was assisted by the fact that the friend whom society had exiled had by then been recognized as an author of fame, association with whom conferred distinction. During the last quarter of a century of his life, Douglas was forever reminding the world of his friendship with Wilde. Three books of autobiography were devoted to the subject and he lost no opportunity of contributing a foreword to any book relating to his friend.

The Ransome case was the first of a series of lawsuits in which Douglas was to be engaged in the ensuing ten years. In most of the others he was a successful litigant, making quite an income from injudicious references to his part in the Wilde *affaire*, until newspapers and authors learned to label him dangerous, not to be touched. Before the end he had lured Ross into prosecuting him in the courts for libel.

Following, again, the example of his father, Douglas goaded Ross into action by accusing him in pamphlets of being "a notorious sodomite," "an habitual debaucher and corrupter of young boys" and "a blackmailer." The case ended inconclusively after an eight-day trial at the Old Bailey, the jury disagreeing. Thereafter Douglas claimed the victory. On the other hand, a widely signed testimonial testified to Ross's virtues above the signatures, among others, of Mr. Asquith, then Prime Minister, Margot Asquith, a dozen peers, and a Bishop of the Church of England. Later Ross was appointed a trustee of the Tate Gallery, a post he held at the time of his death.

The vendetta between Douglas and Ross was only one of the bitterly contested controversies that arose years after Oscar

Wilde had been laid in his grave. There was Douglas versus Harris, Sherard versus Harris, and with even greater acrimony Sherard versus Shaw and also against André Gide. Sherard became a determined controversialist. At first he abetted Ross against Douglas and then, changing sides, joined Douglas against Ross. Frank Harris, whose "Life and Confessions of Oscar Wilde" appeared in America in 1916, was left with his reputation for veracity in tatters. Bernard Shaw emerged without much credit remaining to him for fair dealing in controversy. André Gide, that "egoist without an ego" as Wilde termed him, was seen to be an author who on matters of fact wrote with a novelist's license. Amidst all the controversies Alfred Douglas was popping up with satisfaction undisguised when any of the contestants referred to him in flattering terms either of his good looks or of his poetry. He purred his loudest when he was compared as a poet with Shelley or for his sonnets with Shakespeare. All this is stuff of the highest comedy, fascinating in the extreme, but too long to be related here.

Final publication of Oscar Wilde's writings was deferred until 1949 when the full text of the "Epistola in Carcere et Vinculis" was for the first time made available in England. In 1909 the original MS. had been lodged in the safe keeping of the British Museum by Ross, with the instruction that it should not be made public till 60 years had passed. During the hearing of the Ransome case, it was produced in court but was restored to the custody of the Museum, where it has since remained despite Douglas's demand that it should be handed to him as the person to whom it had been addressed. In 1949 the complete text was printed from a carbon copy of the typescript made according to the instructions Wilde had given to his literary executor. Vyvyan Holland, with a son's pride, wrote an introduction to this the last complete prose work of his father.

By that time the artistic rehabilitation of Oscar Wilde was

complete. He had taken his place amongst his peers of literature in the Pantheon to which admission is governed by rules
concerned with the perfection of art, and of art alone. In that
fane there are many who in their lives incurred the world's
censure. For the most part their frailties and follies have been
forgotten. His have been remembered, and though greater
understanding has come with the passing of the years, they
are remembered yet. With a foreknowledge, perhaps, of his
own fate he summed it all up in an epigram: "Each man lives
his own life and pays his own price for living. The only pity
is that one has to pay so often for a single fault. In her dealings
with man Destiny never closes her accounts."

If, in the Elysian Fields, echoes reached him of the discords
that disturbed his friends, we can imagine that Wilde turned
away with disdain to more rewarding philosophical pursuits.
To toy with ideas had been his joy in life, not to dispute or
argue. He was no controversialist as was Bernard Shaw. He was
satisfied to enjoy the display of his wit without harnessing it to
a cause. Only a part of his felicities were caught in his writings
and were preserved in print. The rest, squandered heedlessly as
he discoursed at the table, was unrecorded and lost. It is pleas-
ing to imagine that he may be discoursing yet and that happy
souls pass hours in Elysium listening to the songs the Sirens
sing and sharing with Oscar Wilde in his table talk.

SOURCES

THE Oscar Wilde literature is already extensive. More books have been devoted to him than to any author of modern times.

The autobiographical sources in his own writings upon which I have drawn are indicated in the text. Not all his letters have been published, and few of them that have appeared have been given in full. The letters are still in copyright and have not been available to me. The main published collections are:

Resurgam, unpublished letters by Oscar Wilde, Clement Shorter (1917).
After Reading, Letters to Robert Ross (1921).
After Berneval, Letters to Robert Ross (1922).
Letters to the Sphinx, with reminiscences of the author by Ada Leverson (1930).
Collection of Original Manuscripts and Letters, a sale catalogue, Dulau & Coy. (1928).
Letters to William Rothenstein (1930).

There are two authors closely connected with Wilde who are the principal source of biographical matter, Robert Harborough Sherard and Lord Alfred Douglas. Neither is completely to be trusted. Sherard sought to record the truth as he conceived it, but as a chronicler he suffers from a lack of critical judgment. He contradicts himself on frequent occasions. His judgment was distorted by his affection for Wilde of whom he wrote in undisguised admiration. He was handicapped, particularly in his earlier books, by his sense of propriety which did not permit him to refer other than in vague terms to Wilde's aberrations. He was, furthermore, swayed by his feelings towards Ross and Douglas. His earlier books were written when he was anti-Douglas and the later when he was anti-Ross. Sherard's works are:

The Story of an Unhappy Friendship (privately printed 1902, public edition 1908).
Life of Oscar Wilde (1906).
Twenty-Five Years in Paris (1905).
The Real Oscar Wilde (1915).
Oscar Wilde Twice Defended (1934).
Bernard Shaw, Frank Harris and Oscar Wilde, with a Preface by Lord Alfred Douglas (1937).

The last named is a controversial book, making a detailed and critical examination of the writings of other authors, marred somewhat by the author's controversial purpose, but containing much biographical matter.

Lord Alfred Douglas is to be trusted even less than Sherard. He had an inability to see facts that were contrary to any of his strongly held opinions. His first book on Wilde, inspired by hate, was a tissue of distortions and prevarications. Later he apologized and withdrew what he had written. In his later years his writings suffered from the bias of a zealous convert to religious faith. His books were:

Oscar Wilde and Myself (1914).
The Autobiography (1931).
Without Apology (1938).
Oscar Wilde, A Summing up, with an Introduction by Derek Hudson (1940).

From the archives of the Douglas family, many letters by Wilde, Lord Alfred and the Marquis of Queensberry, were published in *Oscar Wilde and the Black Douglas* (1950), by the Marquess of Queensberry in collaboration with Percy Colson. Lord Queensberry, grandson of the Scarlet Marquis, contributed much new information and there is also an introduction by Montgomery Hyde.

There is a life of Lord Alfred Douglas—*Spoilt Child of Genius*—by William Freeman (1948).

Robert Ross, it is to be regretted, did not write an account either of his own life or of Wilde's. He contributed a few facts in his introduction to Wilde's works, and wrote a short life of Aubrey Beardsley that is tantalizingly reticent. A book was devoted to him in 1952—*Robert Ross, Friend of Friends*, letters and extracts from his writings edited by Margery Ross. This admirable memorial to a man who gave valuable encouragement to the host of his friends in literature and the arts, yields much information about Wilde, the circumstances of his death, and the publication of "De Profundis" and other works.

Of the books by the close friends, the *Life and Confessions* by Frank Harris is in a class of its own. Many chapters of it have been evidently written up from previous writings by other authors, garnished by Harris's fertile imagination and foisted off as his own. No assertion of fact could be accepted from Harris without corroboration. Harris, in later editions, was given a posthumous introduction by Bernard Shaw that was the cause of a long controversy.

The first detailed account of the trials was published in 1912 under the title *Oscar Wilde, Three Times Tried*. It was compiled by Christopher Millard (Stuart Mason) assisted by the publisher, Cecil Palmer. There is also a volume in the Notable British Trials Series (1948). This was edited by Montgomery Hyde with an introduction which gives one of the best accounts that has been written concerning Wilde. There are valuable appendices on the legal, historical and pathological aspects of homosexuality.

Of the authors who wrote from knowledge or drew on the first-hand authorities there are: Arthur Ransome, friend of Robert Ross, *Oscar Wilde, a Critical Study* (1912); Vincent

O'Sullivan, *Aspects of Wilde* (1936); Charles Ricketts, *Recollections of Oscar Wilde* (1932); André Gide, *Oscar Wilde, a Study* (1905) and *Oscar Wilde* (1951); William Rothenstein, *Men, and Memories* (1931); Anna Comtesse de Brémont, *Oscar Wilde and His Mother* (1911); Leonard Cresswell Ingleby, *Oscar Wilde* (1909), *Oscar Wilde, Some Reminiscences* (1912); R. Thurston Hopkins, *Oscar Wilde* (1913); Sir David Hunter Blair, *In Victorian Days* (1939).

Stuart Mason, with indefatigable industry, prepared a Wilde bibliography (1914). He also gave an account of the controversy occasioned by the publication of Dorian Gray in *Oscar Wilde, Art and Morality* (1912).

The first considerable life of Wilde written outside the circle of his friends and acquaintances was by Boris Brasol (1938). It makes some attempt at a critical examination of the sources and contributes some new information. There is an excellent chronological table.

George Woodcock made a survey of Wilde as a writer and thinker in *The Paradox of Oscar Wilde* (1949) and St. John Ervine offered a *Present Time Appraisal* (1951). These books are concerned with the works rather than the life of the man, but both give an account of Wilde's career.

Finally there is an excellent life of Wilde by Hesketh Pearson (1946) who contributed much new information from original sources. To avoid any possibility of plagiarism I refrained from reading this and now that I have finished writing I look forward to enjoying a book that has won the reputation of being the best life of Wilde available.

Two books dealing with the period of Wilde's career are Holbrook Jackson's *The Eighteen Nineties* (1913) and Richard Le Gallienne's *The Romantic Nineties* (1926). Reminiscences of the period, once Wilde had become mentionable in print, contain frequent references to him. Among these, together with other authors to whom I wish to acknowledge my indebtedness, are:

The Days I Knew, Lily Langtry (1925).
Artists of the Nineties, John Rothenstein (1928).
Oscar Wilde and the Yellow Nineties, Frances Winwar (1940).
Oscar Wilde and His Mother, Anna, Comtesse de Brémont (1911).
Speranza, Horace Wyndham (1951).
Life of James McNeill Whistler, E. R. and J. Pennell (1908).
The Aesthetic Adventure, William Gaunt (1945).
Theatrical Cavalcade, Ernest Short (1942).
W. E. Henley, John Connell (1949).
Autobiography, R. B. Haldane (1929).
Life of Lord Carson, Edward Marjoribanks.
Apologia Pro Oscar Wilde, Dal Young.
Oscar Wilde, H. Davray.
Oscar Wilde Fragments, Martin Birnbaum.
Confessions of a Journalist, Christopher Healy.
Recollections of a Dialogue, Laurence Housman.
Two Deaths of Oscar Wilde, Vance Thompson.